D1596660

Harry Wright

Harry Wright

The Father of
Professional Base Ball

by CHRISTOPHER DEVINE

McFarland & Company, Inc., Publishers
Jefferson, North Carolina, and London

LIBRARY OF CONGRESS CATALOGUING-IN-PUBLICATION DATA

Devine, Christopher
    Harry Wright : the father of professional base ball / by Christopher
Devine.
      p.   cm.
    Includes bibliographical references and index.

    ISBN 0-7864-1561-4 (softcover : 50# alkaline paper)

    1. Wright, Harry, 1835–1895.   2. Baseball managers—United
States—Biography.   3. Baseball players—United States—Biography.
4. Cincinnati Red Stockings (Baseball team)   5. Baseball—United
States—History—19th century.   I. Title.
GV865.W75D48   2003
796.357'092—dc21   2003010994

British Library cataloguing data are available

Cover photographs: Harry Wright ca. 1880s; his Boston Red Caps, 1879
(National Baseball Hall of Fame Library, Cooperstown, N.Y.)

Manufactured in the United States of America

McFarland & Company, Inc., Publishers
  Box 611, Jefferson, North Carolina 28640
  www.mcfarlandpub.com

To Pete Costella and Ryan Puza,
for the glory days.

Acknowledgments

In the area of research, I must thank Halsey Miller, Jr., above all. Through the paperwork concerning the life of his great-grandfather and the stories that he was privy to, I was allowed a unique and authoritative perspective on Harry Wright's life. His generosity with both his time and information is greatly appreciated, and hopefully done justice by this work.

In the area of writing, I thank Madeline Warner, who took the time to edit this manuscript and check my creative grammar.

Professionally, I was offered a great deal of help over the past couple years by the Baseball Hall of Fame, notably Scot Mondore, Pat Kelly, and Andy "Yogi" Zides; my unofficial agent, Evelyn Begley, and our friend, Mike Getz; Darryl Brock, for sharing his expertise; Harry Higham, for his interest in the story of his beloved forefather's colleague.

Personally, such an undertaking would not be viable without the everyday help of my family and friends, whether impacting this project or the circumstances around it. Foremost among them are Donna and Michael Devine, Edith Wilson, Evie Schmidt, Alex Trzasko, Adam "Shibs" Shibley, Robbie "Papi" Talevi, and the long list of good people in and around my hometown of Westfield.

Contents

Preface

To understand Harry Wright, as with any subject, one must first understand his background: the heritage, culture, and circumstances that influenced his life. The surname Wright can be traced to Boernician origin before A.D. 1100, and first found in England in Berwickshire, near the border of Scotland. The name gained prominence in the county and later the nation through widespread migration. By the 1851 British census, the name could be found in 65 counties, including variations such as Wrightman, Wrighton, and Wrightson.

After a heavy concentration in Kent County, the Wright name appeared in Yorkshire, England, the county home to Harry Wright's birthplace of Sheffield. Today England's highest industrial city, the green hills of Sheffield were first utilized as a fortress by the ancient Brigante tribe to fend off invasion by the Romans. The rolling hills, often used today for climbing, overlooked the Don Valley, an ideal view for spotting intruders.

The Norman baron William de Lovetot later erected a wooden castle where the Don River met the Sheaf, and the city grew around this. The castle was later replaced by a stone version in 1270 to house the fourth Earl of Shrewsbury. While living there, the Earl developed a reputation as the city's most prominent resident and commissioned the construction of the Manor Lodge, which was later adjoined to the Turret House. This is where Mary Queen of Scots took refuge when fleeing to England in 1568.

The city's plentiful resources of iron ore, oak woods, and surging rapids allowed for the development of the cutlery trade during the Middle Ages, from which Sheffield gained fame and fortune. By the mid–1800's, it was considered the foremost steel-manufacturing city in the world, a reputation only enhanced in later years by Sheffield resident Harry Brearley's discovery of stainless steel.

1

It was on the banks of this industrial city that Sam Wright met a 21-year-old Irish girl named Annie Tone. While Sam Wright's family history can only be traced to his paternal grandfather, research by his great great grandson, Halsey Miller, Jr., establishes ascendants as far back as the 11th century.

Among the Tones' prominent relations was an Earl, a knighted baron, a beneficiary in Pope Clement V's will, and Bertrand de Blanquefort, the fourth Grand Master of the Knights Templar. The Knights Templar was an exclusive organization founded after the reestablishment of Christian authority in Jerusalem in 1099. The security of the Christian reign was uncertain, and in 1113 nine French knights formed the Knights Templar to protect the city against invasion. After gaining prominence in Jerusalem and receiving approval from the church, the Knights' membership grew exponentially until it encompassed fifteen provinces across nearly all of Europe, with the exception of Scandinavia. At the height of their influence, the Knights counted 20,000 members, among them Europeans of the highest status and pedigree. At the head of the society was the Grand Master, an elected leader who swore to serve as such for life. Blanquefort was elected in 1156 and presided through 1167, the longest serving Grand Master of any of the first eleven. Ironically, the king of France would later vanquish the Knights in 1307 in cooperation with Clement V, the uncle of Blanquefort's great-granddaughter.

The wealth and status accorded to these forefathers was not devolved upon Annie Tone. Her parents, John Tone and Mary Bryan, eloped in 1802 at the respective ages of 15 and 12. Mary would die in 1814 at the age of 30, and John emigrated from Ireland to Rochester, New York, where his eldest brother William worked. He would later return to Ireland to live out his last years.

Sam and Annie Wright waited until seven years after marriage to move to America amid the flood of British Isle emigrants. The nature of their voyage is not known today, but it is quite likely that it was a trial much like the one that others paid for the freedom and prosperity of a new American identity.

There are no records yet discovered to indicate even who traveled on this journey. Some have suggested that Sam Wright actually came to America beforehand and established himself in cricket circles before bringing Annie, young Harry, and perhaps by then, his second son, Danny, across the Atlantic. While this is a plausible explanation, there are no documents to shed light either way except the 1840 census. That record proves that the rest of the family was in America by then, but of course one cannot draw any conclusion from it as to when each member of the family immigrated.

Consequently, the path that the Wright family took to America cannot be discerned through definitive information, but only considered by logic. While it was common for fathers to establish residence in the U.S. before bringing other family members along, this was usually only necessary in the cases of lower income families. In fact, Sam Wright was a graduate of Oxford University who had time to develop professional cricket talent, a game noted for its time-consuming nature, and therefore more accessible to the wealthy. Furthermore, the earliest identification of the Wrights' residence was with Annie Tone's relatives in New Jersey. If Sam Wright waited until he found stability in America to bring over his family, it is unlikely that he would have brought them to his wife's relative's home.

The year of the Wrights' arrival in America was deemed the Panic for 1837. It was not conducive to building a stable prosperity. Two months after President Andrew Jackson left office, his Vice President Martin Van Buren had succeeded to the Executive post. Under Jackson America had seen unprecedented economic expansion. The American System, cooperative in economy despite contradiction in philosophical operation, thrived as planned. The southern states manufactured an improbable amount of cotton, for which it required numerous slaves. Northeastern merchants profited greatly from this system and its trade opportunities. In the west, speculation was booming. Government land sales grew 500 percent over a period of just two years. Canal systems, railroads, and other internal improvements increased commerce and confidence, but at the price of huge state debts covered by British loans.

The British assistance fostered a doubling of state bank charters. Overconfident banking officials issued more bank notes than they had specie to back them up with, and neglected to call in collateral. With similar confidence, Congress mandated that as of January 1, 1837, the states be loaned an equal portion of the $5 million surplus. The states spent the money with alacrity on ambitious projects, but with insufficient responsibility toward repaying their loans. These acts siphoned off the funding of federal money to the state banks and forced them to call in their loans. Coupled with Britain's lowered demand for cotton as a result of it's own sagging economy, the American dollar was hit hard.

The economy of just months before crumbled. Americans lamented the loss of jobs and the closing of banks, while states abandoned internal improvement projects and focused on fighting the repayment of their loans.

It took until the mid–1840's for America to recover. By then Sam Wright had bypassed the crisis by living securely as a professional cricketer. But his son Harry, who was about to enter the workforce himself, was not bypassed by his circumstances. He remained reverent of his father, nostalgic toward his birthplace of Sheffield, and industrious in his trade. These sentiments impacted the direction of his personal and professional life. As will be seen in later chapters, the results were instrumental in his decision to begin playing base ball in the first place, and even to bring his game across the Atlantic Ocean to his ancestral British Isles.

Author's Note

Since Harry Wright's story took place within the framework of 19th century base ball, the author felt that it would be helpful to the reader to encounter Wright's life through the vocabulary of his times. Below is a glossary of those terms which have been applied in the following pages:

Base ball   Common 19th century spelling of the modern "baseball." During the latter third of the century, the modern spelling came into use, as well as "base-ball." All three spellings were used interchangeably.

Captain   Generally a leader of the club in an official capacity on and off the field. A very similar position to manager, entailing more responsibility than the modern sense suggests.

Club   A base ball club. Used to describe an organization of members rather than simply a team of players.

Gate(s)   A portion of the profits made on a particular game.

Grounds   Ballpark or field. Since most early ballparks were open and not enclosed, this early description pertains to an area where games were played. Once enclosure became common and admission fees were subsequently charged, "ballpark" became standard.

Match   A game.

Muff   An error, often pertaining to a dropped fly ball.

Pitcher's Point   Contemporary reference to a pitcher's mound. However, in the mid-19th century, the area from which a pitcher delivered was not a raised mound of dirt, but instead a level box, referred to as the point.

Revolve   Change from one club to another while still under contractual obligation to the original club. This was an illegal action.

Spectators/Cranks   Early terms for what we now know as fans. The term "spectators" was used in the earlier days of baseball, up to the mid–1870's, when "cranks" became common. Approximately a decade later, in the mid-to-late 1880's, the term "fans" came into popular use.

Striker   A batter.

1. A Base Ball Edison

"[Harry Wright is a] base-ball Edison. He eats base-ball, breathes base-ball, thinks base-ball, dreams base-ball, and incorporates base-ball in his prayers."— *The Cincinnati Enquirer*

I.

It had rained ever since they left Cincinnati. Harry Wright knew what this meant for his Red Stockings as he reclined in his seat on the Pullman train. Three of his players— Asa Brainard, Andy Leonard, and Fred Waterman — sang a quartet with newspaperman Henry Millar in the background. But Wright was focused on the numbers rolling about his head.

The club had been all set to go on its Eastern tour two days before on Sunday evening, May 30, 1869, when they realized that there was not enough money for train tickets. All banks were closed for the Sabbath, so Cincinnati Base Ball Club President Aaron B. Champion and Secretary John Joyce solicited some of the available club members for funds. But none came through until Will Noble reluctantly allowed $300 of savings to be borrowed from a stash that his wife had hidden in their house. The Red Stockings left early the next morning for Yellow Springs, Ohio, but the rains cancelled play and the club had no money to get to Mansfield. Millar, who had been given expense money by his employer, *The Cincinnati Commercial*, loaned the $245 necessary to pay the club's way.

The Pullman arrived in Mansfield, Ohio, at 7:00 that evening, and it was not long afterwards that the rain stopped. By that time, the new grounds of the Independent club had been flooded and the Cincinnati Red Stockings' famous tour that would last one year and 57 wins without a defeat saw its first tour begin on Mansfield's shabby Fair Grounds. The Fair

Grounds was not as much of a ballpark as it was an open field, encompassed by trees. Millar noted dryly that the Cincinnatis faced an "uphill fight," not because of the Independents' status as the best amateur club in Ohio, but because the playing surface slanted upwards as it reached the outfield. Five hundred spectators littered the wooden grandstands, whispering as they watched the field, "There's the Cincinnatis."

The Red Stockings marched onto the field in what would today be recognized as the modern uniform but in Mansfield that day was the look of the future. Up until Wright designed the modern uniform in the winter of 1869, the common style was a woolen cap, flannel shirt, and ankle-length pantaloons. The Red Stockings, in contrast, wore white jerseys made of cricket flannel, cut off at the elbow, and highlighted by a bib in the center of the chest with a bright red Old English "C." They donned a jockey-style hat and calf-skin Oxford shoes, but the kicker was their cricket flannel knickers and scarlet red stockings. "It's a bully set for good legs," marveled the *San Francisco Chronicle*. "It's easy to see why they adopted the Red Stocking style of dress which shows their calves in all their magnitude and rotundity. Every one of them has a large and well-formed leg and every one of them knows how to use it."[1]

Wright led his players nine abreast along the first base path. The line continued across the field until every player had stopped at his respective position, starting with the first baseman. Each man ran in for a turn at the bat, swung at 12 pitches, and returned to his station, while someone else hit high fly balls—"fungoes"—to the outfielders. The foreign concepts may well have proved intimidating to the Independents, a fear as much by Wright's design as the innovations themselves. Wright had an analytical mind that enjoyed the head games of management more than the physicality of ballplaying.

Wright's contributions to the Red Stockings—and base ball in general, for that matter—followed that pattern. He was a man who could be behind the scenes even while on the front lines. While he was known as the Cincinnati captain, manager, and center fielder, he operated in 1869 simultaneously as General Manager, Traveling Secretary, and Public Relations Department. He arranged all the games and gate receipts percentages, set up the travel schedule, negotiated hotel and railroad bills, negotiated player salaries, bought equipment, directed the groundskeeping, handled the media, and promoted Red Stockings games. In today's terms that seems inconceivable, but in 1869 base ball operated on a much smaller scale. (After all, who could imagine George Steinbrenner going to a New York newspaperman to ask for money to pay the airplane bill?)

It was a different game, on and off the field.

Most striking, in summation, were some of the subtle differences between the on-field play itself. "If a modern fan could somehow be transported to a match a hundred years ago," wrote base ball historian Harold Seymour in 1960, "he would see a crude exhibition, but he would recognize it as baseball."[2] Under the rules and traditions in play in the 1869 Mansfield game, Seymour's point is illustrated.

After the Cincinnatis finished their batting practice that afternoon, Wright and the Independents' captain came together for a coin flip to determine who would bat first. Once Cincinnati took the field, Wright stepped into the pitcher's point. Though he usually played center field and had Brainard pitch, Wright decided to give him a rest that day in what he expected to be an easy game. His "mound" was a level 6-foot box bordered by iron disks on each side. Instead of a pitching rubber he stood upon a flat, circular plate, painted white. Forty-five feet away the Mansfield striker anchored his back foot on a drawn line perpendicular to home plate, a one-foot circular stone also painted white. Once both pitcher and striker were ready, the latter called out his pitch, either high or low. If the striker called "Low!" and Wright pitched the ball between his waist and one foot off the ground, the umpire — a volunteer with a high silk top hat who could stand either to the side of the plate, in foul grounds, or behind the pitcher — warned the striker to hit what he asked for or get a strike. However, if Wright missed the low pitch, the ump called out "Ball to the bat!" Any successive pitches out of the strike zone were called balls. At nine balls, the striker took his base. This was also the case if three unfair balls were called, which were pitches that bounced before the plate or cleared the striker's head. If the Independent reached base in this way or made a hit with his 3½-foot, 45–50 oz., willow bat, he reached a one-foot square canvas bag planted in the ground with a wooden block. The game was high-scoring, a 48–14 Cincinnati win, as were most games during that era. This was due to many factors: underhanded pitching, limitations on catchers, lively balls, and — most importantly — the fact that the players didn't use gloves. It was considered unmanly at the time, and as a result of their non-use it was common for fielders to make at least one error per game.

The evolution of the game over the past 1⅓ centuries may have been a natural progression, but it cannot be dismissed as simply a product of time alone. In fact, much can be attributed to the players present at the Mansfield game. The 1869 Cincinnati Red Stockings, as the first openly all-professional base ball club, were initially denounced for their conversion. Money had been a constant source or corruption in base ball in recent years, from crooked owners, players, and umpires, to fixed games, to everyday gambling. An open association of money with base ball did not sit well with the public. But the integrity of this club and its leader, Harry Wright, eased professionalism into the status of an acceptable element of base ball. Had professionalism continued in its disreputable path one wonders if the system would have been delayed, or even precluded in the years afterwards.

Even Henry Chadwick, one of the most ardent critics of professionalism early on, later credited Wright with a healthy advancement:

> The amateur class never had nor could have the time to elevate to the necessary practice in the development of skill in the several departments of that professional play admits of…. Hence our game would have stood still and never advanced beyond the point of the amateur displays on the field of the early sixties but for the inauguration of the professional methods started by the Cincinnati Club under Harry Wright's management.[3]

Base ball today is a game similar in its basics to the sport known before the Red Stockings' 1869 season, but remarkably different in the details and traditions developed in the time since. Unlike then, one now sees the practices of doubleheaders, farm systems, pitching rotations, sacrifices, fielder platoons, batting practice, positioning fielders in accordance with the batter's tendencies, fielders backing up one another, throwing ahead of the runner, relieving the pitcher in order to upset the batter's timing, scorecards, the modern uniform, the hit-and-run, hand signals, long-term contracts, endorsements, spring training, and even the concept of teamwork. Why? Because Harry Wright pioneered *all* of these ideas.

In 1999, the Society for American Baseball Research completed a poll that ranked Harry Wright as the third largest contributor to 19th century base ball. Though hindsight is often said to be 20/20, that is questionable in this case. In fact, the 19th century perception of that question was quite different. In a November 1893 edition of *The Sporting News* Wright was noted as the most remarkable figure in base ball. His only competition, according to the paper, was neither Henry Chadwick nor Albert Spalding — named first and second in the SABR poll — but longtime player and manager Adrian "Cap" Anson. It is likely that 20th century achievements and events have persuaded opinions to change over time. Chadwick, recognized as America's original sportswriter, worked in a profession that has gained quite a bit of status in the past 100 years. Sportswriting has since been applauded for its use in popularizing base ball across the country with an in-depth coverage of the game, a style originated by Chadwick. This, coupled with Chadwick's effect on the changes and developments in rules has given him credit as a founding father of the game. Though Wright failed in brief attempts at sportswriting — "Composition is out of my line"[4] he once explained — he was as knowledgeable of, and as instrumental in the changing of, the rulebook as Chadwick. Contemporary sources ranked the two as equals in this regard.

In Spalding's case, much of the reverence for him may have come as a result of his 1911 book, *America's National Game*, regarded as the first history of base ball. This, of course, was a 20th century achievement, not a 19th century base ball contribution. He was also a phenomenal player and powerful base ball magnate who established the successful Spalding sporting goods company. Wright tried his hand at the latter venture, but failed. However, he himself was an acclaimed ballplayer and a powerful executive of sorts in his own right.

Harry Wright, if bested by those men in their areas of expertise, was not truly eclipsed. And as an all-around pioneer, he may have had no match.

Though Harry Wright is not a household name today, he was a

The Father of Professional Base Ball in his grandfatherly days. Harry Wright posed for this portrait in the 1880's. (National Baseball Hall of Fame Library, Cooperstown, N.Y.)

living legend for several decades in the 19th century. Newspapers frequently referred to him as either "The Father of Base Ball" or "The Father of Professional Base Ball." "You make me feel awful old when you say I am looked upon as the 'father of the game,'" he wrote to National League President William Hulbert. "You must look farther and I am certain you will fare better. There is a gentleman in New York, Henry Chadwick Esq. who is richly deserving of the title 'father of the game,' for 'the pen is mighty' and he has invariably used it for the best interests of the game, as we all know."[5]

Wright's ready deference to Chadwick on the matter was graciously returned. After Wright's death in 1895, Chadwick regarded him as the "most widely known, best respected and most popular of the exponents and representatives of professional baseball, of which he was virtually the founder."[6] Quite high praise, indeed. Wright's former employer, Col. John I. Rogers, who he was often at odds with, went so far as to note that "It has truly been said, that so identified was he with the progress and popularity of the game that its history is his biography."[7]

Though the complimentary attitudes of these men may have been heightened in the wake of Wright's death, it was not uncommon to find similar ones during his baseball days. "Harry Wright is undoubtedly the best known baseball man in the country,"[8] declared one paper in 1886.

In 1896, the Reach Guide asserted,

> Every magnate in the country is indebted to [Harry Wright] for the establishment of baseball as a business, and every patron for fulfilling him with a systematic recreation. Every player is indebted to him for inaugurating an occupation in which he gains a livelihood, and the country at large for adding one more industry ... to furnish employment.[9]

Wright's leadership in advancing the professional movement with success and dignity was made possible by his own reputation. Whereas most representatives of professionalism were contract-jumping blackguards and high-stakes gamblers, Wright was one of the first — with pitcher Jim Creighton as the only other inclusion — to disassociate money in baseball with corruption and instead refocus on the link between money and good base ball. He was well aware of what dishonest ballplaying would do to the game. "The clubs now play to win," he assured in 1877, "and when the public know that they will take an interest in the game and attend the contest. When the people get to thinking that either nine are not doing the best they can, they become disgusted with the game and will cease to patronize it."[10] Seventeen years later, he was just as confident. "If base ball patrons leave the game disgusted they are apt not to return again."[11]

Wright had a shrewd mind for business—and regarded base ball as one. In order to drive up demand, he knew that he had to make the supply more attractive. Whereas many owners sought to solve economic woes by cheapening the admission fees, Wright saw a better brand of base ball as the answer. "It is well worth 50 cts. to see a good game of base ball, and when the public refuse to pay that, then good bye base ball. They do not object to paying 45 cts. to $1.50 to go to the theatre, and numbers prefer base ball to theatricals. We must make the game worth witnessing and there will be no fault found with the price of admission."[12]

Wright was generally given the benefit of the doubt in spite of his hardball economic attitude because he was not the archetypal money-hungry executive. Wright was a man of temperate habits who did not swear, drink, or smoke. He banned all beer and betting pool sales at his home grounds, and in fact went so far as to station a police officer in the ballpark while with Philadelphia to put a stop to smoking and insults. Nevertheless, peers admired him for his manner of acting morally without condescension.

Wright was also noted for his honesty, which he carried onto the ballfield even when detrimental to his team's cause. In an 1868 game between Cincinnati and the Unions of Morrisania, the umpire made an erroneous decision to favor the hometown Red Stockings. Wright knew the call was an effort to appease the crowd and so he stepped onto the field and overruled the umpire, in what proved to be a Cincinnati loss.

Years later, with Philadelphia, outfielder Ed Andrews took a 20-foot shortcut inside 3rd base en route to a run. To most onlookers, sneaking this by the umpire (there was only one on the field in those days) was a sign of cleverness. Wright did not see it that way. When Andrews returned to the bench, his manager was pale. "Ed," he said, staring intently into Andrews' eyes, "don't ever let me see you do that again. I don't want any games won that way."[13]

Trust for Wright was so strong that he occasionally umpired National League games while managing other League teams. As *The Sporting News* put it, "There was no figure in base ball more creditable to the game than dear old Harry."[14]

Wright's contributions to 19th century base ball included both specific and general breakthroughs that have been vital to the development of the game and to its establishment as the National Pastime. Many of the earliest milestones in base ball occurred in Wright's presence. He headed the New York nine in the first game at which an admission fee was charged (1858), was the first player to openly receive money for a game (1863), led the first openly all-professional club, the Cincinnati Red Stockings (1869–70), won four of five championships in the first all-professional league, the National Association (1871–75), and provided instrumental direction in the founding of the National League (1876). As Henry Chadwick once said, "To write a full sketch of his career would fill a volume."[15]

In light of Wright's achievements and experiences, the volume that covers them will answer an intriguing question: Was Harry Wright the most important base ball figure of the 19th century? "An opinion settles nothing," he once admonished, "unless the truth of the assertion is either self-evident or demonstrated."[16]

II.

One of the mysteries blurred by the dust of time is the birth of Harry Wright. Almost across the board, his birthdate has been reported since his

death as January 10, 1835, in Sheffield, Yorkshire, England. However, other
sources have cited his birth as occurring in 1832. Wright's fourth daughter,
Carrie, wrote in a 1963 letter to grand-nephew (and Harry's great-grand-
son) Halsey Miller, Jr., that the Wrights came to America with infant Harry
in 1832. Furthermore, Mormon records show his baptism to have taken
place on November 8, 1832, at St. Peters Church in Leeds, England. Both
Wright's name and the names of his parents match up, as does the county,
Yorkshire. However, these records are not always accurate.

Another source suggests a later date. According to Wright's death
certificate, filed after his October 3, 1895, passing, he was 60 years, 9 months,
and 21 days old upon demise. This implies a birthdate of December 13,
1834.

It is most likely, nevertheless, that Wright was, in fact, born in 1835.
In the 1840 New York census, two boys under the age of five were listed in
the Wright household, meaning Harry and his younger brother, Dan. The
1850 census concurred by listing him at 15 years of age. (Of course, in the
same census, father Sam was lowballed at 37 and mother Annie was inac-
curately listed as 37 instead of 41.)

Ultimately, one must consider the matter logically. Most contemporary sources of Wright's day cited the date of January 10, 1835. Had Wright
known this to be untrue, he could have corrected it easily. The thought
that he would have used a false age to extend his career or something of
that nature is illogical and out-of-character.

So if the theory holds true, William Henry (Harry) Wright was born
in 1835 as the first child of Sam Wright and Annie Tone Wright, in the
city of Sheffield, England. Sam Wright was a "fancy wood turner" by trade
born in Sheffield himself. He graduated Balliol College, of Oxford University, before marrying 21-year-old Annie in 1830. The marriage to an
Irish native was upsetting to Sam's English family, especially because of
her uncle Wolfe Tone. Wolfe was an Irish rebel who inspired the line "they
won't shoot me like a soldier, they want to hang me like a dog" in a famous
Irish ballad. He committed suicide in a British prison before they got the
chance.

The three Wrights emigrated to America in the summer of 1836, for
reasons not completely clear. The most likely scenario is that Sam sought
to swap the wood turning business for a place on the St. George Dragonslayers cricket club. Sam began playing for the club in 1837, on the Red
House Grounds located at Second Avenue and 106th Street in New York
City. He would play with it for the next 33 years, until his retirement in
1869. Upon that occasion, Sam was treated to a celebration at which he
was given a fine silver drinking mug and $300. In his time with the club,

Sam built a reputation much like that of his eldest son in later years. His integrity was so revered that "as honest as old Sam Wright" became a household phrase in New York cricket circles.

The parallels between Sam and Harry Wright's careers in their respective sports of expertise are fascinating. Much like Harry would eventually do, Sam became an early professional after participating in his sport's first game played for money. Recalled Henry Chadwick years later, "If I mistake not, this was the only contest at cricket ever played in this country for a money stake."[17] Sam led the New Yorkers to a 140–77 trouncing by scoring a game-high 20 runs.

The Wrights did not know what to expect upon their move to America. An old college roommate of Sam's sent him a pair of hunting knives once he got there. Apparently, as Carrie explained, "he thought [the] United States a wild country."[18]

The pair of "bear knives" sent to Samuel Wright from a friend in Sheffield, England, to protect him in the "wild country" of New Jersey. The knives were later passed down to Harry Wright, then on to his daughters Hattie and Carrie, before coming to reside today with Halsey Miller, Jr. (Courtesy Halsey Miller, Jr.)

Initially, they stayed with Annie's relatives in New Jersey. The Wrights' stay there was brief, for they moved on to Harlem, New York, shortly thereafter. In approximately 1857, they moved to 65 Washington Street, Hoboken, New Jersey, when Sam was given charge of the St. George's Cricket Grounds.

By this time, Annie Wright was about to have her 5th child. Second son Dan had been born two years after Harry, in 1837. Little is known about his life, for Dan moved to the disconnected west in San Jose, California, somewhere between 1861 and 1877. The reason for his departure is unknown. He would marry twice — the first in New York — and have two children, but never attain the status of his three professional ballplaying brothers. As a result, the details of his life are confusing and mysterious. Dan — in his few occasions in public print — was represented as Harry's senior, such as this 1895 recollection of Henry Chadwick: "Harry had three brothers. Daniel — the eldest of the family — and his younger brothers."[19] However, the 1850 New York census listed him as lacking an occupation, while Harry did have one. This is consistent with the difference between a 13-year-old and a 15-year-old at the time, especially given information on Harry's status in 1850.

The birth of George Wright has been clouded by its own mystery. George was born on January 26, 1847, in Harlem. Modern reports, such as the *Dictionary of American Biography*, have listed George's mother as a woman named Mary Love. Whether Love was a creature of fiction or an actual human being is uncertain, but the idea of George and Harry being Hall of Fame half-brothers after all is pure fabrication. The origin of this myth is found in George's August 21, 1937, death certificate, in which house-keeper Sadie Kelly, a non–family member, gave this new information. Why would she do such a thing? "Boston Irish are known for their loquacious imaginations,"[20] notes Halsey Miller, Jr.

Sam Wright, Jr. — affectionately called "Sammy" — was the last son born, on November 25, 1848, in New York City. He was followed 10 years later, in 1858, by sister Mary. Virtually nothing is known of Mary, except that she lived with Sammy as of 1880 at age 22.

With the birth of Sammy, Harry now had a family of six to help support. So in 1849, at the age of 14, he dropped out of the New York Public School system to work for a jewelry manufacturer. Wright's comments on education later in life are surprisingly condemnatory to the uneducated:

> Intelligent, educated and sober men excel in every other walk of life. Will any one say they can not in base ball? There are many excellent players in the League who possess none of these desirable qualities, but does anyone doubt that they could play better if they were educated, and exemplary in their habits? To deny this would be absurd.... An educated man has brighter and quicker perception than an unlettered one.... His correct habits of life will make him as superior physically as he is mentally.[21]

Wright apprenticed in the jewelry business at Tiffany's, in New York, where he worked for several years. He was also a clockmaker in this time. In 1859 his family moved to a brick house facing the back of St. George's cricket grounds. Before work Harry and Dan would get up early in the morning to play cricket and base ball on some open lots to the side of the house, with school-bound George and Sammy. In the wintertime the four cleared off the snow to play on the lots, with hands covered by gloves to avoid the sting of their palms sticking to the bats.

Harry had developed a love for his father's sport, cricket, and joined St. George's in 1850 at the age of 15. He had begun playing the game shortly before this time by participating in games with businessmen on their time off from work. Recalled Wright decades later, "[C]ricket was my first love, commenced when a school boy, and I still retain the old love for it."[22]

Cricket had come to America by the mid-18th century with British colonists. It was not until 1839, when the St. George's Cricket Club was established in New York, that the sport reached popular status. Soon cricket tours were being taken across the country and up to Canada. Wright came along for several of these. In 1859, the All-England Eleven visited America for a series of matches attended by up to 25,000 per game.

But cricket eventually became a casualty of the Civil War. After the Union victory, America sought a patriotic endeavor, not the pastime of another nation; especially not one of Mother England, who had been within one major southern victory of extending recognition to the Confederates.

Sam and Harry Wright, father and son, pose in their cricket uniforms in the 1850s. Harry played for his father's St. George's Dragonslayers before converting to base ball in 1858. (Courtesy Transcendental Graphics.)

However, cricket had little chance of survival anyway because it did not concur with the American lifestyle and tempo. As a matter of practicality, patronage of the game did not work for most Americans. Cricket matches often lasted an entire day, or even two days. Working men did not have the time or the flexibility to do this, so the game's fanbase was restricted to the upperclass.

Jingoists tended to stick more to the theory that cricket was doomed because of its slow pace (which gives an interesting perspective on modern base ball criticisms). "Americans do not care to dawdle over a sleep-inspiring game all through the heat of a June or July day," complained one contemporary writer.

> What they do, they want to do it in a hurry. Englishmen differ materially in this particular. The latter will spend a half-hour over a glass of 'arf and 'arf and an hour conning a column of the *Times*. An American dashes off a whiskey cocktail or snack and reads the *Herald* summary in about three minutes. Thus the reason of American antipathy to cricket can be readily understood. It is too slow and every man is not engaged. In baseball, all is lightening. Every action is swift as a seabird's flight and there is no one who has not something to do.[23]

In 1857 Wright began receiving $12 a week to take on the role of assistant professional of the St. George's club, in addition to his services as its round arm bowler, a position much like Pitcher. His father was already the team's star bowler and club professional. It was in that year that the Dragonslayers moved their headquarters to the Elysian Fields, in Hoboken. The Elysian Fields was really an enormous, open meadow used for a number of outdoor activities, from cricket to boating to picnicking. There were a number of diamonds across the field, uninterrupted by fences.

Harry would often take George onto the grounds to train him at cricket, if not involving him in a game with the older men. It was while coaching George one day that the two looked east of their field to see the New York Knickerbockers playing a game of base ball.

The Knicks are recognized as the first base ball club, established on September 23, 1845. The context of the term "club" in the early base ball sense is radically different from the modern day. The prime recreation of its members was to hold meetings and banquets. The banquets could be club dinners, formal balls, or a number of other activities. When free time opened up between these exercises, the men split into squads and played base ball.

The game has been said to have been introduced to them by club member Alec Cartwright, the 22-year-old "inventor of base ball." But according to recent discoveries by historians such as John Thorn, it appears that Cartwright may only be responsible for having introduced the idea of a ballclub. It was merely another step in the evolution of the game, picking up on the advancements of others. Crude forms of the game had existed around the world for centuries, but it was in this era that the modern guidelines of base ball such as 90 feet between bases, fair and foul territory, and three outs per side were applied by organizations such as the Knicks. The Knickerbockers club, formed in 1842, played under these rules before officially establishing their team in 1845. As more clubs cropped up, the players took the game more seriously, and the game eventually became a competitive occasion instead of a social one.

On June 19, 1846, the Knicks played the first recognized base ball game ever, against the New York Club. The New Yorks had organized just one month after the Knicks and actually played two ballgames by this point. But they were against eight-man cricket clubs, and therefore do not officially count. So they proposed a match with the Knickerbockers the following spring. The Knicks appointed a committee to carry out the arrangements and the two squared off in what proved to be a 23–1 New York Club win.

The Knickerbockers did not play another game until five years later. Nevertheless, by the mid–1850's they were among the four prime clubs in metropolitan competition, along with the Gothams, Eagles, and Empires. Only eight games were played between these clubs in 1855, a clear illustration of the lack of competition in the game. As a result, Wright decided to stay aboard the St. George's Club while learning base ball with the Knicks on his off-days, Monday and Wednesday.

Wright learned quickly and learned well. He had a natural athletic ability that allowed him to make such a transition from one sport to another easy. Noted his son, Harry Wright II, "He gave a superior performance in any kind of physical activity."[24] Besides cricket and base ball, Wright also excelled at fishing, hunting, skating, and track. He did not always look the part, but Wright truly had the build of an athlete. Harry stood at a tall 5' 9¾"—tall, that is by mid-19th century standards—and approximately 157 pounds. He had a firm, lean frame, strong both in the upper and lower body. His chest and hips were nearly symmetrical, 38½" and 38", respectively. His right forearm measured 11½" and swelled to 12½" at the bicep as a result of his religious conditioning techniques of hoisting Kehoe Indian clubs and dumbbells at the gym. One friend described him as a "strong, muscular athlete in full prime,"[25] while another observed him as "tall, good-looking, neatly dressed, somewhat clerical in appearance."[26] He had a well-tanned face featuring a pair of deep, dominating eyes, full of awareness and perception.

The transition for Wright's agile body from cricket to base ball was smooth. After all, the differences between the two were minimal. In the basic concepts of the game, they were, in fact, closely related, which helped the Wrights to adapt. "[Harry and George] face the ball, no matter how hot it comes, pick it up and throw it in with a vim," said the *New York Herald*, "but the others run sideways with the ball, coax it up and then jerk it from under their arm with much show but little effect."[27]

As an all-around player, Wright was a characteristically strategic base-ballist. "He plans and plays and does both excellently," said one paper in 1868; "the others simply play, without plan."[28] In 1872, the *New York Dispatch* called Harry and George "the best exponents of base ball *as a science* in the country. These players know *when* to strike, *how* to strike, and where to put the ball."[29]

His cerebral nature was best applied in the field, though, not at bat. Wright was noted for his efficiency in executing the little-ball basics. He had superior judgment in the outfield and an instinctual knack for tracking down fly balls. Summarily, the *Detroit Post* concluded that "Harry Wright is the finest, safest, best, and least showy player in America."[30]

Wright's love for cricket had been compromised, but not betrayed. The switch was somewhat of a sacrilegious one, especially if construed in the America v. Britain context common at the time. Sam's reaction, though not recorded, is unlikely to have been pleasant. He was, conceivably, the most popular figure in American cricket, echoed by his son in several ways. Like a father planning for his son to inherit the family business, he surely had his hopes for Harry, hopes dashed by the new base ball fad.

It *was* a fad, right? Actually, Wright had found a new passion. Sure, he continued to involve himself in cricket, coaching club members and arranging matches for St. George's. But these were his parting shots; Wright had converted to base ball. "There is no other game that can supplant base ball,"[31] he later said. "Base ball is a game of the people and will always remain so. I have no doubt but that cricket ... will never cope with base ball, which in my opinion is the peer of all field sports yet conceived."[32]

The enthusiasm with which he regarded the game translated clearly to the people around him. "Harry is always full of base-ball," described the *New York Times*. "...However much he may seem to be consulting his ease, word on this favorite theme will send Harry far into the field of base-ball conversation."[33]

The Knickerbocker club Wright joined allowed him to enter the heart of the base ball scene. In the 1850's, metropolitan New York was practically the wingspan of base ball's popularity. The champion team of Gotham was considered the champion of the world; of course, this determination was often made by the New York-dominated sports media.

Each of the New York clubs sent their delegates to a first-ever meeting of the National Association of Base Ball Players, in January 1857. This was the first organization of the game's players and clubs, and was thus hailed by newspapers as a progressive first step toward organizing and standardizing base ball so it could become the first "Native American Sport." (This term, of course, predated the modern context; the xenophobic Know-Nothing party often used it to compliment American-born citizens.) The Knickerbockers' Dr. D.L. Adams was elected President, an appointment representative of the status of the Knicks during that time period. But by the 1858 convention the club's influence was lessening.

The March 10, 1858, meeting, was called by the big four New York clubs, but Adams was replaced as president and no Knicks were elected to executive positions. It was like a major political faction being shut out of participation in drafting the United States Constitution. However, this detachment was not as much a snub as a mutual breakup. The Knicks had a different perspective on the direction of the game than most of their comrades. They looked at the game as a gentleman's sport to be used for entertainment and recreation, not competition. For the first time in the game's history, spectators were becoming rowdy at the games and rivalries between opponents had become intense. The Knicks wanted no part of this trend and gradually receded to its own smaller circle of like-minded, gentlemanly organizations.

Nevertheless, at the time of Wright's alignment with the Knicks in 1857, they comprised a powerful and well-respected club. Wright was dividing his time between their grounds and the cricket grounds, but increasingly he could be found on the base ball field. On July 8, 1858, he played his first game with the club. Though Wright would usually catch while with the Knicks, he played the outfield in this match versus the Brooklyn Excelsiors at Long Island's Fashion Race Course Grounds. The Excelsiors were just establishing their superiority in the game, after a 32–13 defeat of the Eagle nine. By a nearly identical score, 31–13, the Knicks were defeated, despite three great catches by Wright in the outfield.

Twelve days later, Wright returned to Long Island to play the first of the famous Fashion Course Matches. The Matches were a three-game summer series between picked Nines of New York and Brooklyn. Among its many firsts, this series contained the first high-profile games in base ball's short history. A crowd of 4,000 spectators attended the July 20 game, among them "a galaxy of youth and beauty in female form who, smiling on the same, nerved the players to their task, and urged them, like true knights of old, to do their devoirs before their 'ladyes fair.'"[34]

People began feeding into the streets in the early morning by foot, buggy, and even a special trip along the Flushing Railroad. The grounds that they arrived at was picked specially for the occasion, based mainly on its neutral location. It was attractive, but the field itself was coarse as a result of rushed landscaping. The Fashion Race Course grounds were not usually used for base ball, and so the field had been laid out specifically for this game. In order to fund this venture, the grounds proprietor had taken a revolutionary step: he charged admission.

The idea of admission fees was taboo among base ball purists. A game, they argued fiercely, had no place generating business. But even traditionalist Henry Chadwick took a voice in supporting the cause. "[Gate charges are] not relished by the masses," he conceded,

> but by the respectable portion of the community is regarded as a desirable improvement, as by means of the increased price hundreds of blackguard boys and roughs generally are kept out, while the respectable patrons of the game are afforded better opportunities for enjoying a contest.[35]

However, the 50 cent charge that brought in $2,000 that afternoon was not interpreted as a matter of consequence at the time; in fact, most contemporaries noted the series for its effect on the popularity of the sport. The games created such excitement that they convinced many casual followers to become die-hard loyalists.

The game itself was persuasive. It was a see-saw battle from the start, with Brooklyn going up early 3–0. They extended the lead to 10–3 after three innings, but New York recovered to go up 14–11 after five and hold on to a 22–18 win. Wright, the right fielder, made three catches in the field, two on the fly and one on the bound (off of the first bounce, a legal catch), but was shut down at the plate by Mat O'Brien. Despite having played his first game with the Knicks only twelve days before, Wright headed the New York contingent in this match.

However, there were elements of the game that Wright was ashamed to be associated with. During the contest Henry Chadwick overheard a couple of men making a wager on whether Brooklyn 2nd baseman John Holden would hit a home run. The man who bet on Holden's success approached the ballplayer with a proposition. "Jack, I've bet $100 that you'll make a home run in this game, and if you do I'll give you $25."

"All right," Holden responded, "I'll try my best."[36]

Holden soon came to bat against New York's Tom Van Cott and swatted a fly ball deep to right-center. Wright chased after the ball, but it cleared the fence and settled the bet.

Wagers were so heavy on that day that even women — usually the innocent element of the crowd — made conservative ones.

Gambling was the bane of Wright's base ball existence. It constantly dirtied the name of the institution of professionalism that he sought to cleanse. His track record on the issue is spotless as far as history shows. He bet no money, but occasionally put harmless accolades on the line. In 1878, he "name[d] as a wager the ["victory and" scratched out] pride of superiority in the manly exhibition of our National Game."[37] Four years later, he upped the ante to a gold or leather medal in a wager with New York Giants manager Jim Mutrie.

It's ironic that Harry Wright, one of the fiercest opponents of gambling on base ball, provided one of the first known links between money and the game. In 1863, when Wright was preparing to leave the Knicks, the club hosted a three-game series of benefits for him, Sam Wright, Sr., and others. Spectators were charged 25 cents to get in, but for 50 cents they could receive a souvenir stub with a portrait of a player on it. The clubs consisted of nine Brooklyn Excelsiors versus a collection of four New York Gothams, a New York Eagle, one of the champion club of New Jersey, and three St. George's Dragonslayers. Wright, the leadoff hitter, paced his team in batting, with three runs in the third game. Though the benefit was not held exclusively for him, it was Harry who received the $29.65 in profits.

Though this is the first recorded open transaction of money — under-the-table deals such as pitcher Jim Creighton's being excluded — it appears that Wright may have been involved in a similar game two years before. In mid–October 1861 he participated in a game reported by newspapers as a "benefit" for him and his father. Though the 1863 series is often recognized as the first time Wright — or anybody, for that matter — received direct payment for play, the fact that it was designated as a benefit game infers that he must have received money for this as well.

The game was billed as a St. George's v. Base Ball match, but it was really a mix of 18 cricket and base ball players versus 9 base-ballists. Though the former largely outnumbered the latter, their "advantage" turned out to be anything but. Henry Chadwick reported seeing "some remarkably funny scenes ... from the ball being missed where it came down among a ruck of five or six of the eighteen."[38] Wright, who actually played for the St. George's aggregation, avoided the fray by serving as Catcher for most of the game. Given the surplus of team members, Wright was backed up behind the plate by a second catcher, his brother George. Despite the second layer of protection, some pitches still got away, and George had to go chasing after them until impeded by a series of "crinolines," a stiff lady's hoop skirt. According to Chadwick, "Little Georgy Wright must have done some damage to the aforesaid [crinolines] of some of the fair dames, by running ... with his head into them in search of the ball to save a run."[39]

Despite these developments, the idea of mixing money with base ball was still taboo. After all, how could grown men be playing games for money when the Civil War had begun?

III.

Contrary to what one may expect, the Civil War seemed to pass Harry Wright by. It's as if the conflict consumed another country instead of his own, for Wright, as well as his family, did not participate in the war or appear to be directly impacted by it. In other modern writings, his non-involvement has been characterized as a matter of indifference or avoidance, but in fact it was for legal reasons. Wright was a registered alien, not yet a U.S. citizen, as was the case with his father. George was a U.S. resident, but at 14 years old, not yet of age to fight.

The Wright family's sentiments toward the Civil War are undocumented, but even if loyal to their northern region, they may have been inhibited by the position of the Mother country. England's stance was an awkward balance between practical sympathy and philosophical opposition. Its leaders believed that the southern states had a right to secede; but more importantly, Britain needed its cotton. However, the English were averse to slavery, an institution abolished there years before. Yet recognition of the C.S. was never far away, and even war with America was foreseeable. One of President Lincoln's Cabinet members had proposed the U.S. start a war with Britain just to reunite the country.

If Wright was reluctant to join the war effort, there was another reason — he was now a family man. Exactly when he married New York native Mary Fraser is unclear, but this appears to have taken place at some point after May 11, 1861. On that day, Wright took part in a Single v. Married cricket match in which he was a member of the Singles side. The first child of Harry and Mary Wright seems to have been born later that year.

Charles Wright was born in New Jersey in 1861, according to sources including the 1880 census. However, the 1870 census implies an earlier birth by listing him at 11 years old. As proven earlier, censuses are not always reliable and often contradict one another.

In the ensuing four years, the Wrights would have two more children, Lucie Louise (who likely died at a young age) and George William, or "Willy." Somewhere between Willy's birth in New Jersey before March 8, 1865, and Harry's remarriage on September 10, 1868, the marriage to Mary ended. The exact reason for this is not known due to a fire that burned all records that could have explained it, but it may well have been by death. Harry, a devoutly religious Episcopalian, did not believe in divorce, and furthermore their three children lived with Sammy Wright — along with sister Mary — as of 1880. Had wife Mary been capable, it seems reasonable that she would be taking care of the 19 and 15-year-olds at the time, if not Harry.

When the war began in April 1861, base ball hit a standstill. How could young Americans healthy enough to play sporting games not be fighting to save the Union? This was the first time that the country had dealt with such a question, the Mexican-American War having taken place too early in base ball's existence to apply. "At the first glance," one writer conceded, "it would seems as if indulging in sports and pastimes by our young men, was a little out of place when every shoulder is needed at the wheel of the national chariot."[40] Base ball ultimately did continue. Over the years, the game has been looked on as a therapeutic recreation and entertainment during times of war.

This earliest known image of Harry Wright shows him in his younger days with dark hair and a van dyke instead of his usual full goatee. Based on these facts, he likely posed for it in the early 1850's. (Courtesy Halsey Miller, Jr.)

Though the game did not disappear, it certainly seemed to fade away. Attendance at the December 1861 NA convention dipped by half of its 1859 showing, to 34 clubs. Those teams that did stick around reduced their schedules dramatically. The Brooklyn Atlantics took until August 11 to play their first of only 11 games, while the Excelsiors—who lost 91 members to the Union cause—did not participate in a single match.

The Knicks were no different from their New York brethren in cutting their schedule. The Knickerbockers played in a mere ten club matches, five versus other clubs and five between single and married nines. That year they announced that they would only participate in "friendly" games, to avoid the evils of competition. This cutback has more to do with that philosophical distancing from the NA than anything connected with the war effort. By 1863, the Knickerbockers joined with fellow old school clubs such as the Excelsiors and Eagles in all but dropping official competition. So Wright left the Knicks to become a New York Gotham.

The Gothams were actually a slight transition from the Knickerbockers. They were an old-fashioned and honorable club that often presented gifts to opponents after games, even losses. Wright would primarily play shortstop, as well as a little third base with the club. The position of shortstop had evolved greatly in the past several years. Up until Dickey Pearce of the Atlantics revolutionized the position in the 1860's, the shortstop stood in front of the baseline and waited to involve himself by helping the pitcher defensively and cutting off throws from the outfield. In short, whereas today the shortstop is the most active non-battery player in the field, at that point he was the least involved.

Wright joined the Gothams as early as July 21, when he scored five runs in a 26–22 win. He would go on to compile 14 runs in seven matches, an impressive average of two per game.

One of the beneficiaries of this fine play was teammate George Wright. George's rise to base ball stardom paralleled his elder brother, simply with less cricket. George began learning the family business of cricket at 10 years old under the tutelage of Harry and Sam, Sr.; mainly the former. He would bat against members of the St. George's club, using bats specially cut to the proper length by his father. At approximately 14 years old "and not much taller than the wickets" George played in his first professional cricket match, one between the Third Eleven of New York and the Second Eleven of Manhattan. He would go on to become a prominent cricketer and eventually the Assistant Professional of the St. George's club.

But George was beginning to eye the base ball field. "[Q]uite frequently," he later explained, "having heard that I was interested in [base ball], invitations were extended to me to play."[41] And so he began playing with the Gotham Jrs. in 1862 at the age of 15. This was not an outright repudiation of cricket; he would continue playing the games interchangeably. He was soon promoted to the parent Gothams club for a match against the Brooklyn Stars. During that game he played left field, but in fact George started off his Gothams tenure as a catcher. However, "one day a foul tip struck me in the throat and it hurt me so much that I never afterward was able to muster up sufficient courage to catch, and so I went to left field, eventually going to second base and then to shortstop."[42]

In 1865, George rededicated himself to cricket, if only for the money. He became Professional to the Philadelphia Cricket Club, though he played base ball with the Olympics of Philadelphia on every Wednesday, his off-day. Oddly, though, George continued to play with the Gothams— under an alias. Using the name "Cohen," George joined the Gothams to defeat Newsburg's Hudson City Club. It was illegal for him to play for any other club while still obligated to the Olympics. The *Philadelphia Mercury* exposed his revolving in a scathing editorial which accosted the Gothams for not seeking "native talent rather than professional players from rival cities, who cannot be expected to have the welfare of the club at heart as much as our men."[43] The scandal embarrassed Harry Wright more than anybody. He had taken a firm stance on revolvers, recommending that "any player violating a legal contract by signing a second contract with another club … should be expelled from the Association."[44]

When the Wright Brothers were not flip-flopping between cricket and base ball, they were busy pioneering ice base ball. In the winter of 1864-5, George and Harry began playing the game in what was a naturally smooth transition for them. Though they were recognized as two of the premier ice base-ballists around, this was not a result of their base ball skills. In fact, in ice base ball, skating was the most important skill. Since the players were on skates, it was difficult to keep one's footing. This precluded the players from hitting the ball squarely, setting for a throw, or reaching for a passing flyball or line drive. As a result, the best skaters were chosen over the best base-ballists. This was no problem for Wright, who—as son Harry II once said—executed "the most difficult skating designs with ease."[45]

Ice base ball differed little from the grass and dirt game. The difference was in the nature of the field. In anticipation of the wild bounces that the ball would take, the pitcher delivered the ball slowly. The advantage that this slow pace provided for the striker was balanced by the fact that he was swatting a dead ball, one that did not travel far when struck. The dead ball was used to keep it from bouncing incessantly past confounded fielders. Of course, this still happened enough because the pitchers were so easy to lay into.

The game, which had been stunted by the onset of the war after a successful 1860 season, grew quickly in popularity. It soon became a staple in Brooklyn and Troy, New York, before expanding to Philadelphia and Chicago only one winter later. With few other games to compete for popularity, ice base ball was quick to catch on and helpful in promoting the traditional form of base ball.

Base ball was certainly growing by that time, not so much as a wartime activity, but as a recreation certain to explode once the young soldiers were returned to peacetime freedom. The game was invariably found in Civil War prisons, especially because it was so easy to transport the necessary tools. And it provided a necessary distraction from combat for the soldiers. As many as 40,000 soldiers took in a Christmas Day 1862 match at the Hilton Head prison.

Externally, however, the game was suffering. The *New York Clipper* had to plead with the clubs to send delegates to the December 1864 NA meeting. Despite promises that their clubs would automatically be accepted if they just showed up, only 30 did. This was 20 below what was anticipated — or at least hoped for.

The only answer that could save the spiraling game came about in mid–April when the Confederate army gave in soon after the April 9 surrender of Robert E. Lee's troops at Appomattox. Confederate President Jefferson Davis was soon hunted down and captured, along with Southern generals.

The North, enraptured by celebratory spirits, planned a day of Thanksgiving on April 20 to include several ballgames. But all was set aside when they received the news that President Abraham Lincoln had been assassinated on April 14 in Washington's Ford Theater. Opening days in Brooklyn and New York were delayed until May and the season that had been expected to eclipse the vaunted "Furore of 1860" seemed to be buried in a Springfield, Illinois, grave.

But 1865 turned out to eclipse 1860, indeed. The reason was simple psychology. Base ball had hit a nerve by acting as an emotional release valve for a country that had spent the past four years in muted anguish fighting a brutal war and/or thinking of their loved ones out doing so. And in the north, where base ball's popularity was essentially concentrated, the game was a way of getting out the people's excitement and taking part in a patriotic game. In short, it typified the leisurely concept of home that they had nursed for four arduous years now.

To that effect, Henry Chadwick wrote that "For the first time in the annals of base ball, the game has been endorsed as the National game of ball of America, as cricket is of England, and henceforth it will be regarded as a permanent institution of the country."[46]

More games were played in 1865 than ever before — by far. "Never," the *New York Clipper* affirmed, "did a season terminate leaving the public appetite so eager for a further supply of ballplaying to feast on than this has done ... 1865 will be known as the year when base ball was first regularly established as the national game of America."[47]

"This season," another paper said in summation, "the whole country seems to have base ball on the brain."[48] 1865 was a great year to be an American and a base-ballist.

It was an odd time for Harry Wright to pack up and leave for Cincinnati.

2. The Queen City

"Never before in the history of our country has there been such a combination of the muscle and strength of American youth — whose profession is swinging the narrow bat and sending singing through the air
the ball, with the precision of an arrow from a well-trained bow who
have traversed so many miles of mountains, plains, and sometimes
almost deserted country, to grasp the hand of the brotherhood, fully
three thousand miles away, and teach the art and perpetuate the many
rudiments peculiar to the national game." — *The Cincinnati Commercial, August 28, 1869*

I.

In the rear view mirror, the notion is quite ironic. When Harry Wright
left on March 8, 1865, for Cincinnati, Ohio, it seemed that his career in
base ball was over. He had just left behind a steady position in the hotbed
of the country's fastest-growing sport. He was 31 years old and had
accepted a new job as professional cricketer of Cincinnati's Union Cricket
Club. Yet it was, in essence, the first step toward a Hall of Fame base ball
career.

Wright came to Cincinnati like a true Western pioneer: with a family and the promise of work. The UCC paid his way from New York to
Cincinnati at a charge of $79.50 after hiring him to head the fledgling
cricket club for $1200 per year. Back in New York, the base ball crowd was
reluctant to see Wright go. One paper threatened jokingly that "if the
Cincinnatians don't take care of these popular Wrights, we'll 'scourge' 'em
out of the Union."[1]

When Wright took over as Instructor and Bowler of the Unions on
August 2, he began the task of organizing a respectable representative of

29

the ambitious Queen City sportsmen. He in fact reached that point so quickly that in the same year one paper acknowledged that the UCC had already been "brought into prominence." Despite this success, Wright was surprised to find how decidedly base ball outranked cricket in its appeal.

The rise of base ball in the Queen City was really initiated by the establishment of the Cincinnati Base Ball Club on July 23, 1866. The club was founded by 26-year-old lawyer Aaron B. Champion in hopes of promoting the city. In fact, he had only a measured interest in the game itself and the story lines that developed around the club; the only reason those things mattered was because it improved the club and city economy. Once more it must be understood that the club was truly a club. Much like the Knickerbockers, it was a societal instrument governed by membership requirements and a constitution. And since the club was directly funded by the contributors of its 300-plus members, it needed to satisfy and entertain them. What better way to do that than with a good base ball club?

The UCC played on a shabby field at the foot of Richmond Street often called the Lincoln Park Grounds. In 1866, Champion approached Wright to propose a limited use of the grounds if the CBBC and Live Oaks club would put in $2,000 each to revamp the Lincoln Park Grounds.

Wright and Champion hit it off immediately and began speaking often. One day in a conversation, Champion — who was well aware of Wright's base ball status — invited him to switch over to the CBBC. The cricketers had already began to spill onto the base ball fields and practice with their counterparts. So Wright accepted. It was déjà vu all over again.

Wright's motivations were probably practical and financial. He knew cricket would not be nearly as stable as the growing game of base ball. Whether for this reason or another, he was followed shortly thereafter to the base ball field by Con Howe, George B. Ellard, and Sammy Keyes. The new ballplayers provided a new direction for the club and consequently the weaker charter members of the CBBC were grandfathered out.

The new and improved Cincinnati Base Ball Club did not take the field for a game until September 29, 1866. Though it would seem to be at a disadvantage, this was a match of the inexperienced versus the inexperienced. Their opponents in the match were the cross-town Buckeyes, a feisty assemblage of old town ballers. Town ball was a parent game of base ball and, like cricket, a convenient gateway to the new game. The unfamiliarity showed through as the Buckeyes, who somehow managed to win the game, tried to Indian-tag the runners and overrun the bases, like they would have done in town ball.

Despite the fact that the Red Stockings stumbled a step behind throughout the game, in one way they were a step ahead. Though Wright wore civilian clothes in the match that day, he is often credited with having introduced the eye-catching red stockings that became the signature of Cincinnati. In fact, it was George Ellard who took the field on September 29 sporting red stockings along with a white shirt, white pants, and a red cap. He would continue wearing the uniform again for all of the club's remaining four matches. In 1867, this became the club's regular uniform, although they were not adopted officially until the spring of 1868. By that time, one local writer described them derisively as the "Red Stockings"— and the name stuck.

Wright may have been incorrectly identified as the inventor of the red stockings, but his tremendous standing with the club was unquestionable. Despite his relative newness to the Red Stockings, he was unanimously elected captain of the club, which was most likely in deference to his prior status in the game and his clear superiority on the ballfield. Wright was not only the club's best hitter, but also its best pitcher.

Though he was a bowler for St. George's for several years, Wright rarely — if ever — tried his hand as Pitcher for the Knicks or Gothams. But once in Cincinnati, he translated the bowling technique to earn the reputation of "one of the most effective pitchers in the country," according to Henry Chadwick. The reason? He was known as the only hurler in the game who could change pace effectively. In effect, this meant he could throw his "slows" (most likely some form of a changeup) along with dew drops (now known as "curveballs") in contrast to most hard-throwing pitchers of the day. Since Wright's breed was rare in the game, he found that his method worked well in throwing off the strikers' timing.

The new, more strategic style that this presented on the mound curried instant favor among purists. The slows triggered a more scientific game because they were so conducive to pop-ups and grounders, and therefore necessitated a strong defense. The New York Times called for an all-out overthrow of the fireballing trend, declaring "swift pitching is not the style of delivery for a lively and pretty style of ball in which fine fielding is the feature."[2]

Wright's impact on the club was immediate. In 1867 the relative upstart Red Stockings went nearly undefeated, 16–1. This was largely spurred by Wright's rigorous coaching and offensive prowess. In those 17 games, he scored 112 times and legged out 22 home runs. His home runs tended to come in bunches — once even seven at a time! In a June 23 game versus the Holt Club of Newport, Kentucky, Wright not only pitched and won the game but he also racked up seven four-baggers off the helpless opposition. In one of his 1895 obituaries, this was noted to be the highest one-game total in base ball history.

Wright's influence was further felt in the club's attitude. He knew that professionalism was hurt by the stereotype that all pros were drunks and gamblers. But Cincinnati refuted this image with incidents such as a boat ride back from Louisville. After a win in the Kentucky city, the Red Stockings were celebrating aboard nearby a large assemblage of women. The ship captain decided this was a recipe for mischief, so he stepped firmly into their banquet room and ordered that there be no more "undue noise or hilarity," according to sportswriter Harry Ellard.

> With gentlemanly sense of honor the most victorious Red Stockings promised faithfully that the strictest decorum should be observed. This banquet stands on record as being the most unique, as well as the most silent one ever celebrated. Voices moderated to the lowest tone when toasts were proposed, no clinking glasses gave forth a sound, while "Hip, hip, hurrah!" was uttered in the most quiet manner. Champagne flowed freely, but the remarkable repression of ebullition of feeling among the Red Stockings seemed to temper the effect. The captain afterwards made the remark that it was the stillest party he ever saw where so much wine was present.[3]

The Cincinnatis again squared off with the Louisvilles—often called the "Eclipse"—on the Fourth of July. It was on that day that they debuted the new Union Grounds. The Union Grounds was, in fact, the old Lincoln Park Grounds. Once the Red Stockings and Live Oaks began sharing the grounds, the popularity of base ball gradually thrust its exponents into the foregrounds. The UCC plunged into debt and dragged the base ball clubs' prosperity down with it. Finally, the CBBC realized they would have to rid themselves of this weak link in order to become financially stable. So they bought out the cricketers and allowed them to die a slow death.

With the fifth wheel discarded, the Cincinnati management took on an ambitious project to revamp—even revolutionize—the Union Grounds into the "Finest Field in the West." The ballpark was planned out splendidly. Located only one mile from the center of the city, it was easily accessed by horse cars and even by foot.

The grounds itself was advanced, for its time. Above all, its most spectacular feature was the two-story veranda that hung over the first and third base sides. As the Red Stockings became more renowned, attendance surged, and seating was added on the third base side. The next year, a second deck was added.

There were primarily two factors at work in this project. First, Cincinnati was now set to pick up financially on the growth of its team and sport, by charging gate fees at the newly enclosed grounds. It raked in $340 at the first game alone, a substantial sum. But more importantly, as could be seen by that very game, it had a winning team on the field.

The match was supposed to begin at 2:45 in the afternoon, but spectators were so eager to see their new digs that they jammed traffic all the way down Seventh Street in time to see the Eclipse arrive on-field at 2 o'clock. Wright led off the game with a home run. But how many times does it happen in base ball that a player leads the offensive charge with a home run and then begins the next half-inning by taking the mound and giving up a double and a homer to the other team? Well, it happened to Harry Wright. But he bounced back with *three* more homers of his own and the Cincinnatis won the game, 60–24. By this time, they had begun to take on an air of invincibility. That would end ten days later.

The Red Stockings met their mortality as it dismounted the train at 10:40 on the evening of July 13. The Washington Nationals had just trounced the Capitol Club of Columbus 90–10 and were treated to a feast at their hotel before hopping the train car for a brief ride to Cincinnati. There they were to continue their 10-day, 3,000-mile tour. The idea of a tour had been pioneered in 1860 by the Brooklyn Excelsiors when they steamrolled upstate New York with a two-week undefeated trip.

The Nationals tour was set to be slightly longer than Brooklyn's, a three-week venture that they had embarked upon only two days before, on July 11. They set out looking for competition because there was so little to choose from south of the Mason-Dixon Line. The "Champions of the South" were portrayed as skilled amateurs, but they were really professionals in a thin disguise. The club was supposedly made up of federal government employees— mostly concentrated in the Treasury Department — but, in fact, the players did not work there. The Washington club used this as a way to pay the players without subjecting them to recognition as professionals. For example, the Washington Directory stated that George Wright, now the Washington shortstop, served as a clerk at 238 Pennsylvania Avenue; which was convincing until one realized that nothing was there but a private park.

Despite their dishonesty, the Washingtons made a gentlemanly and respected club, professional not just in terms of salary but also in behavior. Naturally, such a club invited the strictest adherence to etiquette and hence the Cincinnati reception of the Nationals on July 13. They were joined there by the rival Buckeyes, with whom they escorted the Nationals by stagecoach to the Clarendon Hotel on Walnut Street.

The next morning the Red Stockings and Nationals took the field in what was essentially the clash of the Champion nine of the west with the Champion nine of the south. Wright stepped into the pitcher's point and held the opposition at bay. After 3½ innings, the score was knotted at 6–6. The Cincinnati crowd became so excitable that they began cheering their hometown club. Wright and the Red Stockings were caught off guard by this showing of partisanship, something frowned upon at the time. They tried desperately to quiet the spectators, but when that didn't work, the Nationals did it for them by rallying to a 53–10 win. It was Cincinnati's only loss of the 1867 season.

The Red Stockings watched closely the next day when the Nationals took on the rival Buckeyes. Since the Nationals were expected to rout all competition along their tour, the Cincinnati clubs decided to determine the superior between the two by seeing who performed better in their loss to the Washingtons; either who allowed fewer runs, scored more runs, or had the lowest margin of difference between scores. How either club ranked the importance of these figures was not decided until after their games. That way, each member could take whatever position best suited his club.

The Buckeyes fell by an 88–12 score over 6 innings. Though their rivals had allowed 35 fewer runs and lost by a margin 33 runs slimmer, the Buckeyes claimed victory because they scored 12 times as opposed to Cincinnati's 10. By the time Washington boarded its boat to Louisville at 6 o'clock that evening, debate was already furious over who had outdone whom. (It's interesting to note that in a match as intense as this, the umpire selected for the Buckeyes game was Red Stockings Captain Harry Wright.)

In spite of the bitterness the Washington visit evoked, ultimately the experience set the wheels in motion for the prominence of base ball in the west. Clubs and spectators alike were charged by the dominating Washington tour to beef up and conquer the base ball world. "In the West baseball has become a mania with the people," declared the *Spirit of the Times* in 1868. "On the other side of the Alleghanies [sic] the ballplayers have worked themselves into an incandescent, and if they even escape melting they are lucky."[4]

Wright and Champion were determined to put Western ball on an even keel with the Eastern brand; and not just any western club, but the Cincinnati Red Stockings had to do it.

II.

In the winter of 1867-68, Champion decided to institute a 10-cent admission charge to the Union Grounds and told Harry Wright to sign as many top-flight base-ballists as he possibly could. So Wright headed east and signed three ballplayers to under-the-table contracts: pitcher/outfielder

Asa Brainard (a former Knickerbockers teammate of Wright's), third baseman Fred Waterman, and outfielder Johnny Hatfield. First baseman Charley Gould was inked as the only native talent, a member of the crosstown Buckeyes.

Later in the summer, the Red Stockings were still looking for a catcher, so Secretary John Joyce and Alfred Gosham traveled to Philadelphia to see a ballist named Johnny Radcliffe. When they couldn't attract Radcliffe, the two decided to stick around and scout for a week. One day, Joyce opted to see a ballgame while Gosham stayed home. One of the first batters he saw was a 22-year-old catcher named Doug Allison, who clubbed a long home run to deep center field. Joyce caught up with Allison after the game and convinced him to sign with the Cincinnatis. He turned out to be quite a find. "Allison proved himself one of the finest catchers in the country."[5]

The Buckeyes wanted just as badly to be King of the West, so they responded immediately by luring second baseman Charlie Sweasy and outfielder Andy Leonard from the Irvingtons of New Jersey, as well as other players. In addition, they leased five acres north of the Union Grounds to build a fine new field. This was really the last link to equality with the Red Stockings. Both clubs now had professionals, both now had state-of-the-art playing grounds; now the superior would be settled on the ballfield.

The Red Stockings took the first match by a 23–10 score on May 23, which set the stage for a Buckeyes must-win in Game Two. It would be three-and-a-half months before they reached that point. Once there, though, the Buckeyes still weren't prepared to handle the Red Stockings. They lost 20–12.

This was a tremendous disappointment for the Buckeyes. They had lost the season series to the Red Stockings and put their very survival in jeopardy. It was not until after the game that the public found out how far the Buckeyes had gone to avoid that.

On the previous evening, September 1, Johnny Hatfield — the club's most productive and least trustworthy member — was ushered off to a saloon by gamblers and loaded up with booze until he was heavily drunk. At that point he was offered $200 and a steady job if he would leave the Red Stockings and become captain of the Buckeyes. The next day, before the game, whispers went about the ballpark until they reached the Red Stockings' bench. Some of the players confronted Hatfield, and he admitted to the incident but insisted that now that the spirits had worn off he had no commitment to the gamblers. But the Red Stockings were not willing to trust him enough to let him play, so Hatfield sulked on the sidelines as the game was played.

The Red Stockings played the game under protest, but not even because of the Hatfield tampering. That morning, they had received a telegram from the Washington Nationals reporting that two of their players had revolved to the Buckeyes for that game and were being paid illegally to do so. These shenanigans were representative of the mischievous nature of the Buckeyes. The fact is, it was the bad character of their players that buried the club, not the bad performance of their players. They were the antithesis of the Red Stockings and even the Washington Nationals that they had sought to emulate. Their players were mostly self-serving and greedy. Their interest was in receiving a paycheck, regardless of what team it came from. And so they lacked the discipline and work ethic that drove their cross-town rivals to prominence.

When the inferiority of the Buckeyes became apparent, the club began to split. Sweasy and Leonard left for New Jersey out of homesickness and star pitcher Cherokee Fisher soon followed. The club's play became erratic and it ended the 1868 campaign with much less direction than when it had begun. So in January, management announced that the Buckeyes would become professional for the 1869 season. Reaction was critical, but three weeks later it was a moot point anyway. Low gate receipts from the base ball season and low skating profits from the winter made it impossible to pay rent on the grounds. So a lawsuit was brought against the Buckeyes, and they lost rights to play at their new grounds. In desperation, the Buckeyes procured the rights to play at the crude Iron Slag Grounds. It would have been difficult to draw there if they were good; but the Buckeyes were a terrible club, and few spectators bothered to patronize their games. Some talk was drummed up of signing professionals for 1870, but in the spring a Cincinnati reservoir owner, Mr. N. Ohmer, leased the grounds to convert it into a summer garden. The club was dead. One Cincinnati newspaper noted that the Buckeyes would have been the best club in the country if Harry Wright was its captain.

The exit of the Buckeyes left the Red Stockings without significant competition. Cincinnati's Live Oaks and Great Westerns were still active, but they had resigned themselves to fighting for the "championship of the home talent." So the Red Stockings were champions of the west. Great! ... Where to go from here?

"Cincinnati" was not the answer to that question — this the Red Stockings understood. They could not maintain financial stability playing ball in the Queen City, because what spectator would want to see the Red Stockings when he knew the nine would invariably blow out its competition?

Increasingly, the idea of a tour seemed to be the answer. Even the Buckeyes had taken one that summer, the first by a western club. The Buckeyes were not compelled to make this historic trip an ambitious one, though, by restricting its travels to six cities, most notably St. Louis and Chicago.

On August 24, the Unions of Morrisania (today a part of the Bronx) stopped in Cincinnati amid their own tour. Much like the Washington tourists of the year before they would lose only one game and have a very successful trip. Furthermore, their shortstop was George Wright. However, this time the Cincinnatis only lost by a much closer score of 12–8. The Red Stockings were not satisfied by this score; their initial goal that year was to compete with the top clubs, and they were not going to give up easily on the opportunity to do that. The Unions were invited to stay another day, and so they did. The Unions later claimed that this was planned to be an exhibition game; that way they could excuse the 13–12 loss to the Cincinnatis.

The reason the Unions cared about distinguishing between an official and exhibition game is because they were trying to win the Gold Ball Championship. At the beginning of the 1868 season, *New York Clipper* proprietor Frank Queen had offered the Golden Ball to the champion club of the year. In order to win the Ball, a club would have to defeat the Unions (who had been declared the 1867 champion, though the Nationals may have deserved it) in a best-of-three series. The Unions were not anxious to defend their crown ambitiously, so they had faced nothing but the easiest of competition until their tour. That's why the Unions were so insistent on recognizing the loss to Cincinnati as an exhibition. Just to be safe, they refused to risk a second loss by avoiding the Red Stockings during a visit to New York that fall.

Convinced by the success of the Washingtons and the Unions' tours, as well as by the threat of their own local predicament, the Cincinnatis set out on a challenging Eastern tour in September of 1868. Harry Wright had begun the season by aiming to put his club on par with the eastern clubs, and that's exactly what he was doing at the season's end.

The Cincinnatis set out by train for Washington. Much like the Nationals did along their way to Cincinnati in 1867, on their way to the Capitol the Red Stockings sang a club anthem, titled "The Cincinnati Baseball Club Song":

> We are a band of baseball players
> From Cincinnati City;
> We come to toss the ball around,
> And sing to you our ditty.
> And if you listen to our song
> We are about to sing,

We'll tell you all about base ball
And make the welkin ring.

CHORUS:
Hurrah! Hurrah!
For the noble game, hurrah!
"Red Stockings" all will toss the ball,
And shout our loud hurrah.[6]

After the trip to Washington, the Cincinnatis continued in a gradual northeastern course, to Baltimore, Philadelphia, and then Brooklyn, where they edged the tough New York Mutuals 29–28. Overall, it was a rather successful tour. The Cincinnatis won 10 of 14, falling to Philadelphia's Athletics and Keystones, the Olympics of Washington, and the powerful Brooklyn Atlantics on October 1.

It was not the only traveling that Wright would do that year. The All-England Club took him as its leader against an American nine. The first game was played on the St. George's grounds in New York, then in Boston and Philadelphia. Wright only participated in the first two. He was beginning to revive his ties to New York, even joining George in opening a sporting goods store in the metropolis. It wouldn't be the last time either one went into that field, but this particular business did not work out.

Wright could use the supplemental income at that point because he was, once again, a family man. Shortly before leaving Cincinnati, on September 10, Harry was married to Caroline Mulford. Once married, she was referred to as Carrie Richardson Wright for unknown reasons. Some have suggested that she adopted this name from a first marriage, but no information is known to support this. Wright's players celebrated the marriage by giving their captain a gold watch inscribed with all of the club members' names, which was wrapped in five $20 government bonds.

Carrie Mulford had been born in Cincinnati, circa 1840. From the best information available, it appears that she was the daughter of Dr. William Mulford, a nationally renowned physician who had helped to establish the Hospital and Sanitary Association during the Civil War. Carrie took his lead early on by caring for soldiers. But she did it in her own way, often by singing to them in her sweet, melodious voice. She was well-educated, a skilled musician, and a popular lady of society. She fit Harry perfectly.

The two were inseparably close, even mentally if not physically. Wright once wrote of a beautiful morning on the Connecticut River that he spent rowing a rented boat and "enjoying it amazingly." In the midst of it he dreamed that Carrie "was with one to enjoy, too."[7] He viewed his wife in the tradition of the time, both in her sentiments and household role. "Ah!" Wright once sighed, "the true rule is that a true wife [will be] her husband's servant in the home [and] queen in his heart.... She becomes the best that he can conceive, promises the highest that he can hope, purges what is dark in him, strengthens what is failing."[8]

Carrie's role as an actual "servant in the home" was limited. As of 1880, the Wrights housed a 24-year-old servant by the name of Catherine Roach. This was not unusual; Brother George's family had two. Carrie was a housewife officially, taking care of their seven children.

An image of the beautiful Carrie Wright. Born Caroline Mulford, she was often known as Carrie Richardson Wright, suggesting a previous marriage. Like questions in Harry Wright's other two marriages, the answer to the mystery may never be known. (Courtesy Halsey Miller, Jr.)

The first, Hattie, was born on March 30, 1869, followed by Stella (1870), Harry II (August 4, 1871), Carrie (January 27, 1874), Albert (December 20, 1874), and William (July 13, 1876). It was a large family; perhaps larger than Wright had anticipated. "At home I am looked on as considerable of a father of base bawlers," he wrote in December 1874. "...I am willing to be considered the father of this little game [Albert], but I wish it to go no farther. Seven is plenty, thank you."[9]

The children of Carrie and Harry were also too much for Mary Fraser's children. There seems to have been a large degree of resentment between the two step-families. For unknown reasons, the Fraser boys did not live in the same household as Carrie's children. In later years, Sisters Carrie and Hattie spoke infrequently of "some family members" who had sold some of their father's memorabilia, an unthinkable violation in the traditions of the family. The items they appear to have sold were a series of detailed scorebooks begun by Wright in 1878, and continuing through a debilitating eye injury in early 1890. He would score every inning of every game he managed in those books, National League or otherwise. At the end of each year, Wright would have the volume professionally bound between leather covers, with the date stamped in gold. Recently, an individual volume has sold for as much as $38,500.

The Wrights never forgot this insult. Before Carrie died, she made her grand-nephew Halsey promise that he would donate the bear knife sent to Sam Wright, Sr. and passed down to Harry to the Baseball Hall of Fame. She was frightened by the thought that it may end up on the memorabilia circuit somewhere.

Base ball and family was rarely a pleasant mix for the Wrights. As his base ball duties increased, Harry got to see his children only infrequently during the season. Once in July of 1886, his Philadelphia Club was rained out of a game in New York, so Wright hopped the earliest train back to Philadelphia and went immediately home once there. He spent a bit of time on the first floor before walking upstairs. After a while, Carried wondered what her husband was doing up there, so she went up and opened the door. "Why, dear," she exclaimed, "what in the world are you doing?"

Harry was taken aback by her surprise. "Why, wifey, I am putting the children to bed."

"Yes," Carrie answered, "but this is one of our neighbor's children — all undressed!"[10]

The two quickly redressed the child and hurried it on home.

Even when home, though, Wright was a busy man, as shown by a brief summation of his day once made to William Cammeyer. Harry began the morning by writing some letters before breakfast, then walked through downtown Boston to the Tremont Gymnasium. He arrived about an hour later and stayed until noon coaching "the boys"—as he affectionately called the players—and ensuring that they were "on their muscle." At 12 o'clock they took a break. Wright read a little of the *New York Clipper* and ate lunch at 1 o'clock. He then dressed for afternoon drilling on catching fly balls and stopping grounders that lasted until 6 o'clock that evening, while playing a picked nine in-between. On his way home, he stopped to pick up his telegrams in downtown Boston. "That is my active each day, pretty much, and sometimes I do just feel a little tired."[11]

Often the work did get to him. "It is all very nice for you to talk about 'prompt' in answering," he wrote jokingly to Cammeyer. "You can sit down in that smug little office of yours, behind a big Sigar [sic] and a little black bottle and scribble away to your heart's content. Now look at me. I'm writing at home in my bedroom, 11.15 o'clock, wife and little ones fast asleep. It is my best chance for writing. I have written three or four letters and have as many more to write, 'yet I am not happy.'"[12]

How did Wright end up getting so busy? one may ask. The reason is that base ball was on a bigger scale at this point, now that it had gone pro.

Four of Wright's children from his first two marriages: George "Willy" Wright, son of Mary Fraser, and Carrie's daughters Stella, Carrie, and Hattie Wright. Why selected members of these two fractious step-families posed together for this picture is uncertain. (Courtesy Halsey Miller, Jr.)

III.

The delegates in Washington for the December 9, 1868, NABBP convention came out with a monumental resolution that was less of an edict than it was a definition. "All players who play baseball for money, or who shall at any time receive compensation for their services as players, shall be considered professional players, and all others shall be regarded as amateur players."[13]

The news was welcomed heartily in Cincinnati — until Aaron Champion thought about it a little more. While the Red Stockings could now openly pursue a superior professional club, in order to do so he would have to ignore   and therefore worsen in the short term — his club's financial woes. Two weeks prior, the Cincinnati club members met at Mozart Hall to form a stock organization. The plan was to raise $15,000 in capital. $7,500 of the stock would go to current stockholders to thank them for their prior contributions. The other half was to be sold to new stockholders at $25 per share. To their disappointment, a meager $3,500 of the $7,500 allocated to new stockholders was sold by that spring. The CBBC needed that money; they were $6,000 in debt and trying to pay off the Union Grounds.

Ultimately, Champion realized that the best way to recover the debt was to build a ballclub with the caliber to generate national interest. To do that, he would have to construct a champion; not just an entertaining club that could draw pretty well, but a champion.

Champion tapped Ellard and Gosham once again to scout and sign talent. Their objective was to ink every man on the 1868 *Clipper* Gold Medal nine. Ironically, Gold Medal right fielder William Johnson left the Cincinnatis after they decided to go pro in 1869. But this was hardly the blow that spoiled Cincinnati's plans. Soon after attempting to crash the market, Cincinnati realized that it wasn't the only free-spender jumpstarted by the NA announcement. Besides, such a star-studded nine could never be kept intact. Players were so greedy now with professionalism in the picture that they rarely allowed team loyalty to get in the way of a bigger paycheck. The team of Champion, Ellard, and Gosham found the inner workings of this game within the game so confusing that they gave up and turned the reins over to Harry Wright.

Wright's immediate reaction was to suspend active efforts and begin studying his newspapers and scorebooks to find the best available men. From time to time, the information *came to him*, though, as young ballplayers would write to him looking for a job. Wright often received such letters throughout the years. Young men would send descriptions of their play with a photo, and frequently ask for advice on how to become a professional. One prospective big leaguer once wrote to him asking how to maintain a career in pro base ball. Wright answered, "In regard to diet, eat hearty Roast Beef rare with ... regularity, keep good hours, and abstain from intoxicating drinks and tobacco.... [B]e a sure catch, a good thrower — strong and accurate — a reliable batter, and a good runner all to be brought out ... by steady and persevering practice."[14]

Once educated on the candidates, Wright decided initially to look no further than Cincinnati. He swiped from the Buckeyes second baseman Charlie Sweasy, left fielder Andy Leonard, and substitute Dick Hurley.

However he did venture to Indianapolis to get the signature of his new right fielder's father. Cal McVey was only 18 years old, but impressive enough to earn a starting spot on the club. Though he was the youngest of the Red Stockings, he was part of a remarkably youthful club. Besides Wright and Brainard, no one on the ballclub was more than 23 years old. But Wright had the foresight to pick ballplayers who not only had the talent to build a successful team but the mentality to handle that success.

For the last link, Wright used a family connection to sign Gold Medal winner and brother George Wright. George had developed into the best base-ballist in the country by this time. Signing him in 1869 was equivalent to signing Alex Rodriguez in 2001. Although he was just entering his prime, he was, according to the *St. Louis Republican*, "The beau-ideal of base-ball players. His fielding exhibits science at every point, his picking, throwing and strategy could not be excelled, and he is plucky in facing balls of every description."[15]

George's play at shortstop was of the revolutionary brand. He was the first shortstop to play between second base and third while stationed at the back edge of the grass, a style that would not have caught on unless he used it to play the position well. "He covered more ground in his position than any other man in the country," recalled Harry Ellard, "and he and Sweasy made a pair that could not be surpassed. He was as active as a cat...."[16] The *Clipper* concurred, "He is very active, a swift and accurate thrower, and especially excels in 'judgment', as it is called, never being bewildered at the most critical moments in a contest."[17]

The latter comment addresses an interesting difference: whereas Harry Wright played the game by studious analysis, George played by his instincts. Though he was flashy at times—"I'd rather be Wright than President" spectators would cheer after an outstanding play—George was considered great because he consistently pulled off the routine plays with ease, like Derek Jeter today. He had a wide range, fine maneuverability, was quick in mind and fleet on foot. As a result, he was the only fielder of the barehanded era to maintain a .900 fielding percentage, and led the league in fielding seven times in the 1870's.

Unlike today, excellent fielders of George's era were considered stars even if they were weak strikers. What made George stand out was that he was a strong striker as well. He had deceptive power for a man of his size — 5' 9"—and would lead the 1869 Cincinnatis with 49 home runs to compliment a .633 batting average. When on the bases, he was a pesky runner. "[He is] full of capers," noted the *San Francisco Chronicle*, "...hopping about like a kitten on his base — now touching it with his hands, again with his feet, then falling across it with his body."[18]

Did George Wright realize how good he was? Yes, and he was often resented for it. People thought he was cocky, "has too much self-esteem," "thinks he is perfect." Otherwise his character mirrored Harry's by most descriptions. Despite that, it is most likely that George carried some level of self-conceit; why else would he wear the *New York Clipper* Gold Medal around his neck every day of the 1868–69 winter?

Part of George's value went beyond base ball. He was the type of personality that kept spectators entertained at the ballpark, using his ambidextrous ability to juggle bats and balls before games, or by mesmerizing the crowd with his sleight-of-hand tricks.

George also attracted the fairer sex to the ballpark with his good looks. He had curly brown hair, deep eyes like his brother, and a precisely shaven face. But, above all, he was noted for flashing his large, white teeth that earned him the nickname "Smiling George"; in fact, George was so cautious about protecting his smile that he often wore a mouthpiece in the field. One may find it quite ironic that one of the first pieces of protective equipment to be used in base ball was there for cosmetic purposes.

Along Cincinnati's tour of 1869, young women went wild for George. Once while visiting a city in the east, the girls there boldly raised their skirts high enough to show ankles covered with red stockings. Despite all the attention he received from the ladies, George was a single man and would remain so for the next few years. Until then, he lived with Harry and his family in Cincinnati. The house was only a ten-minute walk from the Union Grounds, so it was convenient for him. Sweasy, Leonard, and McVey all lived nearby at the Hummol House on Main Street. While in Boston two years later, Wright continued making such arrangements, housing George and McVey. Many of the other players stayed at the Highland House, next door to the Wrights. The charge was $21.00 a month, room and board.

George could easily handle such expenses. With Cincinnati, he had signed for a princely $1,400, the highest salary on Cincinnati's $9,300 payroll. (Harry was just under at $1,200.) While it's easy to sneeze at such figures today (and to toss that A-Rod comparison aside), these were truly enormous salaries at a time when the average American worker was topping off at $2.00 per hour and $525–$750 per year. When one considers that the Cincinnatis were being paid these sums for an eight-month period — March 15 to November 15 — the magnitude of the signing becomes all the more understandable.

Naturally, with salaries so outlandish, Wright took a lot of heat when he announced to the press that Cincinnati would be fielding an all-professional nine. Reaction to the announcement was decidedly negative.

However, under NA rules, the Cincinnatis had been a pro club during the previous season anyway. According to the new by-law, any nine that consisted of a majority of professionals (five) would be regarded as a pro club.

The Buckeyes, like a political party opposition, automatically dug in the heels against the Cincinnati decision. They already knew by the end of the 1868 season that their star had burned out; losing Sweasy, Leonard, and Hurley just gave them a good excuse to turn to amateurism. They tried to use that as a pious gimmick against the CBBC, but the city never responded receptively. People were often intrigued by a moral conquest, but not enough to spend their money on it regularly. However, they would gladly spend money on a good ballgame, and that's why they were so drawn to the Red Stockings.

At first the press regarded Cincinnati as a novelty. The club's professional status qualified them for recognition, but writers tended to treat it as a sideshow to contrast the real championship races. While most attention focused on the New York Mutuals and Philadelphia Athletics, the *New York Clipper* noted, "contestants for the championship ... will have to keep one eye towards Porkopolis."[19] ("Porkopolis" was a derisive nickname for hog-slaughtering Cincinnati.)

It seems that the Cincinnatis were often dismissed out of resentment, just like recent successes of the Florida Marlins or New York Yankees may be or have been downplayed out of contempt for their perceived "spend-to-win" strategies. Newspapers were quick to criticize the Red Stockings, even amid successes. After the club opened its season with a defeat of a Cincinnati picked nine, the *Cincinnati Enquirer* reserved a paragraph to note: "The baseball season for 1869 was opened yesterday by a game between the first nine of the Cincinnati Club and the field. The playing on both sides was very poor. There was quite a large number of spectators present, but the enthusiasm of last summer was lacking."[20]

Excitement picked up for the Cincinnatis' first game against serious competition on May 4 when they played the Great Western Club. Hundreds of raucous spectators followed behind the Red Stockings as they rode the streets of Cincinnati all the way to the Union Grounds in carriages draped with ribbons. The crowd was anxious to see if its nine could hold up against a solid nine, and, to their relief, the Red Stockings did by 45–9 score.

Wright was on the mound that day, as he was from time to time during the season. Most of the time he came on in relief of Brainard in order to throw off the strikers' timing. This was the first time that such a method had been put into use, and it was the conceptual forerunner to relief pitching. Whereas to that point, a second pitcher was used only after the starter could not go any longer — which was rare — Wright looked at the reliever as a strategic weapon for when the right situation presented itself. The move was effective for the Red Stockings. Commented the *Daily Alta California*, "The slow 'twisters' sent by Harry Wright bothered [the opposition] as much as the 'chain lightnings' by Asa Brainard."[21]

Whenever Wright delivered the slows, as opposed to his dew drop or fastball, he would tip off the catcher by flashing a hand signal, then notify the outfielder with one so they would play deeper. When in center field, he also used this method of hand signals to set up the outfield, and to use his own decisiveness to direct traffic. It's interesting to note that while Cincinnati played that season, Wright was virtually the only man to speak in the field. This system of defense was far advanced beyond that of other nines, which left most spectators in awe. "The Red Stockings have arranged a set of orders so brief," marveled the *Daily Alta California*,

> that frequently only the name of the player is called and he hastens to do what is requisite. [An] instance of their alacrity and perfect understanding was given ... when a sky-ball [was] sent between shortstop and right field, for which either might have gone, but the Captain called "McVey" and the right fielder at once put himself in position to catch it, but the Captain also called "Wright" in the same breath, and the shortstop ran and dropped on his knee under McVey's hands, so that if missed by the first it could still be caught before reaching the ground.[22]

Wright also introduced advancements in the defensive game by having his fielders position themselves in accordance with the hitter's tendencies. "In fact," wrote Henry Chadwick,

> Harry Wright would at one time be seen playing almost back of second base, while Sweasy would be nearly a first base fielder, and so they changed about, coming in nearer or going out further just as they judged the balls would be sent to the different batters. It is the lack of judgment like this that outfielders show their inferiority to the skillfully trained Red Stockings.[23]

Of course, not all were willing to accept the change. Cal McVey dismissed it to Wright as "some of your cricket notions, [and] you never see it done by any other clubs."[24] It was not surprising that a pro ballplayer would resent being told how to play his position. In McVey's case, he tended to "get ugly and show his temper," according to Wright. "He says that he has played in the field long enough and knows the striker well enough to know when to change his positioning without being told."[25]

Naturally, Wright wasn't going to please everybody with his methods. But, in the end, it got him results. These stratagems were components of a disciplined philosophy on how to play the game. Usually the players appreciated his style; across the board observers applauded Wright's developments and agreed with sportswriter Tim Murnane's assertion that he was the "originator of teamwork." The Cincinnatis continued these methods to tear through their competition throughout the month of May. In one game against Antioch College the Red Stockings made only four errors while the collegiates suffered through 32. Even against decent clubs like the Kekiongas of Fort Wayne, the Cincinnatis trounced them by a combined 127–15 score over two games. By Memorial Day (then known as Decoration Day) spectators were so certain of the game's outcome that they stayed away in droves. In hopes of putting up a respectable gate, the Cincinnati promotions department — otherwise known as Harry Wright — tried to hype the game into a big draw. To Wright's dismay, the skies were dark and threatening as game-time approached. Three innings into it, the rain began to pour down, and the game — which the Red Stockings owned by a 35–5 score — had to be cancelled. Cincinnati lost $60.

As difficult as the hit in the wallet was to take for a ballclub already in debt, the Cincinnatis took solace in their hopes that they were on the brink of a jackpot. They were going to take a five-week tour of the East, right out to the shores of the Atlantic. It was farther — much farther — than a western nine had ever gone. But it wasn't even this short-term prospect that was supposed to cure the club financially; it was the reputation that it would build. Cincinnati — against the toughest competition in the country — expected not to lose a single game.

On the evening of May 30, Champion, Joyce, and Wright gathered the club at Cincinnati's Gibson House Hotel. Henry Millar was also there. He was to come along with the Red Stockings on their tour so he could telegraph the nine's progress back to the *Cincinnati Commercial* on a daily basis to keep excitement strong in the Queen City.

As soon as the players were assembled, Wright ordered that they stay there, in the hotel, until the train left the next morning. He wanted them to be well-rested and prepared for the trip. (Asa Brainard had already meandered around the precaution by getting drunk before he arrived at the Gibson House that evening.) Champion followed Wright by extolling his men to keep up the good play and rack up the wins. Of course, they anticipated such bland pleas and weren't likely to care, so Champion used the motivational topic of money. The more the club wins, the more the spectators would come, he reasoned. The more people, the higher the gate receipts would be before being divided among the club.

Early the next morning, the Red Stockings entourage left the Gibson House for East Cincinnati. At seven o'clock they arrived at the Little Miami Railroad Station carrying just two dozen bats, two dozen balls, a bottle of antiseptic, and ten ballplayers.

The rains that harassed the Red Stockings through their stops in Yellow Springs and Mansfield cleared up a few days later by the time they marched the streets of Cleveland. Along the way to the Forest City ballclub's grounds women flapped red handkerchiefs at them from their window perches. It seemed that Cincinnati could make a killing there, but they only collected $81.

From there the Red Stockings rode to Buffalo, New York, for an upstate series. A sizable crowd came out for a win in Buffalo, as was the case in Rochester the next afternoon. Three thousand spectators showed up despite threatening skies and an awkward makeshift field on the public square. In the bottom of the first, Rochester's Alert Base Ball Club matched Cincinnati's output by scoring two runs to tie the score. The Red Stockings were just about to take the bat when rain suddenly poured onto the field. This did not last long, but it came down so hard that it flooded the grounds. There were no grandstands to hide under, so the two ballclubs scurried to an adjacent household and asked to stay there until the rain stopped. When it did, the field was soaked. The Rochester groundskeeper saw no point in trying to fix it and suggested the game be called off. But Wright knew the Red Stockings were in no condition to let another gate slip away. He immediately grabbed a bucket of sawdust and ordered his players to clean up the field. Several minutes later Wright walked to the Alerts bench and told them it was okay to play now. The Rochesters were not anxious to comply; at the end of the game they had lost the tie and succumbed to an 18–9 defeat.

In full uniform, the Cincinnatis arrived next at Syracuse's Salt Lake City ball grounds—only to find a meadow of ankle-high grass. The players stood in disbelief looking down at the weeds covering their feet. And that broken fence over there — was that part of the outfield? All of a sudden a shot rang out. The players dove for the ground and looked to the side. Two men were in the outfield carrying hunting rifles. One bent over to pick up the bird that had just fallen heavily before him, and stuffed it in a bag.

Wright picked himself up and walked over to the men. He introduced himself and explained what his team was doing there. "What is happening here?" he demanded. "Where is the Central City club?"

The hunter shrugged. "I don't know. No one said nothing to me about a ballgame. The grounds are being used all day for a pigeon shoot."[26]

Did Wright hear this man correctly? He had scheduled this game back in April. Maybe he missed the cancellation notice. In any event, he took the opportunity to give his men a rest. For 35 cents per man, he took them to a local health spa on Onondaga Lake. Where he got the money to do this from is anyone's guess.

Perhaps Wright was emboldened by his anticipation of the following game in Troy, New York, at which the Cincinnatis ended up making $281 in gate receipts. Ten thousand spectators had turned out to see them defeat the powerful Troy Haymakers 38–31. From there, the tour made its way through Albany and into Massachusetts, first Springfield and then Boston. The three games the Red Stockings played at the Hub, on the Boston Common, Riverside Park, and then in Cambridge, made for one of the first times the city had seen a professional brand of base ball.

On June 14, the Cincinnatis were scheduled to play Yale University in New Haven, Connecticut. But the game was rained out and Wright again had to turn to Millar for a loan to pay the club's way to New York City. The Boston games had brought such small returns that all profits from the Troy victory had been exhausted. But the club needed to get to New York City. See, all of Cincinnati's games to that point — with the exception of Troy — were ones they were supposed to win. The tour would be insignificant unless the Cincinnati pros could prove themselves against the principal ballclubs of New York, as well as Philadelphia. The Cincinnati faithful knew this as well. They were so anxious to know the outcome of the New York games that they gathered at hotels, cigar shops, and newspaper offices to see Millar's telegraph reports.

With the enthusiasm building at home and nearly as strong in New York, Wright and Champion were expecting the New York tour to replenish their depleted funds and cover the entire Eastern trip. But the more the rain fell, so did attendance. Only 1,500 showed up to see the Cincinnatis take on the favored New York Mutuals. Despite the marketability of the matchup, it's understandable that so few would attend. The winds were vicious and the clouds still leaden. It didn't look like this would be much of an afternoon for base ball.

As it turned out, the thousands that would otherwise have come missed a game that one paper declared "never had its equal and probably never will have." Mutuals pitcher Rynie Wolters kept the Cincinnatis at two runs through the seventh inning, whereas they were usually in the dozens by that point in the game. Brainard, with his motion the *New York Tribune* lauded as "beautiful, easy, and true," kept the Mutuals at bay with only one surrendered run going into the top of the ninth. The Mutuals led off with a double that aroused the slackening crowd. Sweasy watched another one fall in the same place, just over his head, for a single. Another hit drove in a run and the spectators got rowdy again. Before the game they had hollered at the Cincinnatis, "Wait 'til you play the Mutuals— they'll show you a thing or two!" Now, for the first time in eight innings, they believed it.

Dave Eggler popped the next pitch to 3rd base. As it descended, Wright shouted from the outfield "Two, Fred, two!" Waterman let the ball drop and flipped it to George, who had just dashed over to cover 3rd. George caught the ball and fired to Sweasy at 2nd for a double play. This play, usually executed by George Wright, would today be a victim of the infield fly rule and thus the double play would be nullified. This play, in fact, is the reason why the infield fly rule was created. As a result of the double play, the crowd died down and Cincinnati ended up escaping the inning with the tied score intact.

The Red Stockings began the bottom of the ninth with both a bad break and a good one. First Leonard tried to take second after a fielder misplay, but was caught in a rundown. Then the Mutuals allowed Brainard to get to 3rd on an overthrow to 1st. Catcher Charlie Mills kept a close eye on Brainard as he inched down the line while Sweasy stood at the bat. He kept such a close watch that he allowed a passed ball and, consequently, the winning run. Under the contemporary playing rules, the game was required to continue until the 3rd out was recorded, at which point the score stood at 4–2. "What a contest!" Chadwick exclaimed. "The Red Stockings are popularizing the game in the east like no other club has before!"[27]

The Cincinnatis lounged in the lobby at Earle's Hotel in New York City that evening, accepting repeated congratulations from admirers and reporters. Champion hushed the crowd and cleared his throat to address the crowd; he had just received a telegram from S.S. Davis.

ON BEHALF OF THE CITIZENS OF CINCINNATI, WE SEND YOU GREETINGS. THE STREETS ARE FULL OF PEOPLE, WHO GIVE CHEER AFTER CHEER FOR THEIR PET CLUB. GO ON WITH THE NOBLE WORK. OUR EXPECTATIONS HAVE BEEN MET.[28]

The players cheered loudly at the reading of this and drank several toasts until Captain Wright became afraid that they'd drink themselves into a loss in the next day's game. So he sent them to bed.

Contrary to the optimism of the Cincinnatians expressed in their telegram, the Red Stockings had not met expectations, but exceeded them. The Mutuals defeat was an upset, if only because Cincinnati was a western upstart and the Mutuals an established New York powerhouse. As a result of the surprise and the improved weather on the following day, a crowd between 10,000 and 12,000 swarmed the Capitoline Grounds. Some who wanted to see the game had to line up their carriages and wagons at the end of a hill near the outfield. An estimated amount of hundreds more hung onto trees to get a good view. One man even hung off of a church steeple with one hand gripping a lightning rod and the other holding a set of glasses to see the game.

Betting was heavy among the patrons there. One man ended up making $10,000 after riding the changing tide to wager in favor of the Red Stockings. Those who did side with the Brooklyn Atlantics, in money or in sentiment, were unusually vocal. Some feared the taunting would escalate into rioting. "We fear that eastern prejudices will be thoroughly aroused," wrote one Cincinnati sportswriter, "and resort will be had to all kinds of trickery to defeat our boys."[29]

For all the excitement, the game turned out to be anticlimactic. The Cincinnatis went up 5–0 after the 1st inning and scored 13 in the 2nd. From there, they cruised to a 32–10 win. Henry Chadwick observed, "While the game with the Mutuals rather astonished those who consider themselves posted in ball matters, the Atlantic match completely astonished them."[30]

"Our boys feel decidedly sick,"[31] groaned the New York Telegram after the Cincinnatis completed their sweep of the New York City elite with a 24–5 win over the Brooklyn Eckfords. Finally the Red Stockings were now being recognized as a legitimate top-rate nine. The Spirit of the Times exhalted the Cincinnatis as

> the only true exponents of the game today.
> Full of courage, free from intemperance, they have conducted themselves in every city they have visited in a manner to challenge admiration, and their exhibition of skill in the art of handling both ball and bat call for unexampled praise.[32]

The Red Stockings' conduct had indeed been commendable, and this helped to polish the image of the club. Not always were the Red Stockings on good behavior. When the club arrived in Buffalo at the beginning of the Eastern trip the players were tired. It was four A.M. As the carriages pulled up to take them to the hotel, Brainard convinced Fred Waterman to go see the town, and presumably get drunk. Wright immediately scolded Brainard, one of the older members of the club, for being a bad influence. Brainard listened to the speech, nodded obediently, and did it anyway.

So the Red Stockings were not as innocent as portrayed by newspapers that swore these fine gentlemen drank nothing "stronger than lemonade."

Sure, that may have been true of the Wright Brothers, but the rest had their own mischievous inclinations. If the newspapers can be trusted, however, the players did keep this in check.

> The players eat and go to bed according to routine. Breakfast is discussed from 7 to 8. A light luncheon of tea and cold meats is eaten shortly after noon — but no heavy dinners are allowed before a game. After the game, the young men appear in the next evening dress, and treat themselves to a square meal. Retirement to bed at a comparatively early hour is enjoined.[33]

How credible are these accounts coming from the romanticizing media? Certain instances bear out the gentlemanly image, such as a May 1870 game versus the College Hill BBC. After winning handily, the Red Stockings were invited to a Professor Wilson's home to eat lunch and chat — with about 20 college girls. The boys — George in particular — had just spent all day trying to impress them with daring steals of home and such, and thus "No over-persuasion was required for the boys were gallanted by the young ladies to the table."[34] Despite the obvious connection, the players maintained exemplary conduct throughout the afternoon. The only ruckus came about when Captain Wright told his men that it was time to leave.

After making such a name for themselves in New York, the Cincinnatis traveled on with a win in New Jersey before moving on for the final serious test in Philadelphia. First they discarded the Olympics of Philadelphia by a 22–11 score. But that wasn't the game that mattered. Now that Cincinnati had toppled the Mutuals, base ball enthusiasts were anxious to see them take on the other titan of the NA, the Philadelphia Athletics.

Approximately 25,000 spectators — a record crowd at the time — came to the game at the Athletic Grounds. Much like the Atlantics game, thousands of other lined up their carriages and wagons along the outfield grass. The game was heated even during the selection of the base ball. Wright wanted to use the lively ball of George Ellard's, but the Athletics insisted on a dead ball. Though Wright often relied on scientific hitting, he knew the slugging Red Stockings could pull the important game out with a ball conducive to their strength. But the Athletics won the argument because they had used the lively ball in their last game with the Cincinnatis. Now that a half-hour had been exhausted in settling the issue, the two nines began play.

Back in Cincinnati, the people were anxious. "Imagine two thousand people in and around the Gibson House waiting for the score," marveled the hotel proprietor Al G. Corre in a telegram that night. "Every minute roars and yells go up…. Oh, how is this for high?"[35] There was much occasion for cheering that day as Cincinnati shot ahead with a nine-run 6th inning to lead 17–3 and end up winning 27–18. Local newspapers compared the Red Stockings to a Chinese magician for their educated fielding techniques. But most talk was of the symbolism of this win — Cincinnati had solidified its position as the best ballclub in the nation. They had beaten all New York and Philadelphia competition handily (with a 45–30 win over the Keystones of Philadelphia the next day), the only close call being the 4–2 Mutuals match. The *New York Clipper* compared the tour to General Sherman's march of 1864.

The undefeated record of the eastern tour provided the coup de grace for the Red Stockings — a financial success. In reality, that is why management funded the tour. Cincinnati had been stumbling before it got to New York, but the Big Apple set them back on their feet with a healthy $4,474 profit. All told, the club came out $1,000 in the black. Perhaps most significantly, this helped Wright to establish the 50-cent admission charge as an acceptable standard. Other club officials shied away from such a high tax for fear it would alienate patrons, but the New York and Philadelphia games proved that people would pay double the normal rate to see an attractive game.

Before the Red Stockings could return home, they had some less consequential stops to make

Harry Wright in the Cincinnati Red Stockings uniform that he first conceived, circa 1869. The style of knee-length pants and stockings lasts to the uniforms of today. (Courtesy Transcendental Graphics).

in Baltimore, Washington, and Wheeling, West Virginia. Naturally, they won all these games, but it was their reception in these cities that proved interesting. In Baltimore, 5,000 spectators were in attendance; this was much lower than other Red Stockings games, but a record crowd for Baltimore. When the Red Stockings arrived in Washington, they were met by a throng of greeters sent by the Nationals club and driven to their hotel by horse-drawn coaches. Hundreds of Washingtonians lined the streets to cheer them and 8,000 showed up to watch their game, including government officials. Much like the Brooklyn man that stood on a church steeple, one spectator watched the game from atop the State Department.

After the game, the Red Stockings were treated to the privileges of Washington celebrity. First, a team portrait was taken at the studio of revered Civil War photographer Mathew Brady. The next morning, the players were invited to the White House by President Ulysses S. Grant. This was the first time a president recognized a base ball nine in such a way. Each player entered the room separately and was introduced to President Grant. "I believe you warmed the Washington boys somewhat yesterday,"[36] he noted, puffing on a black cigar as the players burst into laughter. Grant was the first president to really acknowledge base ball as an activity of some importance to the country. Even after Cincinnati's undefeated streak was broken a year later, the President sent a telegram two weeks later reading, "The San Dominican Treaty is dead, but the Red Stockings Base Ball Club still lives. In this I find consolation."[37]

The Red Stockings' stay did not last much longer before they left the White House to march down Pennsylvania Avenue, singing their club song and getting ready to head back West.

IV.

The song picked up in Cincinnati, when the Red Stockings arrived at the Miami Railroad Depot. Five thousand Cincinnatians fired off guns and fireworks, threw money, waved banners, and sang the club song. The Red Stockings had just given them two important things: civic pride and lots of money. "I don't know anything about base ball," acknowledged one grateful Cincinnatian, one of several at the ballpark later that day that had never before watched a game. "But it does me good to see these fellows. They've done something to add to the glory of our city." A friend nearby interjected excitedly, "Glory, they've advertised the city — advertised us, sir, and helped our business, sir."[38]

Cincinnatians by the hundreds followed behind the Red Stockings' caravan of carriages covered with flowers and ribbons, singing alongside the Zouave band that played "Hail to the Chief" in honor of Harry Wright. Streamers floated down from the building tops all along the way to the Gibson House.

Once inside the hotel the players tried to pacify the audience by appearing briefly on the balcony. They soon returned inside to eat lunch and prepare for their game. At two o'clock the Red Stockings returned to the streets and paraded to the Union Grounds to defeat a picked nine. Prior to the game, the president of a local lumber company and member of the CBBC presented the Red Stockings with a 27-foot long, 1,600-pound base ball bat.

That evening, a banquet was held at the Gibson House. Flowers, flags, and bunting adorned the walls, and one wreath was hung for each of Cincinnati's wins on the Eastern tour. At the entrance of the room, a red and white banner read "WELCOME HOME, RED STOCKINGS." After dinner, speeches were made by businessmen, politicians, and club members. Champion spoke last. "Someone asked me today who I would rather be, President Grant or President Champion of the Cincinnati Base Ball Club." He paused to glance at the players. "I immediately answered him that I would by far rather be President of the Base Ball Club!"[39] The crowd responded with a loud cheer and once more broke into the club song before wrapping up the evening with a lively rendition of "Auld Lang Syne."

More than anything, this was a night of civic — and especially Western — pride. In reaction to such displays, the Eastern counterparts became resentful and sought to discredit the Cincinnatis. The locale of a ballclub, they argued, was nominal; it was the source of its players that characterized a nine as Eastern or Western. Since only McVey and Gould were Western natives, this made the Red Stockings a truly Eastern nine. Cincinnati had to concede that fact, but they justified their Western identity by claiming the players as adopted sons. What did that mean? The majority of the Cincinnati nine had played in relative anonymity elsewhere; it was only under the leadership given by Harry Wright and other Cincinnati club members that these players became productive contributors to a first-class ballclub.

Perhaps out of their bitterness, or perhaps just a fear of defeat, the Eastern clubs initially refused to return the visit made by the Red Stockings, as would have been customary. The Washington Olympics were the only ones to respond immediately, by playing in Cincinnati on July 2, 5, and 13. The Red Stockings disposed of the Olympics in all three games. In fact, their only true competition of the month came from the Forest Citys of Rockford.

The Cincinnatis started the game by scoring three runs, but the Forest Citys responded with four in the 2nd. For the rest of the game, each team matched the other tit for tat. In the 8th inning, Rockford pitcher Al Spalding connected for a key hit to spark a five-run inning. He shut down Cincinnati in the bottom of the inning, and Wright did the same to Rockford in the top of the 9th. Trailing 14–12, Wright singled with one out in the bottom of the inning and advanced to 3rd on a Leonard single. While inching off of 3rd, Wright signaled to Leonard for a double steal. On the next pitch, both men took off and slid in safely to make it a one-run game. The seemingly impermeable Spalding kicked the dirt in frustration as the crowd celebrated. Brainard followed with a double and Sweasy drove a hot grounder towards left field. Shortstop Ross Barnes dove, but he could not reach it. Brainard rounded 3rd and crossed home in a shower of confetti.

Shortly after this game, the Red Stockings left for a three-game tour of the Midwest. They scored easy victories in Milwaukee, Chicago, and Rockford before returning to Cincinnati for a three-week home stand. Finally, a northeastern team returned the visit of the Red Stockings by coming to Cincinnati; of all clubs, the negligent Syracuse nine. In the first game, the Red Stockings won easily by a 37–9 score, but the second game was more complicated.

With Brainard reeling from another long night out, Wright took the mound against Syracuse. He proved rather ineffective as the two clubs headed into the 8th in a 22–22 tie before the Red Stockings broke through with 13 runs in their next at-bats. But soon the light began to wane and the Cincinnatis knew they'd better go down quickly before the game had to be called off and their rally negated. With little hope of surmounting their new deficit, Syracuse sought to let the game be called and take the tie instead of a loss. And it seemed that Syracuse had the advantage since it was yet to record an out in the top of the inning. When Wright struck out for what was ultimately the only time that entire year, Syracuse complained excitedly to umpire Joe Doyle that it was intentional. Doyle quickly calmed them down and restored play. After two singles, Syracuse was pacified. Then a grounder was hit to their third baseman for what seemed to be the first out; but he turned the tables on Cincinnati by purposely throwing wide of 1st base to extend the inning. Unwilling to continue engaging this war of wills, the Syracuse captain ordered his nine off the field. Doyle did not accept Syracuse's decision. He promptly ordered them back to the field, but the team would not listen. At this point, Doyle called the game a forfeit in favor of Cincinnati, a 36–22 win.

After a bout with the Brooklyn Eckfords, Wright decided to give his men a week off at the Yellow House resort in Yellow Springs, Ohio. After all that had overtaken their lives in the past few months, the players needed a break; and perhaps it was the interruption that rejuvenated them for the rest of the season. Or perhaps it took them too far away and cost the Red Stockings their only blemish of the 1869 season.

Suspicions were heavy on the morning of August 26. There were rumors that two or three Red Stockings had been bought off, and when Brainard gave up six runs in the 1st, the whispers grew louder. Four of the runs had come with two out, on muffs by Waterman, McVey, and Leonard. It was this type of suspicion that deterred several other clubs from playing the Troy Haymakers. Some swore never to play Troy again, despite their drawing power and usually stiff competition. Wrote the *Cincinnati Commercial*, "The Haymakers, while strong players, are not of good reputation. [They are] in the hands of New York gamblers ... [who] are used like loaded dice and marked cards."[40]

The Cincinnatis came back with 10 runs of their own in the top of the 2nd, but Troy responded equally, as it would continue to do throughout the game. By the time the 6th inning came, the two were tied at 17–17. Inevitably, the close score had come with some controversy. In the 2nd, umpire John Brockway had mistakenly called a Cincinnati runner safe at home when he was obviously the third out. Six runs came across after that. In the top of the 5th, Troy catcher and captain Bill Craver tried to bully Brockway into changing his ruling on a steal of second, but the umpire stood fast. Haymakers President John McKeon threw aside his chair at the scorer's table and stormed onto the field. While pumping his cane in Brockway's direction, he threatened that if any more close plays were called against Troy, the team would be called off the field. Wright knew that McKeon was looking to set up a walk-off if the Haymakers went ahead or tied up the ballgame, so he tried to head McKeon off at the pass by offering a different umpire. McKeon refused, which only confirmed Wright's suspicions.

In the top of the 6th, Cal McVey fouled a couple balls towards Craver behind the plate. On the second ball, Craver caught it on the short hop of a third bounce and thrust his arm up with a handful of dirt. "How's that?" he grunted. Under the rules of 1869, the batter would be out if his foul ball were caught on the first bounce, or "the bound," as it was called. Brockway was so sure that it had bounced more than once that he simply laughed at Craver. "It bounced three times!"

Though Craver had no case, he had the passion to tempt Brockway to be convinced. His eyes bulged and the veins cut through his neck. "You're blind as a bat!" he hollered. "You've been calling plays against the Haymakers ever since the game began!"[41]

As Craver rampaged, McKeon again stepped forward and ordered his nine off the field. The Haymakers began grabbing their equipment and heading towards their omnibus as the crowd assaulted them with catcalls and heavy objects like bottles, rocks, and vegetables. The Haymakers scurried for their places on the coach and sped away as fast as they could, trailed to the Gibson House by an angry mob. Wright and Champion had tried to convince McKeon to call them back, but he ignored them and left the Red Stockings alone on the field.

With the Haymakers gone, Brockway climbed a chair near home plate and made an announcement to the crowd. "The Union Club of Lansingburgh, New York [the official name of the Troy Haymakers], having withdrawn from the game, I decide the Cincinnati club has won the game." Brockway even personally penned this decision into Wright's scorebook. So how could there be any dispute that Cincinnati had won? At the time, there was little, except on the part of the Haymakers. At the 1869 NA convention, a motion in Cincinnati's favor was put forth to officially resolve the result as a win and not a tie. However, the league Judiciary Committee dissented and kept the 17–17 tie. The basis for this judgment is not known, but with the Haymakers involved one wonders how they may have influenced the decision process.

Additionally, the NA delegates voted to have Cincinnati return the $1,000 in gate receipts that they had withheld until an apology was issued to Brockway. Though McKeon pretended not to need the money, Cincinnati was their biggest draw, and the profits from this could have covered nearly all of their traveling costs. But Chadwick pointed out that the NA's decision had to be approved by the Judiciary Committee. In the summer of 1870, the Haymakers settled the issue by sending an apology to Brockway, and the money was restored with interest.

Immediately after the game, the fury was still strong. The Haymakers were so frightened of the Cincinnatians that they hid upstairs at the Gibson House while McKeon spoke to the press and citizens from the coat room entrance. Craver's catch, he said, was just the tip of the iceberg. Brockway had been making partisan calls for the hometown Red Stockings all day.

Cincinnati didn't buy it. The Buckeyes immediately canceled their game with Troy for the next day and joined with the Red Stockings in boycotting the Haymakers until Brockway received an apology. "We have plenty of games to play and can go right on with our tour,"[42] McKeon shrugged, feigning indifference. The Haymakers left the city for Washington as soon as they could.

The Buckeyes and Red Stockings had formed an unlikely alliance.

Now that the Red Stockings had succeeded in crippling their rival's prestige, they sought to bring them back to some level of prominence. Perhaps this was done to provide profitable competition for Cincinnati without having to go on tour. An August 31 game designed to encourage funding for the Buckeyes defeated all these purposes. After a 103–8 thrashing by the Red Stockings, it had become apparent that they would have to become a traveling club.

V.

Wrote William J. Ryczek, "Like Alexander the Great, the Red Stockings were quickly running out of worlds to conquer."[43] Local competition was unfruitful and the Eastern clubs didn't want to come west. So the Red Stockings themselves went west.

Champion had been speaking with San Francisco grounds proprietor William Halton about coming to California. The brand of base ball played there at the time was the outdated version taught by old Knickerbockers members and other transplanted Easterners. A visit by the Red Stockings provided an opportunity to update their play and generate interest in the game, much like the Washington Nationals' ambassadorship to the Midwest in 1867. Financially, the tour looked promising. Clearly, the Red Stockings would sweep all its games against the inexperienced Californians, but interest would be high. The Pacific Coast had never before been visited by a major league club; now they were to be visited by the best in the country.

On September 14, Cincinnati boarded a Pullman train bound for St. Louis to meet up with Halton and play a couple games. Pullmans had come into use in 1865, and quickly gained prestige as the most advanced commercial train in use. Unlike most trains, they had three-tiered sleeping quarters so the players wouldn't have to forego sleep, as they would on most other trains. There were luxurious rooms for smoking as well, but none for dining; the players had to pay expensive fees for bad food at whistle stops along the way. Henry Millar condescended that

> The Crestline way of washing down dust is to offer the wayfaring man sundry shreds of juiceless ham, and peach pies that are chiefly remarkable for their resemblance to circles of raw dough filled with white.... Nothing but the irrational thing they call hunger (which is not hunger, but impatience) could induce a man to lacerate such provender with his teeth.[44]

Once back on the train, the players passed the time by singing, reading, and hunting. The latter was Wright's idea. He picked up his gun and poised it on the windowsill, taking aim at the antelope, buffalo, bison, deer, and prairie dogs that caught his eye. His aim was poor, though, due to the constant shifting of the train cars. "The cars zig zag in such a manner that is the next degree from impossibility to stand erect while on board," wrote Henry Millar. "Then not only do they zig zag, but they jump up from the tracks."[45] While traveling through Iowa and Nebraska on the return trip, the passengers saw piles of crashed train cars scattered near the railroad tracks.

But the most intense fear was towards the American Indian tribes that inhabited the area. Attacks by these groups had just been reported in Montana, Nebraska, and Kansas, and the ballplayers had no cause to feel exempt. As Ryczek noted, the natives had about as much respect for the game of base ball as Americans had for their traditions. Fortunately, General George Custer had just been sent out west to take care of the problem.

The Red Stockings arrived in Sacramento on September 23 unscathed. Ballplayers were often considered good luck charms on a train because it seemed that accidents never involved them. Henry Chadwick once reported an instance in which a lady was boarding a train with her escort, a man named Harry. "How about that tunnel, Harry," she said, uneasily. "I feel awfully nervous." Harry quickly dismissed her concern. "Oh, you need not fear a bit, we have a baseball team on the train."[46]

The route to Sacramento had not been a pleasant one. The Pullman had stopped to switch to the Central Pacific Railroad at Promontory Point, Utah. Just four months prior, on May 10, the Central Pacific had been linked with the Union Pacific at Promontory Point to complete the first transcontinental railroad. Once on the Central Pacific, all baggage had to be taken out of the sleeping cars and stored elsewhere. All on board wore the same clothes for the two days necessary to reach California. Along the way they encountered "a succession of barren, dried-up [lands], covered with alkali dust, and occasionally intermingled with clotted ponds of stagnant water."[47] One player called it a "grand and effective scene, composed in a measure of telegraph poles, dry land and sage bushes."[48]

Once the Pullman arrived in Sacramento, the players took a brief trip by steamboat along the Sacramento River to San Francisco. San Francisco Association of Base Ball Clubs President John Dunkee met them there, along with selected members of the Association and 2,000 eager base ball enthusiasts. Six luxurious stagecoaches waited to take the Red Stockings to the downtown Cosmopolitan Hotel. The enthusiasts followed alongside in a parade.

The reception by the San Franciscans was enthusiastic. Champion had to decline an elaborate banquet to be hosted at the hotel that night. His players had come to play, he explained, "and did not wish to make any superfluous show of themselves." Instead, they ate a quiet lunch with Halton and a few others. In the next few nights, the players did venture out to the opera and the state fair. Despite this good treatment, according to Millar, the entire squad was homesick. "'Tis not because they are many thousand miles away from their favorite city, but more because their disappointment in this place is so great.... Without a single exception, it would be a most difficult task to persuade any of them to remain any longer than their engagements call for."[49]

The San Franciscans had high expectations for their visitors. "The Red Stockings, it is said, will open the eyes of those who consider themselves 'base-ball sharps' as they make the game so much superior to the old style, that they bear the same relations as chess and chequers."[50]

The Red Stockings began their games by easily defeating the Pacific Coast champion Eagles twice. On the night after the first game, the Eagles showed the gentlemanly manner of the old New York clubs by taking the Red Stockings to the Alhambra Theater to watch a play.

The ballplayers then switched gears with a game of cricket won almost exclusively on account of the Wright brothers (George produced 53 of the 118 runs himself) before beating up on the Pacific Club twice and then the Atlantic BBC once. The defeat of the latter was so lopsided, 76–5, that the *San Francisco Chronicle* published its box score under the headline "Suicides Yesterday."

Seeking a competitive game, the Red Stockings divided up into squads of the Harry Wrights—comprising the Wright Brothers, Gould, Allison, Sweasy, and four Californians—versus a set of nine others, including Brainard and the rest of the Cincinnatis. The Wrights won 20–7, the closest match of the Western tour; but despite the lack of competition, the tour was actually quite successful. Four thousand spectators attended their 13 games and made the Red Stockings $1,000, which accomplished their first stated objective of the tour. The second was met as well. Interest in base ball was cultivated in California, as the Red Stockings had helped to do nationwide. A significant portion of the breakthrough number 1,000 ballclubs was located in California.

After a game on October 4, the members of the Eagle, Pacific, and Atlantic clubs saluted the Red Stockings with a banquet in the Pacific Hall at the California Theater. A number of toasts were made by the San Franciscans, ranging from the heartfelt to the humorous in nature; the latter, of course, was of the watered-down 1869 brand. "Our National Game," one deadpanned, "may we never think it Wright to let our exertions in its support come to a short stop."[51]

Another one was dedicated "To the best Captain any club could have." The crowd immediately exploded into cheers and calls for Wright to make a speech. He blushed at the attention and thanked them for the compliments, but declined to make a speech. When the people insisted, he rose reluctantly and spoke a few words that were "inaudible to the reporters' gallery." Wright's sheepish attitude toward speeches can be considered either humble or insecure, but it most likely was a blend of the two. "[W]hen it comes to making a speech or writing an article for publication I'm a failure," he once explained. "On the field, with bat and ball, I feel, or rather did feel, quite at home. When it comes to wielding the pen — I wish I were other men. That's all."[52]

The banquet ended after one o'clock that morning. Later that day the Red Stockings boarded a train for Sacramento. From there, they retraced the old route through Nevada and Utah, before trekking through Wyoming on the way to Omaha, Nebraska. At a 45-minute layover in Cheyenne, George Wright and 17-year-old Cincinnati substitute Oak Taylor jumped off the train to look at a plant shop to find a certain type of flower they had been collecting throughout the trip. "All aboard!" the conductor suddenly hollered and the train whistle blew. But no one knew where George and Taylor were. Champion ran to the conductor to tell him to hold up while Wright ran about frantically in his trademark linen duster, a hat he wore so much that some believed he slept with it on. Soon enough he found them and the trio raced back to the train while the other passengers yelled angrily for them to get on board and stop delaying the trip. The players laughed hysterically at the sight and made fun of them for it throughout the trip to Omaha.

One writer's favorite story of Wright's train travels came later in his days with Cincinnati. The train had stopped for a layover in Pittsburgh and Wright sat down at a railroad restaurant to get a piece of pie. When he bit into it, the pie tasted rather cold, so he called over to the waiter, judged by a newspaperman to be an Ethiopian man. In his light British accent, Wright ordered "Take this pie to the fire and 'eat it."[53] The waiter obligingly strolled over to the stove and ate the pie.

When the Red Stockings arrived in Omaha shortly after the layover in Cheyenne, they were surprised at how badly they had underestimated the knowledge and excitement of the enthusiasts there. Champion had rejected games in Stockton, Denver, Cheyenne, Laramie, and other moderately-sized cities because he didn't believe they could produce a gate receipt to cover the club's travel costs.

A sizable crowd turned out for the game that day, including Grant's Vice President, Schuyler Colfax, and other notable generals in the west to check on railways and Army outposts. Wright impressed the distinguished crowd with a four-hit game en route to a 65–1 win. The score was so skewed that towards the end the spectators turned their attention to a pair of dogs growling in the stands. Lulled by the blowout on the field, they began encircling the two dogs to encourage a fight. Champion was both upset and humiliated that there was more attention focused on a dog fight than his club's game. He stomped over to the umpire and threatened that if this was not stopped, he would call his nine off the field. He was quickly obliged and the game was resumed.

Wright followed his performance in Omaha with two more four-hitters to make three in four games. After having played one more game in Nebraska, one in Quincy, Illinois, and a finale in Indianapolis, the Red Stockings pulled in to the Cincinnati train station late in the evening of October 16. Surprisingly, there were fewer people there to receive them than on their return from the East. Perhaps the novelty had worn off. But there were still hundreds of citizens that paraded behind their coaches all the way to the Gibson House, and the celebration looked much the same as it had three months prior.

As winter set in, Cincinnati scrapped to salvage whatever momentum its base ball fever had left. October 18's game against the Philadelphia Athletics was billed as the "Last Grand Game of the Season." The game attracted 8,000 spectators, mostly covered in blankets to protect against the October chill. The two clubs rewarded their bravery with a tight 17–12 ballgame taken by the Red Stockings.

After a short trip to Louisville on November 3 the Red Stockings returned to Cincinnati on the 6th for the last game of the season. The game started at one o'clock instead of the usual three o'clock to adjust to earlier hours of darkness that came with the fall. Despite the lingering winter coldness that also joined it, 7,000 spectators came to see the Red Stockings close out their undefeated season with a 17–8 win over the Mutuals. "The closing game of the 1869 season," Wright noted in his scorebook, and added above his initials the conquering victory cry of Julius Caesar: "Veni! Vidi! Vici!"

Wright's pride in the season just completed can be easily read between the lines of that scorebook. On other occasions he refused to write anything so bold as "Veni! Vidi! Vici!" After the last scheduled game of the 1878 season was rained out, he penned this simplistic entry: "No game. Very cold and windy. Stockholders failed to put in an appearance. Nine all on hand and disbanded for the season. 'Champions of the United States' for the sixth time since the organization of the club in 1871."[54] A victory cry for his personal viewing was a statement of restrained ecstasy from a man who was known to only sheepishly tip his cap after an outstanding play in center field.

Wright's deviation from his usual pattern can be attributed to a pride that he had never before faced. His club had become the only professional nine to ever play a whole extended season undefeated, though the exact number of wins accumulated in that time has never been settled. Newspaper accounts have listed the wins as ranging from 57 to 61. Some modern accounts have even inflated this figure to 69. Wright was the only one to concede a tie to the Mutuals and magnanimously lower the win total to 56. His method was to only count wins against NABBP opponents. Since picked nines did not fit under that umbrella, he did not recognize them. Some have looked at this as a condemnation of the picked nines as weak opponents, when in fact they were stronger than several of the NA clubs Cincinnati faced. Wright actually denied them because they were temporary; only established ballclubs were considered for the win column.

Therefore the official record of Cincinnati for the 1869 season included 56 wins against NA nines and one tie. Victories also were accomplished at the expense of several picked nines. Should they be recognized in the Cincinnati win total? The best illustration to judge this by today's perspective would be to ask if a win by a major league club against a minor-league affiliate should be counted on its season record. Of course it shouldn't. So the record officially stands at 56 wins and one tie; in rational consideration, it stands as 57 wins, no ties, and no losses.

Along the way the Red Stockings traveled 12,000 miles from coast to coast, scoring 2,396 runs and averaging a 40–10 win in each game. They spent $29,724.87 and took in $29,726.26 in gates, making for a profit of $1.39. In the sense that they had possibly the best season in history, this was a financial failure; in the sense that they avoided finishing in the red, it was a success. Regardless of finances, the Red Stockings had completed what the *New York Clipper* declared "The greatest achievement since the healthful and exhilarating pastime was first incepted."[55] Historically, the Cincinnati season has been regarded with this reverence, which effectively negates the disappointments of the ballclub directors. "No club in the United States, nor, in fact, all the clubs put together, have done so much toward creating a furor for baseball and making it so pre-eminently a national pastime as the Red Stockings,"[56] *The San Francisco Chronicle* said at the time.

VI.

Henry Chadwick recognized the Cincinnatis as the national champions of 1869. "The result of the season's play places the Cincinnati Club ahead of all competition, and we hail them as the champion club of the United States."[57]

But the claim to a championship title in 1869 was a nominal one. There were no divisional winners, no playoffs or World Series games; the champion was in the eye of the beholder. The only somewhat organized method of determination was the confusing Gold Ball Championship, which Cincinnati refused to entangle itself in.

The Gold Ball was more a test of the champion club's keep-away skills than base ball skills. Once the Eckfords got it they did their best to avoid threatening competition before losing to the Atlantics on November 8 after considerable haggling to even set a third game up. Once the Atlantics won it they dealt with the Red Stockings in the same way that the Eckfords had; having lost to them once already, they delayed a potential second loss until the season was over. Secretary Joyce reminded the Atlantics that they had vowed a return match to Cincinnati after the Eastern tour visit, and after a while, the Brooklyn representative wrote back to decline because some of their players couldn't get out of work for that length of time. (The Atlantics were still feigning amateurism.) Joyce even offered to come to Brooklyn to settle the series but he received no answer. Finally on November 11 he received a telegram from Brooklyn proposing a game one week later, on Thanksgiving Day, November 18. It was well-known that the Red Stockings' contracts ran out on November 15.

Any championship system run by self-serving champions was bound to lose credibility once the proper alternative appeared. Inevitably, the emergence of the undefeated Red Stockings reduced the Gold Ball to a championship of New York. Said the *Spirit of the Times*, "For any other club to set itself up as champion in the face of such a record as has the Red Stockings is preposterous."[58]

Cincinnati also refused a three-team, six-day tournament to figure out the national championship in 1870. The tournament was discussed early in the season and continued to be considered throughout. But the idea made little sense. A championship tournament involving three ballclubs (the Red Stockings, Athletics, and Mutuals) shut out every other club in the country from a chance at a title. Why would the teams bother to try? Why would people bother to attend their games? And if the tournament took place early in the season — as it was originally proposed — how could anyone be certain that the best three teams of 1870 were playing for the championship? It would not be the first time nor the last time that the superior nine did not emerge until mid-season.

The sphere of competition had expanded by 1870, thus forcing base ball observers to reconsider the New York-oriented championship focus (until the Yankees began winning titles 50 years later). Some of this expansion came about in hopes of emulating the success of the Red Stockings, while some organized to dethrone them. The Chicago White Stockings were established on October 12, 1869, to do both. The club was outspoken about its desire to become the top nine in the West, "one that will not allow the second-rate clubs of every village in the Northwest to carry away the honors in baseball,"[59] according to management.

One of Chicago's first moves was to try to lure George Wright away from Cincinnati with $2,600. George chose to stay put for a slightly lower salary of $2,500, a $1,100 raise. All of the players received a raise for the 1870 season, bringing them in the $1,500–$2,000 range. Despite other lucrative offers in the market, Cincinnati retained each player, although Sweasy came close to leaving.

One must remember, contracts only ran from March 15 to November 15, so in the meantime the Wrights oversaw the Union Skating Park until springtime rolled around. Excessive rains had flooded the Union Grounds by this time, sending Wright and Champion scrambling to prepare the field for pre-season play. On April 18, the Red Stockings had their first game before a meager 400 spectators. They defeated a picked nine by a 34–5 score before boarding a steamboat down the Ohio River to Louisville and then onto New Orleans, Louisiana.

Joyce had gotten the idea for a southern tour after New Orleans' Southern Base Ball Club came to Cincinnati in August, followed by the Lone Stars of New Orleans. He suggested that the Cincinnatis travel south, but there was not enough time left in the season to keep its existing commitments and schedule another tour, so the club decided to go in the spring of 1870.

This was the first time a ballclub had toured the south before the season began, and therefore it is tempting to consider it the first example of spring training. But, as will later be shown in Wright's development of the practice, spring training is a concept and not a function. When done with the intention of getting out the rust of winter and fine-tuning the team's play for the season, that is spring training. In the case of the 1870 Cincinnatis, they were looking for a lucrative tour that fit conveniently into the confines of their schedule.

While this *was* the motivation, it is certain that Wright regarded the tour as somewhat of a warm-up for the season. He counted training as a high priority throughout his managerial career, one of the most ardent practitioners among his colleagues. Wright's preferred locale for training was the gymnasium. In 1878 he wrote that his players

> receive[d] orders to be at the Gymnasium for exercise from 10 to 12 A.M. [sic] and 2:30 to 4 P.M. This will consist of throwing, pitching running and jumping, swinging light clubs and dumb bells, rowing, pulling light weights, and in fact doing a little of everything to keep them going and assist in making them supple and active. When the weather is favorable they will meet on the grounds in the afternoon at 2:30 for practice. This will comprise a half-hour's indiscriminate throwing, batting, and catching; then they will assume their regular positions in the field, with, say two, taking alternative turns at batting — 8 strikes each, all hits counting — to be relieved by two others in turn until all have been at the bat. With three men at the bat, the bases can be run as in a game, giving two or three outs to each batsman. No loafing or shirking should be permitted, and yet the Manager or Captain must study the temperaments of his men and be guided accordingly from commencement to end, in his judgment as to what should and should not be done.[60]

In spite of his patronage of the gymnasium, Wright still ranked game-style practice ahead of all other forms of training. "Give me ten day's practice in the field and the other teams can have their month's practice in the gymnasium," he told the *Sporting News* in 1887. "In my opinion one day on the field is nearly as good as one week in a gymnasium."[61]

The Cincinnatis arrived in New Orleans to take the field on April 25. They were greeted by a chilly reception unlike California or New York. The Civil War had ended only five years before and New Orleans was still occupied by Federal troops. In the shadows of the shanties of the Reconstruction-era ghost town, the Cincinnati tour must have come across as a cruel joke when the Northern nine swept a five-game series in the Crescent City by an average 44–5 score.

While in New Orleans, Wright was tempted by lucrative offers to play games on the Sabbath. Sunday ball was a controversial issue throughout the 19th century, especially as early as 1870. But in New Orleans it was no big deal. However, Wright was not at all in favor of the idea; in fact, in 1891 he turned down a managerial post with the Brooklyn ballclub simply because they accepted the practice.

For practical and philosophical reasons, he was opposed. On the practical basis, he acknowledged that crowds were larger on a Sunday, but he believed this only drew away from attendance on Friday, Saturday, and Monday. Therefore, the club gained little or no advantage at the cost of a moral sacrifice. Wright especially valued this principle because he was a practicing Episcopalian. He attended church regularly and even brought the whole Red Stockings ballclub to a service while in Philadelphia on the 1869 Eastern tour. It was not the only time that these two aspects of his life blended. He once conceded to a friend, "Even in church yesterday I had base ball all mixed up with the prayers and sermon."[62]

After six days in New Orleans, the Red Stockings took a steamboat up the Mississippi to Memphis, Tennessee, and Rockford before returning to Cincinnati. On May 30, they embarked again on an Eastern tour beginning in Cleveland, then on to upstate New York, Massachusetts, and New York City. The trip did not start as smoothly as the year before. On the train to Cleveland the roof of the car ahead of the Red Stockings burst into flames and sent its passengers scrambling back to cramp the players. The brakeman took care of the fire, but the train reeked of smoke the rest of the way.

The club rode out of Boston on the way to Worcester by stagecoach on June 9. When they arrived at the hotel in Worcester a score of enthusiasts swarmed the lobby to greet them. Wright and Gould appeased them by discussing base ball while the other players sneaked upstairs. The people continued to speak with them for a while, and one offered to reward Gould for his attention with a bottle of champagne. He thanked the man for the offer, but declined.

When the Red Stockings took on the Fairmount BBC at Worcester's Driving Park the next day, many wondered whether Brainard had accepted such an offer as Gould had turned down. He staggered on the mound to a 3–0 deficit, leading many to believe that he took the field drunk, before Cincinnati bailed him out with a 24-run rally just in time to beat the rain. The downpour that canceled the game had begun as a drizzle the evening before and continued through to cancel Cincinnati's next game in New Haven, Connecticut.

The Cincinnatis returned to New York City on June 12 to play a four-game series to begin against the Mutuals the next day. In contrast to the previous year's experience, the Cincinnatis were expected to "win all the games played, because the New York nines [are] not harmonized," according to one New York paper. When the ballclub arrived at Brooklyn's Union Grounds at three o'clock that afternoon, 10,000 spectators were packed into the grounds. "It's the Cincinnatis!" some yelled, as the small town spectators had the year before. "Here come the Red Stockings!"[63] The Cincinnatis looked to be as strong as the previous year when they easily defeated the Mutuals 16–3.

After three days of rain, the skies finally cleared up for Cincinnati's game against the Brooklyn Atlantics on Tuesday, June 14. It truly felt like a June afternoon, sunny and humid in the mid-80's. An estimated 20,000 spectators came out for the game, though not all paying customers. Noted the *New York World*, "Hundreds who could not produce the necessary fifty-cent stamp for admission looked on through cracks in the fence or even climbed boldly to the top, while others were perched in the top most limbs of the trees or on roofs of surrounding houses."[64] The Atlantics claimed that only 5,000 of these people had paid for tickets, just as the Mutuals had allegedly lowballed the estimate of the previous day's crowd. Cincinnati figured it had been swindled out of $1,000 between the two games.

The Atlantics had a reputation similar to the Mutuals as a troubled, disreputable ballclub. But, in this case, Brooklyn's bad image was a product of the combative attitude of its players. Captain Bob Ferguson was known as a gentleman off the field and a tyrant while on it. He had an offensive way of dealing with his players, often yelling at them during games. Concluded the *Clipper*, "He is a bully who most players are afraid of and consequently none respect."[65] The club in-fighting came to a head in an early May practice when one of his orders was ignored by a player and Ferguson stormed off the field.

The atmosphere within the Atlantics was still tense when Cincinnati came to town, leading some to believe that they were in no mindset to win such an important game. Others thought that if any team in the east was going to do so, it would be the Atlantics. The 32–10 drubbing they had endured the year before was known to be misrepresentative of the club's capability.

The Red Stockings took the early lead and exchanged it with the Atlantics until going up 5–4 entering the bottom of the 8th. With one out, Brooklyn third baseman Charlie Smith shot a line drive out of Allison's reach in left field for a triple. Joe Start followed with a sharp hit to McVey in right when he cut the ball off in time to force a close play at home. All Allison had to do was catch the ball and reach down for the tag, but he missed the throw and the score was tied at 5–5 going into the 9th inning.

Both sides were held scoreless in the 9th to keep the score a tie after a full regulation game had been played. One of Brooklyn's biggest gamblers, Mike Henry, then stepped onto the field to demand that the Atlantics walk away. He wouldn't lose any money on a tie, but he would on a loss. Ferguson was leaning that way already. If the game ended in a tie the players could pocket their share of the gate receipts and then make $300–$400 off of a rematch. Ultimately, his decision may have been made for prestige and the drawing power of it. Noted the *New York Tribune*, "To have played a nine inning game with the famous Red Stockings and tied them with so small a score as 5–5 ... seemed the very acme of fame."[66]

Wright sprinted in from center field furiously, and soon he was joined by Champion. The two argued with umpire Charley Mills about the validity of this walk-off. Wright knew the rules stated that a tied match was to continue "unless it be mutually agreed upon by the captains of the two nines to consider the game as drawn." Wright knew that Mills deferred to his knowledge of the rule book, but he had to consult the impartial Henry Chadwick first. The group walked over to Chadwick's seat where he was watching the game from that day in his hometown of Brooklyn. Chadwick concurred on the conditions of a tie, and now the decision was up to Wright.

Somehow Mills got the impression that Wright had consented to the tie, and he began walking to his coach. When the spectators saw this, a good number of them began to cross the field to leave. Someone reached Mills just as he was getting in his wagon to inform him that Wright wanted to continue. Mills immediately dismounted the coach and hurried back to the field to recall the Atlantics. Ferguson was reluctant to continue but careful not to incur a forfeit. He rushed to the Brooklyn clubhouse and brought his men back to the field.

Back in Cincinnati, thousands of loyalists crowded around the Gibson House in electric tension. "During the progress of the game people stood by the hundreds in the streets and around the newspaper offices," described one Cincinnatian, "watching the result with an interest equal to that manifested during the [Civil War] when waiting for the news from the front."[67]

The skies were darkening by the time the two clubs took the field for the 10th inning, 25 minutes after they had finished the 9th. The delay did not faze the pitchers, but it may have gotten to the hitters. Brooklyn held the Red Stockings scoreless in the top of the 10th, as did Brainard in the bottom half, thanks to George Wright's patented double play with one out and a man on 3rd. Brainard opened the 11th with a double, advanced to 3rd, and scored on a McVey sac fly. George Wright added an RBI single to put the Cincinnatis up 7–5 and seemingly put the game away.

As lines of spectators left the grounds in disappointment, Charlie Smith came to bat and stroked a single, then advanced to 3rd on a wild pitch. The crowd surged with newfound excitement as one of their steadiest hitters, 1st baseman Joe Start walked to the plate. Once in the box, Start connected with a Brainard pitch and sent it arching high to McVey in deep right. McVey drifted back towards the outfield boundary lined with spectators, hoping to cut the ball off on its first bounce. As he was about to reach it, a man suddenly shot from the crowd and tried to wrestle McVey from getting to the ball. Reports have since become part of lore that the man jumped on his back, but shortly before McVey's death in 1926 he attested that no sort of interference had seriously impeded his pursuit of the ball. McVey threw off the man's grip of his shoulders and picked up the ball. As a policeman hustled over to swat the man with his billy club, McVey made a long throw straight to 3rd to hold Start there with a triple. The score was 7–6 with none out.

John Chapman grounded to Waterman for the first out, which brought up Bob "Death to Flying Things" Ferguson. Facing a situation similar to that which had put the Atlantics away in the 10th, Ferguson decided to bat lefty in order to keep the ball away from George Wright. It was also a ploy to affect the Red Stockings psychologically. This was one of the first notable instances—if not the first—of switch-hitting in base ball history, and it was sure to throw Brainard off a bit. Instead of a pop-up, Ferguson laced a single through the right side of the infield to tie the game again.

The crowd began to roar louder than they had all day. The club that had last defeated the Red Stockings, in October of 1868, now had a chance to do it again. Ferguson was on 1st, only one out had been recorded, and the Cincinnatis were vulnerable. Brainard delivered the ball to Brooklyn pitcher George Zettlein, who smoked a sizzling grounder between Gould and the 1st base bag. Gould managed to stop the ball, but could not get an out. George Hall followed with a grounder to George Wright at shortstop that seemed like an inning-ending double play. But George's toss to Sweasy at second got away and trickled into no-man's land in right field. McVey tore over to the spot where the ball had bounded as Ferguson sprinted from 2nd and on towards home. McVey scrambled to pick up the ball and throw, but Ferguson crossed the plate with the eighth and winning run.

The two clubs played out the inning, as the rules dictated. Afterwards, the Red Stockings left the grounds slowly to a thunder of jeers. "The yells of the crowd could be heard for blocks around and a majority of the people acted like escaped lunatics,"[68] reported the *New York Sun*. Interestingly, the New York papers were more apt to acknowledge interference on the McVey play than Cincinnati was. Under a heading of "Defeated by a Brooklyn Crowd," the *New York Herald* empathized with the Cincinnatis for having to play "against the crowd, together with the opposing nine, that the crowd interfered with long-hit balls, and that they received nothing like a fair showing to win."[69]

The Cincinnatis did not rely on these irregularities; Wright's only recorded sentiment on the loss was that he felt satisfied with the quality of play. Champion seems to have concurred. After the game, he returned to his hotel to write out a telegram to the Gibson House:

NEW YORK, JUNE 14

ATLANTICS 8, RED STOCKINGS 7. THE FINEST GAME EVER PLAYED. OUR BOYS DID NOBLY, BUT FORTUNE WAS AGAINST US. ELEVEN INNINGS PLAYED. THOUGH BEATEN, NOT DISGRACED.

A.B. CHAMPION
CINCINNATI BASE BALL CLUB[70]

The news was received mournfully in Cincinnati. After finding out about the loss, several city businesses covered their buildings in black. Initially, the reaction was overly dramatic, but soon the citizens inevitably accepted the mortality of the Red Stockings. "It becomes the good people of our Queen City, to bear with philosophy the fact that the famous Red Stockings at last have been vanquished," wrote the *Cincinnati Commercial*, "no doubt the burden is grievous to be borne, but in the varied affairs of human life, the contemplative mind may find other things fully equal in importance to a first-class game of base ball."[71]

The most significant impact of the Brooklyn victory over the Cincinnatis was not the existence of the blemish itself but the psychological effect on future play. The shield of invincibility that had regulated the psyche of each Red Stockings player in threatening situations had now begun to crumble. Conversely, the cynical supposition on the part of their opponents that a close game or a tie was as near as they could come to victory had also withered away. These clubs— no matter how small— now believed for the first time in a full year of Cincinnati dominance that they had a legitimate shot at winning.

Despite the crack in their confidence, Cincinnati remained resilient. "No defeat or series of defeats will destroy the Cincinnati Base Ball Club,"[72] Champion assured in a letter to the *Cincinnati Commercial* upon the club's return to the city. In the immediate aftermath of the loss to the Atlantics, this seemed to be the case as the Cincinnatis rolled over the Unions of Morrisania, the Resolutes of Elizabeth, and the Brooklyn Eckfords.

On June 18, however, the stability of the Cincinnatis was in question. Brooklyn was still celebrating the success of the Atlantics four days after the event, and, much like celebrations of Red Stockings successes, the whole city seemed to share in the festivities. The Brooklyn Stars were going to challenge them that day, and the city took on the perspective that because it was a Brooklyn team involved, they were sure to topple the Red Stockings. The *New York Daily Tribune* covered the event like a royal procession:

Up the Brooklyn hills the over-taxed horses labored, and conductors elbowed through the crowd while drivers and passengers vied in energetic remarks.... The scene at the Capitoline was a lively one. The sun shot down its intense rays upon the immense crowd without pausing to make any distinction of age, sex, or color....[73]

Future Hall of Famer Candy Cummings was on the mound for the Stars. Cummings, the man who is credited with developing the curveball, didn't find his pitches particularly effective that day, but they were enough to keep the game close. After six innings, the score was tied at 11–11, but in the 7th Gould broke it open with a three-run homer to lead Cincinnati to a five-run rally.

Four days later the Cincinnatis arrived in Philadelphia to play the Athletics before an estimated 15,000–20,000 spectators. This massive crowd proved that whatever aura had been extracted from the Red Stockings mystique with the Brooklyn loss, people were still attracted to their games, if only because they believed their club would deliver the second loss.

The Philadelphians' hopes seemed justified when the Athletics went up 11–4 after two innings. At that point, the Red Stockings realized that Brainard would not be able to carry the team that day, so they would have to kick in the offense. Seven runs in the 3rd inning tied up the game and began a see-saw battle that came to 25–21 Red Stockings after seven. The Athletics quickly conceded two outs to open the bottom half of the 7th, but then a run scored and two men were put on base for Dick McBride. The usually light-hitting pitcher hit a three-run homer to tie up the game and set off a raucous celebration in the crowd. Cincinnati finally responded in the top of the 9th with a single, error, and a double to go ahead 27–25. Brainard managed to nullify a leadoff double by putting down the Athletics for the win.

The Red Stockings capped off the tour with a defeat of the Keystones of Philadelphia, then two wins in both Baltimore and Washington. By the time the club played its final game versus the Washington Nationals on July 29, the players were worn out. George Wright had wrenched his knee in the previous day's game and Allison's hand was raw from catching Brainard's fastballs for a month. In desperation, he covered his disjointed fingers with what the Cincinnati commercial described as a "buckskin mattress." Allison's use of a glove was a first in pro base ball. Gloves were considered unmanly at the time, and that is probably what drove Allison to discard it after the game.

One of the most outspoken critics of the use of gloves was George Wright, who nearly 50 years later scoffed at the daintiness of gloved ballplayers. "The players did not have gloves to protect their hands," he recollected proudly to the *New York Sun* in 1915, "consequently more skill was required to catch the ball, because with the greater weight there was danger of severe injuries unless a hard hit or thrown ball was handled perfectly."[74]

The Red Stockings left Washington immediately after the Nationals game and took the train to Cincinnati. They arrived back home a full 24 hours earlier than expected, so nothing formal was set up like after their two 1869 tours. A few young boys were collected at the depot, and after a while several notable Cincinnatians filtered in after hearing the news. The Red Stockings mingled for a bit before mounting their coach for the Gibson House.

On July 1, the ballclub officers—$7,200 richer as a result of the eastern tour—threw a lavish banquet for the players at Pike's Music hall. The prideful club members had taken to heart Champion's declaration that the Cincinnatis were, "Though beaten, not disgraced." Each speaker acknowledged the loss but hastened to add a positive slant to his assessment of the ballclub. Said one member in a speech, "I feel satisfied that although they were beaten on one field once, that thing cannot be done again ... and having a Champion at their head, I think they will see to it that this thing does not happen again."[75]

The Red Stockings nearly proved him wrong the next day versus Rockford. Cincinnati started off at a disadvantage when George was forced to umpire the game instead of playing shortstop, due to his injured knee. Cincinnati started well, but then allowed Rockford to slowly creep back into the game. After going up 10–3 early, the Red Stockings' margin dissipated to 14–10 after eight and then 14–13. Cincinnati held on for the win, but over a week later, on July 11, the Forest Citys tied them at 16–16 with an eight-run 9th inning rally. At that point, the umpire waved his hand at the sky to call the game off on account of darkness. Across Cincinnati, an unforgiving shockwave swept through the base of their bandwagon.

After narrowly defeating the inferior Harvard BBC at home by a 20–17 score—Millar noted that though this provided a "majority of the tallies, nobody would claim it as a victory"[76]—the press began to turn on the Cincinnatis. Certain newspapers alleged that the ballclub had deliberately allowed the Forest Citys to inch closer on the July 2 14–13 win so they could build up interest in the Fourth of July rematch. The *Cincinnati Gazette* owned the toughest criticism: "The team that charges fifty cents to see a good game of ball and then makes no attempt to play it properly is just as guilty of swindling as the man who stands on the corner and passes off [fake] watches on a victimized public for gold ones."[77] Snickered another writer, "Their grand games take place abroad, but they reserve their milk-and-water contests for this city."[78]

The only loyal supporter locally was the *Cincinnati Commercial*, largely due to Millar's close ties with Wright and Champion. The paper was reluctant to take on the accusatory tone of its colleagues, and in doing so ignored the obvious. Late in the season, the paper half-heartedly held to its claim that "no dissension exists in the nine."[79]

In fact, strong divisions did form on the Red Stockings between Wright's disciplined faction — his brother George, McVey, and Gould — and the rowdy dissidents— Brainard, Sweasy, Leonard, Allison, and Waterman. According to Champion, "There was a great deal of jealousy between [the two factions]. The one side claimed that the Wrights were always assuming certain privileges exclusively for themselves, and the Wrights maintaining on the other hand that they were only performing their duty."[80]

The problems with the latter group varied, but generally the issues revolved around a relaxation of the personal standards of behavior that had established the credibility of the ballclub the year before. Brainard had made a practice of destroying himself, whereas Sweasy did his worst damage to the team by corrupting Waterman and Leonard. Of Sweasy, Wright later wrote, "His influence over Leonard came near ruining him. Andy had a narrow escape."[81]

On the field, Sweasy also came under fire for alleged indifference. "There is no doubt that 'Sweas' can play second base when he tries,"[82] noted the *Clipper*. The most intense criticisms were reserved for Allison. "[Allison's] lazy antics are utterly without excuse," asserted the *Gazette*, "and he does not gain any credit in indulging them."[83] Most writers attributed this flaw to an inflated ego. According to the usually cautious *Commercial*, "Mr. Allison's organ of self-conceit has been terribly enlarged this season.... The public expects work, and no fine airs, and no exhibition of crooked temper and exaggerated self-importance."[84]

Was the Cincinnati press backlash warranted? According to an outside eye, the *New York Clipper*, no.

> [There have been] unjust comments [by] the Cincinnati papers on the play of the nine in games wherein the Reds have not been able to sustain their high reputation for invariable success. The fact is, the Cincinnatians have become so puffed up with the great success of their pet club that they have lost sight of the existing fact that the natural progress of the game and the effects of energetic rivalry have led to the organization of nines pretty competent to hold their own against the strongest.[85]

Unfortunately, any hopes of adopting this rationale in Cincinnati were erased by further losses. On July 27, the Red Stockings took on the Philadelphia Athletics at the Union Grounds. The latter built up an early lead and kept the Red Stockings at bay until late in the game. In the top of the 9th, with Cincinnati trailing 9–5, George Bechtel muffed Sweasy's line drive and allowed a run to score. Brainard, who had began on 1st base, inexplicably stopped at 2nd when he could have easily made third and perhaps home. Sweasy, who had been running hard with his head down, ran right in to Brainard near 2nd base. Second baseman Al Reach picked up the ball and tagged Sweasy on the ground for the 2nd out. To end the game, George Wright took an unheard-of called 3rd strike, and Cincinnati had lost, by an 11–7 score, its first home game since August 24, 1868. This was closely followed by a near-loss to the Mutuals in which the Cincinnatis surrendered an eight-run lead, rallied to tie it up, and then won on Gould's homer in the 9th.

One of Cincinnati's worst losses was sustained nine days later when George Wright was injured in a game against the Haymakers. George crouched his body as he neared 2nd base on a steal when baseman Billy Dick lost his balance and fell heavily onto Wright's leg. George collapsed to the ground and passed out. When he regained consciousness moments later, he could not put any pressure on the leg and had to be helped off the field by teammates. From there he was rushed to a local doctor who found a torn ligament that would put George on crutches until his return in October. He would end up missing 16 of the team's 74 games and re-injuring his leg in an on-field collision with Harry on October 22. In the meantime, he was replaced aptly by Leonard, while substitute Harry Deane took over in left field. But the nine was hurt by the absence of George's leadership, as well as his offense and defense.

Only 2,500 spectators bothered to show up for the game despite the addition of a new grandstand only days before. But Champion had assured only six days before to the club members that all was well. At the club's monthly meeting at Mozart Hall, the president read an extensive account of the Red Stockings' financial history and current state. The debt that had been incurred between 1866 to 1869, he reported, had not even been erased by the previous season's success. After the last paycheck was handed out for the 1869 season, the club was still $1,000 in debt. He had to take out private loans just to fund the Eastern tour of 1870. But it proved to be a good investment because $10,000 had been made, over $7,000 in profit — significantly better than the $1.39 of 1869. At this point, he was happy to report, the Cincinnati ballclub was $4,200 in the black, and he would back it up with a committee to audit club records.

Having said that, Champion then announced that he would step down as President. Secretary Joyce and Director Thomas Smith resigned as well. His reason for leaving was that he couldn't handle the long hours and heavy responsibilities of President. Now he could pursue his law practice and run for Prosecuting Attorney in Cincinnati, a course which seems curiously similar in hours to his job with the ballclub. Obviously, Champion was putting a good face on an ugly situation. He was abandoning ship before it sank.

Clearly, Champion knew the Cincinnati ballclub was in trouble. He most likely figured that if the club went south while he was at the helm, it could hurt his image in Cincinnati that he had worked so hard to cultivate. Club members who either denied to themselves the inevitability of the collapse or dreaded that Champion's resignation would expedite it, begged him to remain as President, but to no avail. The organization had lost its leader at exactly the point when it most needed leadership.

The feel-good moment of the Red Stockings' season when the club rallied from a point of adversity to reclaim its championship never happened. Instead the club began taking its damages in bunches. On August 26, the Cincinnatis were in Portsmouth, Ohio, to take on the Riverside BBC. To everyone's disbelief, the Riversides were leading 27–23 going into the last frame. Pitcher Fitzsimmons easily retired McVey and Gould, only to have his shortstop muff Waterman's pop fly that should have ended the game. Instead Waterman was on first with an error and scored as a result of singles by Allison and Harry Wright. Leonard seemed to have let the Riversides off the hook with a high fly ball to left. The fielder had a beat on the ball but lost it in the sun. As it dwindled down toward the ground he stabbed with his glove and made the catch, according to the umpire. Wright immediately ran off of his base to demand from the umpire an appeal. The two walked out to the left fielder to ask if he had made the catch cleanly, and surprisingly he admitted that he had not. The game was resumed with a Brainard single to load the bases. Sweasy capitalized by slugging a deep fly ball toward the center field fence, which center fielder Rodwich sprinted after but could not reach. All four runners crossed the plate for a game-winning grand slam.

Aboard the steamship *Fleetwood* that night, Sweasy celebrated the victory in his usual fashion. He and a couple other unidentified teammates got drunk that night and ended up fighting over the breakfast table the next morning. The three finally stopped once the ship captain threatened to pull the boat over and throw them off.

The newspapers quickly got a hold of the story and publicized the players' misconduct to the humiliation of the ballclub. Sweasy was expelled by the club executive board upon return to Cincinnati on the grounds of "disgraceful conduct." New President A.P.C. Bonte used Sweasy as an example in his pledge to rid the Red Stockings of all "intemperate, insubordinate, and disorderly members." Yet only 24 hours later Sweasy was reinstated by Bonte. According to Bonte, this was an isolated incident that Sweasy apologized for and promised never to repeat. Most likely, the decision was based on two less noble reasons. First, Bonte was being besieged for use of excessive punishment among the Cincinnatians, and secondly, the Red Stockings had a big return match with the Atlantics coming up that week.

Sweasy received an excellent reception that day from the meager 6,000 spectators present. Given the gravity of this rematch, management had expected a crowd perhaps twice that size. Sweasy acknowledged the cheers as he ran to 2nd base by touching his cap bill several times, then hit a homer and scored three in the 14–3 Cincinnati win to further appease the crowd.

After the game, Champion emceed an on-field ceremony that was rather symbolic in nature, to revive senses of pride in the Red Stockings and also stress the need for good behavior among the players. Holding a red silk banner, he spoke to Wright and the ballclub.

> I have the honor on behalf of a number of ladies of our city, to present you this beautiful banner. These ladies desire in this token to express to you not only the pleasure they have felt in witnessing your play, but also wish to testify their approbation and delight that you have made the word [sic] "Red Stockings" which is placed on this flag on which the name is written, and that no stain shall ever be put upon it by your action, but that it may remain white and unsullied as now.[86]

Wright responded in kind, picking up on the subtleties of Champion's admonition.

> On behalf of this nine, I wish to say to these kind givers of this flag, that we sincerely thank them for this gift, and also thank them for their kind feelings— thoroughly appreciated by us— which induced it. We shall always carry this banner with us and, though it may not on every occasion float over a victorious ball field yet it shall ever wave over us as victors over all temptations.[87]

By the end of the next month, Wright's statement was disproved. Though he was correct that the Red Stockings would not always be victorious on the field, Sweasy also faltered off the field once again. In the rubber match of the Red Stockings/Atlantics series, Cincinnati was beaten once again on a 9th inning Brooklyn rally allowed by four errors and a passed ball. Afterwards, Sweasy and an unidentified teammate walked into a local saloon in full uniform and got badly drunk once again. This violated club policy, broke Sweasy's earlier pledge to clean up his act, and brought yet another black eye on the organization. But nothing was done.

In the one-and-a-half month lapse between Brooklyn games, Cincinnati had managed to release its grasp on prestige that otherwise would have compelled Bonte to more seriously discipline Sweasy. Besides an October 15 loss to the usually manageable Forest Citys, the Red Stockings lost two critical games to a team and a city they loathed: Chicago.

When the White Stockings came to play the Red Stockings, it was, as the *Cincinnati Commercial* aptly noted, "emphatically Chicago vs. Cincinnati."[88] Customarily, clubs would be referred to in the 1870's as "the Chicagos" and "the Cincinnatis." The *Commercial*'s connotation shows the level of the rivalry; this was truly a match of city against city, to see who was the giant of the west. In order to accomplish its goal of becoming the national champion, the White Stockings first had to supplant the Red Stockings as champion of the region.

Chicago induced frequent and well-publicized matchups by inflaming the other city with arrogant belittlement. "If [the Red Stockings] ceased to be victorious, who would ever hear of Cincinnati?" one paper prodded. "Cincinnati has been chiefly known as the place where the Red Stockings ate hash."[89] This type of baiting was not exclusive to the Cincinnati rivalry. It was actually a regular strategy of playing on the emotions of the opposition. Attacks on lesser clubs like Cleveland were just as insulting, if not more. "Bah! Let Cleveland get into better business," one writer chided. "Her club can't play baseball. Her reporters can't report a game.... As it were, Cleveland would be better off to keep her youngsters at home sawing wood, selling newspapers, pitching pennies, running on errands for widows, and the like."[90] On the other hand, the paper asserted, "Chicago succeeds in everything it undertakes." Ryczek was most likely correct in attributing this overcompensation to mere insecurity.

Despite the transparency of Chicago's bravado, its insults were effective. Even the usual politeness of Harry Wright was superseded by a lasting resentment for Chicago. In the fall of 1871, the White Stockings' excellent season was derailed by the Great Chicago Fire. Left homeless and financially broken, they were unable to fulfill several commitments for late season matchups, including one with Wright's Bostons. Harry quickly wrote a letter to the club president with requisite sympathy and a bitter undertone. "We are all very much disappointed at your not being able to give us a game here, as I have no doubt but it would have paid you well. All the large posters were ready to be distributed...."[91]

Chicago won the first match of 1870, on September 7, by a 10–6 score.

The Chicago press unsurprisingly refuted inclinations to be a gracious winner.

> Our Cincinnati friends ... were routed, horse, foot, and dragoons, and not a Porkopalian has heart left to tell of the defeat.... [I]t was necessary in order to teach the Cincinnatians a wholesome lesson. If they will profit by it, and learn that their place is on a back seat, Chicago ... in time may accord them the place of second best.[92]

In fact, the White Stockings did make room in the front seat of their carriage home for a small pig with little red stockings to represent Cincinnati. A sign on the pig read "PORKOPOLIS, SEPTEMBER 7, 1870." The more interesting passenger on board was the game's umpire, William Milligan — or was it Al Harbach?

Umpire William Milligan was not regarded well for his performance in the game of September 7. The *Cincinnati Gazette* noted that "We badly think Captain Harry Wright could have made a worse selection.... The umpire is a very nice sort of man but he knew precious little of baseball. His decisions were given in a weak and faltering sort of voice and only after much hesitation."[93] Perhaps Milligan was indecisive because his calls were blatantly biased. Cincinnati newspapers noted his frequently erroneous calls and his excessive delay in beginning to call balls on Chicago pitcher Ed Pinkham. The plausibility of Milligan's bias was fueled by the revelation that he not only traveled abroad with Chicago to Cincinnati, but also lodged with them at the Gibson House.

After a few days of speculation, whispers began to circulate that umpire Milligan was actually West Philadelphia Club teammate Al Harbach. When Harbach heard this, he angrily refuted the charges and pointed out that Milligan was a "blackguard" anyway. He had tried to throw games, Harbach alleged, and been kicked off the West Philadelphias, which wasn't even an NA club in the first place. Since each umpire of an NA game had to be a "member in good standing," Milligan was clearly invalid. But Cincinnati refused to protest the game and the outcome stood.

A month later, the Red Stockings traveled 14 hours by train to Chicago for a rematch at Dexter Park. Fifteen thousand spectators greeted the Cincinnatis with catcalls and another pig on a cart before bidding them farewell with another round of taunts after the White Stockings won 16–13. Wrote the *Cincinnati Gazette*, "The umpire was against us, the weather was against us, the pestilential air of one Chicago River was against us, the Chicago nine was against us and last but not least, the score was against us."[94]

The game had actually been very close — 8–8 entering the 9th — before Chicago broke it open with an eight-run rally. Wright had just taken over for Brainard on the pitcher's point in the 8th, but the other players called on him to put Brainard back in, which was legal at the time. Brainard got shelled for four runs before Wright reinserted himself, only to give up four runs himself. Three years later, Wright still rued the day of that game. To a friend he lamented, "I would like to play that game over again on Dexter Park."[95]

With the second defeat of Cincinnati, the *Commercial* noted, the Chicagos were now the champions of the west. On November 1, they played the national champion New York Mutuals in Chicago. The Mutuals had taken a rather sizable lead in the game when umpire Tom Foley began calling balls repeatedly against them, including a dozen consecutively at one point. Angrily, pitcher Rynie Wolters slammed the ball down on the ground and stormed off the field, prompting Foley to declare a forfeit. According to the Mutuals, they didn't take this game very seriously because it was only an exhibition.

Before the Mutuals left Chicago, they agreed to meet the White Stockings in another exhibition game, after playing the Red Stockings the next day. Once the Mutuals arrived in Cincinnati, they telegraphed the White Stockings that they were all set for the exhibition when a telegraph was received asking for the Mutuals to meet them in Chicago. The Mutuals were repulsed by this shenanigan in addition to the frustration of the forfeited game. In disgust, they left for New York immediately after the game with the Red Stockings without notifying Chicago.

Since the White Stockings hadn't heard back from the Mutuals, they were all set to board the train for Cincinnati on the morning of November 3 when they received a wire from the Mutuals hotel the night before to inform them that the ballclub had left for New York. With that, the Chicagos avoided the Red Stockings by proposing financially impractical arrangements and simply settled down as champions for the season. Of course, Cincinnati had just beaten the Mutuals 23–7 for the second win since New York had won the championship from the Atlantics on September 22, thereby giving it a claim to the title. As one writer said, "It would take a Philadelphia lawyer to find out which was the champion club of 1870."[96]

The Mutuals defeat had been Cincinnati's final home game of the season. Only 2,000 spectators showed up to see what was ultimately a prestigious event for the Red Stockings. Apathy had been the new bandwagon for Cincinnatians since the mid-summer when the club began showing its mortality. "Disappointment and chagrin marked the visage of every man, woman and child in Cincinnati who had the interest of the team at heart," noted the *New York Sun*, "and gloom ... spread over the team.... [T]he Reds had not been a great financial success, the enthusiasm in Redland petered out as the season waned."[97]

Certainly the poison for Cincinnati was not a dreadful season, for it was 68–6 with one tie and arguably the Gold Ball champions. The problem was that expectations had been raised to a nearly unsustainable level given the invincibility of the 1869 season. One questions if Cincinnati would even have continued supporting the Red Stockings well had they not lost in 1870 either. It seemed that the city wore through fads quickly; the novelty had begun to run its course anyway. Otherwise, how could such a precipitous drop in attendance occur in a matter of weeks?

Bonte frankly told Wright that fall that the ballclub could not afford to bring the champion nine back. The money simply wasn't there. Support had dropped so sharply to the injury of the club's finances that in the off-season lumber from the Union Grounds had to be sold to repay losses from creditors. Ballclub directors estimated it would take $16,000–$17,000 to keep the club intact. Add groundskeeping, uniforms, equipment, and advertising, and 34 games would have to be played at a profit of $500 each in order to stay afloat. This was all but impossible.

On November 21, Wright opened his morning newspaper to find the following announcement to the editor:

> Dear Sir.—According to custom the Executive Board reports to the members of the CINCINNATI BASE BALL CLUB its determination in reference to the baseball season of 1871. We have had communication with many of the leading baseball players throughout the country, as well as with the various members of our former nine.
>
> Upon the information thus obtained, we have arrived at the conclusion that to employ a nine for the coming season at the enormous salaries now demanded by professional players, would plunge our club deeply into debt at the end of the year.
>
> The experience of the past two years has taught us that a nine whose aggregate salaries should exceed six or eight thousand dollars can not, even with the strictest economy, be self-sustained.
>
> If we should employ a nine at the high salaries now asked, the maximum sum above stated would be nearly doubled. The large liabilities thus incurred would result in bankruptcy or compel a heavy levy upon our members to make up a deficiency. We are also satisfied that payment of large salaries causes jealousy, and leads to extravagance and dissipation and good feeling necessary to the success of a nine.
>
> Our members have year after year contributed liberally for the liquidation of the expenses incurred in the employment of players. We do not

feel that we would be justified in calling upon them again, and, therefore, for the reasons herein stated, have resolved to hire no players for the coming season. We believe that there will be a development of the amateur talent of our club, as has been displayed since we employed professionals, and that we will still enjoy the pleasure of witnessing many exciting contests on our grounds. We take this opportunity of stating that our club and grounds are entirely free from debt; and, deeming it our first duty to see that they remain so, we pursue the course indicated in this circular.

For the Executive Board,
A.P.C. Bonte, President[98]
Will Noble, Secretary

Initially, some thought this announcement was a ploy by club management to retain the current nine at lower salaries. They had in fact been negotiating with several of the players, plus Rockford pitcher Al Spalding. But the talks did not go very far because Cincinnati couldn't put a competitive offer on the table. As long as management was skeptical about attendance, it would not commit to high player salaries.

In a more candid statement, Bonte told one writer frankly, "You can wave the Star Spangled Banner, and talk about the glory of the Red Stockings, and the nine that meets with no defeat, but you must put your hands in your pocket and pay the bills. You can't run the club on glory."[99]

Bonte knew reaction would be emotional, and most likely he would be regarded as a scapegoat while the Captain was sainted with nostalgic admiration. When Wright inevitably left, the President would take the blame. So Bonte, with a calculated shrewdness, went on the offensive to reverse the roles of scapegoat and saint.

3. Dynasty in the Rough

"A man he seems of cheerful yesterdays
And confident tomorrows."
— *From a poem by William Wadsworth, used by The Sporting News to
describe Harry Wright*

I.

A.P.C. Bonte led with the most serious charge ever levied against Wright's integrity. According to the President, Wright was at the head of a conspiracy to extort increasingly higher pay from ballclubs across the country and hopefully double all base ball salaries by 1871. He did this, according to Bonte, by demanding to see *all* professional contracts before the players accepted them.

Newspapers apt to distrust ballplayers and find a sinister reason for the abrupt combustion of the Cincinnati ballclub clung to this theory and snowballed it into a personal and professional attack. "Harry Wright as a captain," spat the *Cincinnati Chronicle*, "is a fraud." In concurrence with this assertion, an unidentified club director — not Bonte — told the *Cincinnati Times* that Wright's leadership had been overrated. It was, in fact, Champion and Joyce that engineered the club's glory days, according to the director. As Ryczek notes, this was "quite an accomplishment for two men who never set foot between the foul lines."[1]

"[The Wright Brothers] are good players beyond a doubt," Bonte clarified to the *Times*, "but the papers have been so loud and extravagant in their praise that, to be frank, their heads are turned, and they seem to consider that we can not get along without them."[2]

The *Cincinnati Commercial* remained loyal to the Wrights. "The Wright brothers need no defense,"[3] the paper insisted, but then provided

84

one anyway. The newspaper railed against the allegedly jealous executive board and reminded readers that the board did not speak for all of Cincinnati. As far as the belittlement of Wright's contributions as Captain, he was capable and intelligent enough to start his own champion from scratch. "Such distinguished citizens as Champion and Joyce assume to be baseball men. But for the skill of George and Harry Wright and Gould and the rest, they would never have been heard of." The *New York Clipper* supported the *Commercial*. "[Wright] was known only to cricket when he came here, and he has done more than any single man to build up baseball in Porkopolis."[4]

Wright stayed rather quiet throughout the whole controversy. Eventually, he spoke with the *Commercial* about his disappointment in the disbanding of the ballclub. He told the *Commercial* that, with the exception of George Wright, all the players would have re-signed, given "reasonable terms." Indeed, Gould and McVey had rejected lucrative offers from other clubs for the opportunity to stay in Cincinnati. George had been singled out by his brother because it had been known since the eastern tour in June that he wanted to leave and become Captain of his own professional club. Just that month, November, he had met with Ivers Adams, a Boston businessman who was setting up a ballclub there to bring championship base ball to Boston for the first time.

Boston was the only major eastern city not to put forth a serious contender for the national crown. The sluggish development in base ball in the city can not be attributed to a lack of interest, but rather a lack of financial backing and suitable grounds. The first club to form in Boston was the Elm Tree Club in 1855. Participants played what was known as the "New England Game": 60 feet between bases, 35 feet from the pitcher's point to the batter's box, 10–14 men in the field, and soaking—commonly known today as "Indian-tagging"—was permitted. Two years later, a former member of the Gothams club, E.G. Saltzman, introduced the "New York Game"—predecessor of the modern style—and sparked immediate interest in the game. By 1860, the New England Association governed 32 base ball clubs in the region.

The Boston Common was primarily used for Boston games because it was the only level grounds that could hold a large crowd. But because it was public property, permission was needed to play on it. Before play began in May 1869, the Common was rendered unusable for ball playing, leaving the Boston clubs to find new grounds. Delegates of city ballclubs decided eventually to build a field in the South End in an ideally accessible field location. In the fall of 1869, all city government candidates in favor of improving the field, generically christened the Union Grounds, won their races, defeating all candidates opposed. The surface of the Union Grounds was smoothed, a new fence was constructed, and capacity increased threefold to 3,000.

Now that Boston finally had a top-rate ballpark and a competitive natural market to thrive in, it needed an excellent nine to represent it. George Wright was offered the post of manager, but he did not believe a man could both direct and play for a successful club. Oddly, he suggested that Adams talk to brother Harry instead, who had every intention of playing and managing again.

Wright met with Adams in late November at Boston's Parker House. He was offered a $2,500 salary to take on the roles of manager, captain, secretary, and center fielder, as well as to control all scheduling, and negotiate all financial situations. Wright seemed willing to accept, but debated the decision for a few days. Finally, Adams sent him a telegram saying that he needed Wright to make Boston a success. Wright wired back to accept.

The Boston Red Stockings were not officially established until January 20, 1871. (Wright had taken the liberty of carrying over the Red Stockings name to the consternation of many Cincinnatians. When the Queen City entered the National League in 1876, he would return the name to its birthplace and begin calling Boston the Red Caps.) Initially, Wright wanted to set the club up as an amateur one even though Boston backers had already supplied $15,000 to cover expenses, including salary. Rockford pitcher Al Spalding convinced him to remain professional, and Wright immediately signed him and the old Cincinnati faction, George Wright, Charley Gould, and Cal McVey. Next Wright and Spalding went to Rockford to sign second baseman Ross Barnes and outfielder Fred Cone. All these players were recruited with swiftness and foresight.

Why Wright was tempted to shirk professionalism is a confusing uncertainty. Perhaps he had been scared off by the roller-coaster ride of trying to maintain the economy of a salaried ballclub, or perhaps the public scrutiny had simply exhausted him. Professionalism had undoubtedly gained acceptance over the past two years, but there was still considerable resentment of it. As late as January 1874, the *New York Clipper* ran an editorial to claim that

> [Professional ballplayers] … forget, for one thing, that the services for which they are so liberally paid, is one [sic] that hundreds of thousands of people are only too glad to indulge as relaxation from either mental or physical labor. They also forget that they are actually paid for doing that which is not only an enjoyable excitement to them, but also a service which in every way works to their physical advantage in giving them sound and healthy bodies…. [It] will not do for professional ballplayers

to regard themselves in light of everyday toilers in the world of industry, as they generally do.[5]

But the justification used by Albert Spalding could hardly find a rational refusal. "How could it be right to pay an actor, or a singer, or an instrumentalist for entertaining the public, and wrong to pay a ball player for doing exactly the same thing?"[6]

The ideologies of the two factions clashed within the National Association. Before its meeting at the Grand Central Hotel in New York on November 30, one paper predicted that "Unless this convention takes such action as will conserve only the amateur interest it will be the last convention held of the existing nines."[7] Only 26 delegates were present to represent the 221 clubs. After sifting through trivial matters, Cantwell of Albany — who the previous year had proposed a resolution to reinstate a contract jumper who admitted to having thrown games — stood up to introduce a resolution to condemn the hiring of professional ballplayers as "reprehensible and injurious to the game." This immediately set off the partisan firestorm that had been expected. Above the noise, Cantwell repeated the accusation that all professional contracts went through Harry Wright. Chadwick immediately stood up with a copy of the *Cincinnati Gazette* in which Wright passionately denied such a conspiracy. Several other delegates then stood up to defend Wright. Embarrassed at the unbalanced support of Wright, Cantwell rescinded his claim, or at least held it back. But his speech brought the most important issue to the forefront: Would the NA continue to accept professional membership? After a lengthy debate, a vote was taken that favored the professional by a 17–9 margin.

The amateur element of the NA was not about to accept that decision, nor would it be heard in disagreeing with it. Borrowing a suggestion from Chadwick, the amateurs left the NA to its professional majority and seceded to form its own league without the stain of professionalism. "Friends of our national game," Dr. Joseph Jones of the Excelsiors pleaded, "we appeal to you to aid us in our attempt to restore this pastime to its former high status."[8] The Amateur National Association created little interest in a market where patrons did not often care about pro or amateur labels, but sought the quality of play that social clubs could not provide. The Association folded in 1874 with a reported balance of $4.05.

On St. Patrick's Day of 1871, the day after the ANA was officially established, the NA met for a pre-season league meeting at the Collier's Room in New York City, a saloon on the corner of Broadway. Much like the November meeting, some tedious issues were discussed in the early part of the meeting, but it was obvious that the delegates were up to something.

Chadwick could see it coming. He wrote in the *Clipper*, "If the convention fails to organize a regular association on Friday night, their meeting will have been a failure."[9]

The meeting was opened by J.W. Schofield, a member of the host Troy club. He quickly turned the platform over to Philadelphia Athletics representative James Kerns, who was named NA Chairman. Kerns wasted no time in declaring that the pros' hand had been forced by the previous night's action of the ANA and a committee would have to be selected to formulate a response. The delegates chose Schofield, Harry Wright, and Mutuals secretary Alex Davidson. The three convened in a separate room for a brief period of time before returning with the expected recommendation to establish an all-professional league called the National Association of Professional Base Ball Players.

The response from the delegates was one of eager approval. But now that the decision had been made, the rules for operation needed to be established. The playing rules for 1871 were the same ones agreed upon at the NABBP that past November. As far as schedules, there were none. Western representatives were left to set up their own schedules, while easterners could play it by ear. Somehow each club had to play a five-game series against all of the other league members to qualify for the championship.

The guidelines for the championship created two major problems. First of all, not all clubs were willing to play some of the others. For example, Troy and Chicago refused to schedule a game because the two clubs were feuding. Also, teams like Troy and Philadelphia did not want to waste time and money by traveling west to play smaller clubs like the Kekiongas of Fort Wayne or the Forest Citys of Rockford.

The question also arose of whether the championship was given to the club that won the most games or the one that won the most series. And once a series was won, did the participants keep on playing until all five games were done or quit since the set had been settled? One of the NA's biggest problems was that it never answered this question decisively.

Any club that sent in the $10 entry fee to Wright by May 1 was eligible for the championship. The fees were used to buy a championship banner to be hang outside the recipient's grounds. Nine clubs entered competition for 1871: Boston, Chicago, Cleveland, Fort Wayne, New York, Philadelphia, Rockford, Troy, and Washington.

The entry fee wasn't always as simple as it may sound. In 1873, Hicks Hayhurst of the Philadelphia club forgot to send it in by the time Wright mailed in the list of NA clubs for the season to the *Clipper*. Hayhurst immediately sent the fee to Wright along with an angry letter. Harry responded with an unusual bite.

> What you mean by saying "you feel it to be your duty to *not neglect*" [paying the fee] any longer, as there seems to be a disposition to make capital of it; I cannot understand. Ten dollars is not amount to "make capital of," and you had but four days more to attend to "*your duty*" and "*not neglect*" such a trifling mission as entering for the championship. What I did was merely to send to the *New York Clipper* or other papers, a list of the clubs entering for, or as contests for the Championship, as the rule directs me to, nothing more. As to the games you have played counting or not counting as championship contests is none of my business and I have not made it such. If you think what has been published about your games is *my doing*, you are mistaken.[10]

Confusion was the norm in the NAPBBP, or as it was usually known, the NA. Instances such as these with entry fees, or mid-season uncertainty about how a championship was determined, on-the-fly scheduling, and other enigmas were not clarified by the league government before the inaugural season. That would not have been such a problem if they were taken care of promptly. But instead the NA had a habit of procrastinating and refusing to solve problems, without sufficient explanation. Often inaction could be attributed to a conflict of interest, such as Kerns' simultaneous involvement as President of the NA and President of the Athletics. Would he have the integrity to separate his interests and rule unfavorably against the Athletics? Would people trust him? It was the same reason that the position of Commissioner of Baseball has been kept out of the hands of club owners— until former Milwaukee Brewers owner Bud Selig took over recently as Judge Kenesaw Mountain Landis rolled over in his grave. Bottom line, there was no respected authority to deter corruption in the NA, and therefore corruption thrived.

Ryczek, in his study on the NA, *Blackguards and Red Stockings*, wrote in the summation of the National Association:

> While the players were professionals, management was strictly an amateur proposition. The full name of the NA, the National Association of Professional Base Ball Players, was prophetically descriptive, as it was truly a league of players, not of clubs. Managers merely provided a stage upon which players directed, produced, and performed. Many were unforgettable characters who marched to the beat of their own percussionist, and some did not always act in the best interests of their team. Indiscretions were overlooked, talented athletes were afforded numerous chances, and (not surprisingly) very little profit was recognized by any of the stockholders.[11]

II.

Harry Wright returned to Boston after a long "absence from the city" in mid–April. He had been on vacation since March, most likely in his beloved Florida. Wright didn't mind the Boston weather, though he once complained "The seasons here are very backwards."[12] "The country looks beautiful, but I would prefer Florida just now for all that," he wrote in 1878. "An Alligator hunt would just set me up."[13]

Upon return, the Boston club began training at the Tremont Gymnasium for two to four hours per day. Wright decided to keep the club at home though Chicago and New York toured the south. By mixing the gymnasium routine with outdoor games, Wright had his men in good form for their first game against the Washington Olympics.

In an intentionally storybook fashion, the inaugural NA schedule was set to open with the Red Stockings versus the rival Olympics. Washington was built around the dissident Cincinnati faction of Sweasy, Brainard, Allison, Leonard, and Waterman. Captain Sweasy chose to continue on the unpleasant note of the previous season by boasting that he was capable of defeating the Red Stockings with even the amateur Olympic club. However, Sweasy would not have the opportunity to see this through until August, when he returned from a bout with rheumatic illness. By that time, Washington had sunken into the second division anyway, and in a profound disappointment to the league, the franchise ended up folding in June of 1872.

The opener was supposed to be a spectacle to begin the NA season, but instead it was rained out until the next day, Friday, May 5. The actual inaugural game, as it happened, pitted the Forest Citys of Cleveland against the Kekiongas of Fort Wayne —*not* what the league had envisioned.

On Friday, the skies were threatening once again. Between the blankets of gray sneaked patches of blue sky, but not enough to cause much optimism. Around noon, though, the sun broke through for the first time in two-and-a-half days, and umpire H.A. Dobson called for the game to begin at 4:50 that afternoon. Dobson was chosen as a last-minute replacement for Hayhurst, who never showed up. The *Clipper* correspondent was hardly ideal for the job of administering such an important game in front of the "elite of the city," including foreign and domestic government officials. Dobson had lost a leg during the Civil War and had to use his crutches to hustle into position on close calls. In the 8th inning, he was knocked down by a line drive that smacked directly into his one leg. His biggest problem was that his decisions were erratic. Instead of calling a ball for every three pitches outside of the strike zone (as was the rule then),

Dobson did so for every *one*. This resulted in 18 walks on Brainard's part and 12 for Spalding, a rather high total in those days, as it would be today.

The *Clipper*, which did not mention that Dobson was an employee there, declared Dobson's work a "great umpiring job." Even though Boston won 20–18, the *Boston Herald* boldly questioned Dobson's integrity. Wrote the paper, "[W]e sincerely hope that he may never field the position in any first class match again."[14]

Boston hovered around the .500 mark for the first half of the season. It was a disappointing record caused mostly by injuries, such as George Wright's incurred on May 9 in a game against the Troys. He was chasing a high pop up into shallow left field when he and Fred Cone collided. The incident looked rather harmless, but in fact George had hit his knee in just the right spot to trigger his old affliction. This injury would keep him out of 16 of Boston's 36 games and plague the shortstop for the rest of his career.

Harry Wright was initially optimistic about his brother's recovery. One week later, however, he conceded that "It is doubtful if George will be able to play in either [the upcoming Tuesday or Saturday's game] as he is slower than I expected, and without him, we could not expect the good fortune we [have] had."[15] A month later, he was on crutches and "very lame not being able to run at all."[16]

Soon McVey got hurt in Rockford, Cone — who had escaped harm in his collision with George — fell to injury, and Dave Birdsall did as well. In light of these and several other minor injuries, Wright decided to cancel all of Boston's games for a while, "unless the injured mend." Injuries were an acceptable excuse for canceling a game in those days, especially in the case of a club like Boston, which carried only 10 players. With no set schedule to stray from, Wright was not breaking any rules, although perhaps agitating his fellow club secretaries.

It was neither the first nor the last time he got on the nerves of his colleagues. Wright would again pull out of a scheduled match with the Mutuals on July 17 because "several players of our nine are in no condition for play."[17] In 1878, he irritated an official of the Milwaukee club by forgetting to pay an umpire. "I told [Wright] when I met him at the depot that I was glad he was going to have you as it helped me out," wrote the official to the umpire, "all he done was laugh and we went on about something else. He must think I am a fool if I am going to help him out with his expenses."[18]

Most of the time, Wright enjoyed an amicable relationship with other ballclub officials. Playfully, he taunted Brooklyn's William Cammeyer in September 1874:

We are coming, sister Mary, we are coming bye and bye,
Get ready sister Mary, for the time is drawing nigh.[19]

Overall, this seems to be consistent with the rapport Wright enjoyed with his colleagues. Even in his absence, others spoke well of him. Chadwick once recalled overhearing a conversation between New York Giants' President John B. Day and Al Spalding, then an executive with the Chicago White Stockings. "They never tired of pressing their opinion of [Wright] and I was led to believe that either of these distinguished magnates would cheerfully pay his funeral expenses were he to suddenly drop dead."[20]

Indeed, "Harry Wright is said not to have a single enemy among ballplayers," remarked the *Sporting News* in 1887. "They all like him and the cause is very simple. He is an honest hard-working manager, rules his men with an iron will, but never asks from them any thing he would not do himself. He sets an example to his men and they follow it."[21]

On the Fourth of July, Wright returned to the site reminiscent of his most favorable and unfavorable moments, Cincinnati. In the months since Bonte announced that the CBBC was going amateur, he, the Vice President, and the club Secretary all resigned after a December meeting at which the executive board decision was overturned. The members now wanted to raise $5,000 in capital to field a professional nine. If that amount was to be raised by New Year's Day 1871, they would scrap the idea and go amateur after all. But the club's aspirations fizzled and by the end of the season the CBBC had disbanded. In April 1872, the club was reduced to holding an auction at the Union Grounds in which it sold off all memorabilia from the 1869 season.

It seemed that the money had been emptied out of Cincinnati. The July 3 and 4 matches with the Olympics—the "Old Reds" v. "Blue and Red" as Wright deemed the matchup—failed to realize the profit necessary to pay the travel costs out there. "We did not draw well," Wright lamented, "there being no local interest in the game."[22]

Money problems were being felt across the National Association. In August, the league's first victor, Fort Wayne, had to drop out after contract-breaking and money shortages. With Fort Wayne gone, the field of competition for the NA crown grew smaller. (The Brooklyn Eckfords replaced the Kekiongas but were not eligible for the championship because they did not enter by May 1.) Cleveland and Rockford were both distant, while Troy sunk into mediocrity after a fast start, and Washington and New York joined them in the league's second division.

Meanwhile, Boston had turned its season around. On September 2, the batters took advantage of the "Five-Inning Wonder," "Uncle Al" Pratt, by scoring 23 runs in the 8th and 9th innings to beat Cleveland. Three days later, the Red Stockings overcame the formidable White Stockings with a Charlie Gould grand slam to continue a five-game winning streak.

By the end of the month, Boston was in the heat of the pennant race. On September 29, the club took on Chicago in an important game that was sure to significantly affect the championship. Boston was in the hole for most of the game, but pulled to within 10–8 with two outs in the 9th inning. With men on second and third, Barnes skied a ball deep into left field that went foul by only inches. Fearlessly, Zettlein came right back at Barnes with an identical pitch. And he smacked it deep to the same spot as before, just foul. Again, Zettlein matched his pitch, but this time Barnes could only pop out to end the game.

With that win, Chicago pulled into a tie with Philadelphia for 1st place on September 30. That day's standings read as follows:

	Wins	Losses	Winning %	Games Back
Philadelphia	19	7	.731	–
Chicago	19	7	.731	–
Boston	19	10	.655	1½
Troy	14	12	.538	5
New York	17	15	.531	5
Washington	16	15	.516	5½
Cleveland	10	19	.345	7½
Fort Wayne	7	21	.250	13
Rockford	6	21	.222	13½

But the standings were not as straight-forward as this table seems to indicate. Many questions arose at this point, in mid-season, about how the championship was to be determined. Was it by the winner of the most games? loser of the least? winner of the most series? loser of the least series? After a series was won, should the clubs play out their five games? And how were the games with now-defunct clubs to be factored in? Rockford had been playing with two revolvers and therefore had to forfeit several of their games. As for the forfeits of long-gone Fort Wayne, would its games be counted for and against other league clubs that were still in the race? Would games against its replacement, Brooklyn, count toward the championship?

In early October, a rather belated timing for such a decision, the NA hierarchy tried to simplify the rules for determining the championship. Now it would be decided by the winner of the most series. If there was a tie, the winner of the most games would go ahead. That's why Philadelphia was ahead of Boston in the standings:

	Series Won	Series Lost
Chicago	5	0
Philadelphia	4	1
Boston	4	1
New York	2	2
Troy	1	1

This method was more agreeable to Harry Wright, who opposed determination by winning percentage. "I think the championship rules are imperfect in regard to deciding a tie between two or more clubs. How can there be any best average in championship contests when to tie, the clubs must play, and win and lose the same number of games as the rule as amended now reads?"[23]

The use of winning percentage, though confusing and, according to Wright, inadequate, would have benefited the Bostons tremendously. A week after the series chart was published, the *Clipper* ran a set of standings guided by winning percentage:

	Wins	Losses	Winning %	Games Back
Boston	24	12	.667	–
Philadelphia	24	13	.649	½
Chicago	24	14	.632	1
New York	21	20	.512	5½
Washington	19	21	.475	7

Sensing a need for compromise, Championship Committee member Nick E. Young decided that *now* the championship would be decided by the team with the best record, but games played after a series was decided were to be excluded. The standings now read:

	Wins	Losses	Winning %	Games Back
Chicago	10	5	.667	–
Philadelphia	10	7	.588	1
Boston	12	9	.571	1
Troy	7	8	.467	3

Since Chicago was at the top in both the series and winning percentage-based standings, it was clear that no matter what the standards ended up being, Chicago was the team to beat. But all that was erased by the Great Chicago Fire that swept away 17,000 buildings and left 150,000 residents homeless that fall. Only two players on the White Stockings didn't lose their houses, while Lake Front Park — Chicago's new field — went up in flames.

Reluctantly, the club decided to keep playing, but not well enough to win. The league's strongest franchise folded after the season with $4,800 left in back salaries and only $2,000 in capital.

Boston was the recipient of a couple of good breaks to end the season. First, Troy catcher Bill Craver arrived with his team on October 7 expecting a rainout. But Wright insisted that in spite of the gray skies, the teams would still play. Troy, a co-op club that made its money on portions of gate receipts, was frustrated by the meager rainy day crowd it was being forced to accept, and gave up the lead early in a 12–3 loss. Then in Boston's last game, the New York Mutuals forfeited because pitcher Rynie Wolters was absent.

These two games helped Boston to finish at a healthy 22–10 in championship play and 29–12–2 overall, "four [losses]," Wright noted, "when playing their full nine." This record was good, but not good enough to surmount either Philadelphia or Chicago for the championship.

To Wright's dismay, the champion Athletics chose to hang the inaugural NA pennant in a Philadelphia saloon. Wright looked at the pennant as a symbol of NA prestige, and for it to hang in a bar—the very birthplace of negative ballplayer stereotypes—was infuriating. "If we had them," he wrote of the pennant to Hayhurst,

> I should fly them both in all the grounds we would play next season ... and consider your club entitled to do the same ... I must say, that I was sorry to see it stated in the papers that the flags would be on exhibition in a drinking saloon. I think the proper place is or would be the Athletic club room, or some place where *all* that wish could go and see them. To elevate the National game we must earn the respect of all; and now the Athletics are Champions—the first legal and recognized champions of the United States. They will be looked up to as the exponate of what is right and wrong in base ball, and will have it in their power, to a great measure, to make the game a success—financially and otherwise. (Which it was *not* last year.) I trust that you will excuse me making these remarks, but I do it, knowing that you will do all in your power to gain the desired result.[24]

Despite its championship, Philadelphia decided to restock its club in the off-season. Several players were eased out of the lineup due to injuries and replaced by free agents—so to speak—from other clubs, such as the young Adrian Anson, often called "Baby" and later known as "Cap."

Wright resisted pressure to respond to Philadelphia's activity by perceiving his club's situation with a calm rationality. He realized Boston was basically getting a different team from the previous season since the players that had been sidelined with injuries were now healthy. Therefore he took a conservative approach and restricted his acquisitions to outfielder Fraley Rogers and Andy Leonard, back from the fallen Olympics.

Wright feared the players would not be ready for the season. They could not play ball outdoors until April 29, and not regularly until several days later. "It has been very cold here," he wrote earlier, "too cold for outdoor exercise.... There is five feet of frost in the ground, so you can imagine it will be some time before the 'green turf' will be in condition for us to play upon. All the boys are here ... *enjoying* themselves in the Gymnasium ... I have been busy with the boys."[25]

After the regular season was open for a couple months it was apparent that there was a large gap between the stock and co-op clubs. A stock club was a team funded by club members that paid the players in an annual salary. Judging by how much the club collected in the pre-season, it could gauge the ceiling for salaries and shop for talent accordingly. But a co-op club made its money on gate receipts from individual games, dividing profits among the players. Since the club had no idea how much it would make prior to the season—and profits alone were what determined salaries—it did not have the luxury of working within a set budget when signing players in the off-season. Therefore co-ops committed less money and had a distinct disadvantage when trying to lure in available players.

The disparity that this created was clearly illustrated in the NA standings of June 3:

	Wins	Losses	Winning %	Games Back
Boston	9	1	.900	–
Philadelphia	6	1	.857	1½
New York	8	4	.667	2
Troy	11	4	.733	2½
Baltimore	10	5	.667	2½
Cleveland	4	7	.364	5½

Guess where it was that the co-ops began showing up? The second tier—after that sharp .303 drop-off—began with Cleveland and was followed by Middleton (Connecticut), the Olympics, Eckfords, Atlantics, and Nationals.

Naturally, clubs began to drop out, and at an alarming rate. Six out of the eleven clubs that began the NA season folded by its end. This held all sorts of financial implications on the league, especially when it deprived successful clubs of profitable home games. Wright was furious that his friend Nick Young's Baltimore club refused to play out the last two games of its series with Boston. Philadelphia would not replay a tie, as it was supposed to, and Boston did not complete its nine games series—raised from five in off-season rulings—with the Eckfords, Haymakers, Middletons, Nationals, and Olympics.

With play infrequent, scheduling was light during August, usually a peak month for base ball. According to the *Clipper*, on July 6 the Red Stockings "went to camp on the island in Boston Harbor to shoot, fish, bathe and recuperate generally for the fall campaign."[26]

The club was in excellent shape at 18–1 just two weeks before and coming off of a 15–game winning streak. Seven of the nine regular players were hitting .314 or better. The exceptions were Fraley Rogers and Harry Wright. By the end of the season, there was speculation that Wright would quit playing and even managing, to be replaced by either Rogers or Spalding. Instead, the rumor stated, he would take care of the finances alone. But, in fact, Wright was playing fairly well that season. Chadwick pointed out that he "took the lead in assisting to put players out from center field; his returns being very quick and effective."[27] At one point Chadwick even noted, "Harry Wright was so active that he seemed to be renewing his youth."[28]

For its 19th straight victory, Boston knocked off Troy by a 17–10 score. Troy was playing well but was financially incapable of carrying the high salaries it took to play well. After a July 23 match in Springfield, Massachusetts, against the Mansfields of Middleton, Connecticut, the Haymakers folded their prominent, though controversial, franchise.

With Troy out of the race, the championship was up for grabs between Boston and Philadelphia. By this point, Boston had already taken a commanding lead in first place, as opposed to the volatility that had characterized the race thus far. After surrendering its first loss to Philadelphia, Boston surged ahead. The rivalry with the Athletics was immediately revived. "There is a great deal of interest manifested in your return game with us," Wright penned to Philadelphia's James L. Hamill. "...There is a great deal of enthusiasm in base ball, and it would be as well for you to come while the fever is on."[29]

On July 27, the two clubs clashed again in what was an important matchup especially for the Athletics. If Philadelphia wanted any shot at remaining competitive with the proven force of the Red Stockings, this win was essential. Philadelphia responded in an odd way by making several positional shifts that showed little confidence in the lineup that had carried them well thus far. The catcher, first baseman, and shortstop slots all had new tenants, the latter of which, Denny Mack, had no prior experience there. Despite that, Mack made no errors and pitcher Dick McBride shut the Bostons down on four hits to salvage Philadelphia's aspirations.

Yet three weeks later, Boston had distanced itself distinctly from Philadelphia and the rest of the pack. On August 18, the top tier of the standings read as follows:

	Wins	Losses	Winning %	Games Back
Boston	29	3	.906	–
Philadelphia	19	5	.792	6
New York	20	12	.625	9
Lord Baltimores	21	13	.618	9

After Boston defeated Philadelphia 16–4 on September 4 it seemed that it had put its rivals away. But after two losses in one week to the Mutuals, the Red Stockings seemed to have opened the door just enough for an invasion. The two met again on September 9 for perhaps their best match of the year. The crucial game was tied at 5–5 in the 9th when rain fell and eventually canceled the game. The Bostons had effectively won the championship. When it was finalized weeks later by the season's end, Boston had won decisively by 7½ games with an .830 winning percentage.

As a result of what was essentially a two-horse race, attendance lagged in 1872. In order to boost profits and interrupt the tedious cycle of repetitive matchups against the same clubs, Wright had prepared an extensive Western tour for that August. Between the 13th and 29th of that month Boston toured through Oil City (Pennsylvania), Cleveland, Upsilante (Michigan), Detroit, and up to Canada through London, Guelph (a small town on the fringes of Toronto), Ottawa, Ogdensburgh, and Montreal. The Canadian leg of the tour was the most successful. Boston outscored the Canucks by a combined 524–48 score, winning some games by 66–1, 64–0, and 68–0.

Still Wright was disappointed. He had warned the Canadians that he wanted to play good competition in order to encourage adequate gate receipts. "I can assure you," he wrote to Cammeyer on July 16, "we prefer a good game and big receipts to 'Hail Columbia,' 'Won't go home till morn,' and all that sort of thing you know."[30]

The pomp and circumstance was there, but not the "good game and big receipts." Despite guarantees by the Canadians, scarcely enough money was made to pay the traveling expenses. Attendance continued to slump throughout the season, so in October Cammeyer put up a $4,000 to hold a tournament between the Bostons, the Philadelphias, and his New York Mutuals.

Ironically, it was Cammeyer's Mutuals that cost Boston its biggest payoff of the year. On May 30 the two were scheduled to play at the Union

Grounds before what Wright ventured to guess was the "largest crowd that had been on a ball field in Boston. There had been over 800 tickets sold at [one sporting goods shop], and as many more at the grounds where we stopped the sale, the place outside being crowded and all along Tremont Street wherever they could get shelter. I am afraid it will be sometime before we have such a crowd again."[31]

Fortunately for Boston's effort to salvage the crowd, the game was rained out. On their way out, the people were informed that the game would be made up the next day. Little did Boston know that the Mutuals had decided to head back to New York, "but the idea of them having left the city or intending to leave was not entertained for a moment," Wright remembered with incredulity. When he realized that the Mutuals had abandoned him, Wright was livid. One can almost see it in his handwriting as he tried to efface his anger with gentlemanly restraint: "We feel that the Mutuals did not act honorably with us, and treated us shabbily in leaving the city in the manner they did, half an hour before the time fixed for calling the game [on], and without sending word to the grounds, giving us any notice whatever."[32]

Wright's letters to Cammeyer were not typically this hostile. Wright had many close base ball relationships, but was not consequently passive enough to overlook a raw deal. Most of the time his correspondence was characterized by his usual cordiality and sometimes even his dry humor. One such letter was written in 1873 after a humbling loss to another club:

> Excuse me for not answering you promptly. I have not forgotten you, but — well — let me see, I believe we had a little game here yesterday with some foreign club. I have not seen the morning papers so [it] may possibly have beaten us. Bad dream, that. Now I want to dream that we played the Mutuals Wednesday May 7th [which was two weeks later] and — we — they — after a severe struggle — did — great excitement — immense crowd — &c. — &c.[33]

The tournament was a financial and functional failure. The first game between the Bostons and the New Yorks ended in a 7–7 tie to set up a New York/Philadelphia game the next day. The two clubs went into extra innings this time, all the way to the 12th to give the Athletics a 9–7 win. Instead of taking the day off and enjoying this, Wright made what seems to be a rather unwise move. He set up a game with the Brooklyn Atlantics for the same day, and paid for it with a 5–3 loss. Losing to a club not in the tournament detracted from the façade of elitism that gave the tournament whatever precious prestige it had mustered. The act alone of playing elsewhere while the tournament was going on was a slap in the face. If the tournament were so important after all, shouldn't that be all that mattered to base ball spectators? That's why all other base ball virtually stops for the World Series. Perhaps most injurious of all, the Brooklyn game split the already thin gates being reaped from the tournament. Neither game made much money. In desperation, Cammeyer held a throwing contest to attract attention, won by Hatfield with a record 133 yards.

Boston's slide after the Brooklyn loss continued with another to Philadelphia. The latter went on to beat New York the next day and set up a championship with Boston. In yet another close game, the two were tied at 10–10 after 12 innings, when the game was called on account of darkness. This put New York into contention and started the tournament back up.

Boston again made it to the championship against Philadelphia, but rain and injuries prompted Wright to call for a cancellation. No championship was decided, although Philadelphia eventually claimed it after a subsequent tournament, and little profit was realized. $1,500 was distributed to each of the three clubs, as, according to rumors, had been decided weeks before.

Boston's financial troubles had not been resolved by its championship season (the nominal tournament notwithstanding). The club was $5,000 in debt, due primarily to salary payments, and it was seriously questioned whether Boston would be around for 1873. Then in October, a destructive fire swept across the city and made the situation even worse. Players were on the verge of leaving for greener pastures, or at least those not made of quicksand. It was Wright's job to try to hold on to them all. He assured them that if he did not believe in the club's viability, he would not still be around. If worse came to worse, Wright would move the club back to Cincinnati where the city had already welcomed a return of the Red Stockings.

Such speculation did not last very long. On December 11, 150 BBBC supporters assembled in Brackett's Hall in Boston to officially revive the ballclub. A new management would come in to assume the club's debt and sell new stock to raise money for 1873. The salary problem was resolved by a new system in which players would receive salaries incrementally throughout the season, a variation on the co-op idea. Instead of being paid strictly in divisions of every gate earned, players would receive a salary determined periodically by the current welfare of the club. This gave the players an incentive to play well, for it would help control the money flow of the ballclub that ultimately landed in their pockets.

Wright had told Barnes that he had lost sleep at night because he was so concerned about potential player departures. In the end only McVey,

Rogers, and Gould left, the latter two for retirement. Gould retired to get away from his feuding with Barnes and to help take care of the Wright & Ditson Sporting Goods Store. In February 1871, George Wright had moved the store he and Harry had opened in New York to Boston and took on a new partner named Ditson. At first, George had a tough row because there were not a lot of popular sports at the time. He tried to change that by becoming the first company in America to produce tennis balls. Still it was difficult to make a profit in the early years and George was forced to use his large base ball salary as a life support system for the business.

Eventually Wright & Ditson grew to be a successful company until George sold out the late Ditson's stock to Spalding in the 1880's. He would end up merging with the Spalding Sporting Goods company and A.J. Reach before leaving the business in 1925.

In the 1870's and '80's the store on 391 Washington Street became what one paper described as the "general resort of all lovers of base ball."[34] George also used it to employ old friends like Gould. After Gould returned to manage Cincinnati in 1876, George eventually filled the spot with Andy Leonard, who remained there until his death in 1903.

In 1872, George also added a family to his life when he finally got married on November 25 to a 23-year-old daughter of Irish immigrants named Abby Anna Coleman. George and Abby had two daughters and two sons: Elizabeth Adelaide (1875), Georgia Hall (1878), Beals Coleman (1879), Irving Cloutman Wright (early 1880's). The two sons went on to have illustrious tennis careers. After graduation from Harvard, Beals won national titles in both singles and doubles competition, and was eventually inducted into the Tennis Hall of Fame. Younger brother Irving also became a doubles champion and won the Canadian championship three times. Later in life, he took over the Wright & Ditson operations for his father and also became President of the Leywood Cricket Club for whom George had once played.

III.

Boston stumbled out of the gate in 1873 with another loss to the lowly Atlantics. The club failed to maintain a consistent pattern of play over the next few months, as did several brethren throughout the league, including the Athletics and Mutuals.

By mid–July the Red Stockings were 8½ games behind the upstart Philadelphia White Stockings. Along with swiping the nickname of the late Chicago club, the Philadelphias—as they were commonly referred to—also took several players from the crosstown Athletics. It appeared that the Bostons had been displaced by the Philadelphias as clear-cut champions. The Boston press began to turn sharply on the club, in a way painfully reminiscent of Cincinnati only three years before. The writers and public alike gave up on the Red Stockings for the season, with a mood expressed in the July 26 *Clipper*: "[I]t is evident that [Boston] will not be the champions this year. Indeed, if they do not show improvement in September, they will hardly reach second place."[35]

The inexperienced members of the Philadelphias took this opportunity to become complacent. After a summer break for rest at Cape May, New Jersey, the club lost five straight before rebounding to win 8 of 10. But their misstep came just as Boston hit its stride. With a stretch of six wins over the defenseless Nationals, the Red Stockings began a 26–5 run to close out the season, while the White Stockings were 9–14 after Cape May.

The Philadelphia/Boston rivalry proved just as strong as two years before, even with a new representative of the former. "[T]he base ball fever is running high here at present,"[36] Wright noted of interest in Boston. On September 15 the two clubs met at the Jefferson Street Grounds in Philadelphia. The Red Stockings were drained and dispirited after a grueling 14-inning game against the pesky Atlantics, a loss to the Mutuals, and the long train ride to Philadelphia. Against pitcher George Zettlein, Boston rapped out 15 hits but was tied 5–5 in the 9th. Then Leonard came through with a double and sparked the Bostons to a 7–5 win. This raised their record to 27–13, .001 ahead of the Lord Baltimores for 2nd place and four games back of the Philadelphias.

Boston rolled along with defeats of the Atlantics and Mutuals. The Mutuals then took down the Philadelphias. Their chances began to look uncertain, yet the *Clipper* insisted that "Philadelphia will almost certainly win unless they fall flat on their faces in the next four weeks."[37] By employing that very method, the Philadelphias surrendered the championship. On September 29 they lost to the rival Athletics, a team they had dominated that season. Then two days later the White Stockings lost to the Nationals, setting up a dramatic showdown with Boston the next day.

Four thousand spectators came to the Jefferson Street Grounds in the faint chill of early October. Initially, the Bostons looked vulnerable by giving up four runs in the 1st inning on account of defensive weakness. However, the offense brought Boston into the lead, 7–5, after three innings. Then on a Spalding pop-up with two men on base, Treacey and Wood allowed the ball to fall between them. While the two argued in the field, George Wright and Barnes raced in to score. Later that inning, Wood punished himself for another error by spiking the ball into the ground and allowing another run. When darkness cancelled the game shortly afterwards, Boston was officially in first place after avoiding defeat for nearly a month. By going 12–1 in September and finishing up October 11–3, Boston won its second consecutive championship relatively easily.

The Philadelphias quickly tried to salvage the title by claiming that the Bostons had illegally used a player named Bob Addy. Wright had replaced outfielder Jack Manning with Addy for the Western tour in August. Wright anxiously sought the experience of the veteran Addy and asked him to "Telegraph you will join us in St. Louis and we will go … raising the "standard of the mighty Reds higher and higher."[38] Addy thought this gave him a better chance of being signed for 1874, so he accepted.

The Philadelphias, for whom Addy had played early in the season, claimed that he had played with the Rockford nine as recently as the Fourth of July against Chicago. This meant that if he had played for Boston in mid–August, Addy was guilty of violating the 60-day rule, a provision prohibiting any player from participating in a professional game within 60 days of his last one with a different club. Wright adamantly supported this rule, and it would be hypocritical for him to violate it knowingly. If he did, under consequences that he had already supported, the Boston club would forfeit all its games involving Addy, and therefore the championship.

The decision fell to the League's Championship Committee, a three-man board that included Wright. He was joined by Hicks Hayhurst of the Athletics and Dick McBride of the Philadelphias. This situation highlights the ineffectiveness of NA management; two-thirds of the panel had a conflict of interest. Obviously, Wright wanted to see Boston keep its championship, and McBride wanted to disqualify Boston so the Philadelphias could take the title instead. Hayhurst, the swing voter, resented the Red Stockings because they were the league juggernaut, and begrudged the Philadelphias for raiding his team before the season. The committee was a picture of inaction. Attempts were made to move the process along and get a ruling, but the committee made excuses and delayed the process instead. Eventually, Wright pleaded his case convincingly to Hayhurst, explaining that Addy had a sworn affidavit attesting that the game in question was a pickup game and not a professional one. Hayhurst reluctantly sided with the Bostons and certified them as the repeat champions by a 2–1 vote.

The Red Stockings also made a lasting impact with their Fourth of July game. Finances had recovered that season from the off-season instability, and Boston made up its debt with a spring tour through the South, promising stockholders good gates sooner rather than later. By June 21, Wright reported that "professional games are proving so attractive and remunerative."[39] In order to sustain that pattern, Wright devised an idea for Boston's July 4 game against the unattractive Resolutes of Elizabeth, New Jersey. Instead of one game, they could play two and charge admission for each. Boston was shut down by pitcher Hugh Campbell in the opener in an 11–2 upset loss, but charged back with a 32–3 drubbing in the rubber match.

In the time since the Fourth of July, 1873, the doubleheader has become a staple of base ball, even if its popularity has waned dramatically in recent years. It was a typical Wright innovation, something creative which earned his club extra money and thereafter profited the game as a financial attraction and a longstanding tradition. Wright next turned his vision to something not as much of pragmatic conception as an optimistic and yet hopeless personal quest.

IV.

In every man of ambition, there is a passion to achieve one goal that justifies the wingspan of his activity. This is often known as a pet project. Usually it is the architect's way of reconnecting his present endeavors with the roots of his character. The 1874 British tour by the Boston Red Stockings and Philadelphia Athletics was Harry Wright's doing. It was his pet project. And it was done to connect him with some vestige of his younger days, perhaps to justify the career he had rejected his father's hopes to pursue, by convincing the very country from which his father's game had emanated to switch from cricket to base ball.

On January 5, Wright sent a confidential letter to Athletics President James M. Ferguson. It was the first known mention he made of the trip and he requested that Ferguson keep the matter hushed for a while, "until all preliminaries are all arranged." "The Boston club has opened negotiations for ... the long talked of trip to England and give exhibitions of our National Game," he wrote, alluding to speculation since 1869 that a Red Stockings club would tour Europe. "To accomplish this successfully it is necessary that another club should accompany us, & we give your club the preference."[40]

Wright's described his objective for the tour to be to "have a pleasant trip, see all we can of the 'Mother Country' during our brief visit, and, if possible, make our receipts cover expense."[41] The latter statement — if not merely an attempt at dry humor — is a significant break from Wright's usual operation. From time to time, he would take a chance with the finances of a game, but only when solicited. For Wright to suggest a trip that he didn't believe would give his club a profit — especially in difficult financial times such as these were — signals an atypical motivation.

His true intent was better represented in a letter two months later in which he stated that "My ambition is to play cricket on English soil."[42] Wright's desires for the trip consistently fit a "do it while I can" theme. He wanted to visit England and spread the game there personally, but opportunities were fleeting because his last days on the ballfield were nearer at hand and Wright, at age 39, knew that he was slowing. 1873 had been his last season as a regular outfielder, and George Hall was hired to spell him in center field for the '74 season. Wright was cognizant of the inevitable, but he did not agree to move on. In regards to putting himself on the shelf he wrote, "that is all very well but 'I am no such man.' I will have eight men that will make up for my poor play at the bat, when it is poor, and in the field when it is not first class, and what is left to be made up I think I can succeed in making good.... [In regards to retirement,] No sir. Couldn't think of it."[43]

Anxious to set up the tour that

Wright poses in his Boston Red Stockings uniform in the waning days of his playing career and the heyday of his managerial career. (National Baseball Hall of Fame Library, Cooperstown, N.Y.)

Wright believed would leave his greatest mark on the game, he dispatched Al Spalding as Ambassador to England on January 17. The selection of the 23-year-old Spalding took many people by surprise. It seemed wiser to send a more savvy club official, not a young player. But Spalding had developed a close relationship with Wright, and the two frequently exchanged advice, so Spalding knew better than most what his manager desired from the trip and how he wanted the arrangements worked out. Spalding did have some executive experience behind him, especially early in his career when he became so well respected as a member of the under-16 Pioneer Club that he soon became its president. The team was so competitive that it even defeated the Rockford club, prompting the Forest Citys to sign both he and Barnes to their nine immediately. Wright believed that Spalding would "create a very favorable impression not only as a representative of the two clubs, but as an American Base Ball Player and a professional."[44]

Spalding arrived in England on January 29. His progress was slow initially, but he managed eventually to get his job done. On February 27, he played the first base ball game held in England, against an opposing nine headed by Secretary of the Surrey Cricket Club and *London Sportsman* cricket editor Charles W. Allcock. With his nine cricketers against Spalding and his eight, Allcock did something that NA clubs had done only 33 times over the previous season three seasons in defeating Spalding.

The next evening Spalding met with Allcock to hire him as an agent to promote the tour on the time between Spalding's return and the ballclubs' arrival. According to Wright, "As our agent you have full authority to make or arrange games, securing grounds on the best terms possible, with guarantees when possible, our object being to give exhibitions of base ball playing professionally, not cricket playing." Spalding believed that Allcock was as competent of serving well in this capacity due to his "ability, and the interest he has shown and expressed in the undertaking."[45] But above all, Allcock was valued for his contacts in the British sporting world, as cricketer and newspaperman, to help in both setting up matches and adequately promoting them.

To Wright's dismay and Spalding's discredit, Allcock failed. As soon as Spalding left England, Allcock was seriously injured in a soccer match and thus hindered in his efforts to commence communication outside of England. However, once recovered he still did little. The British were known to patronize any entertaining sport that was simply marketed properly and well-organized. But Allcock neglected to even post an advertisement in the Liverpool and Manchester newspapers. He even tried to set up games for the 28th and 29th of August. The problem, Wright had to remind him, was that they would be leaving England on August 27. Allcock tended to take most of the blame for the financial failure of the European tour. The *St. Louis Democrat* attacked him as a "fat, good-natured, lazy but gentlemanly person who had never seen a game of baseball played in his life."[46]

The problem — though the *Democrat*'s latter assertion was technically incorrect given the February 27 game — was that Allcock was not alone in never having witnessed a true professional-brand base ball game. In order to familiarize the English with base ball, Wright proposed that Chadwick write a book on the game to be sold in Great Britain for six cents apiece. Wright also sent along clippings from newspapers to describe the game and the Boston and Philadelphia players. The articles got brief recognition in the *London Daily News, London Sportsman,* and certain Liverpool papers, but overall exposure was less than Wright had anticipated. He sensed that Allcock was not doing enough as Agent and, though restraining his doubt with a confident approval of Allcock, he occasionally micromanaged portions of the operation to salvage the potential success of his project.

In mid–March, Spalding returned to the States with a tentative schedule of games and a report on the productivity of the trip to England. In hopes of heartening Wright, he overemphasized British interest in base ball, thereby raising unwarranted expectations. One displeasing note to Wright was that Spalding had spoken too highly of American cricket abilities and agreed to several matches along the British tour. Wright had wanted this to be a base ball trip, with occasional cricket matches that would not be a significant detraction from the focus on the American game. Wright masked his fear to Allcock as deference to British expertise, while actually it was an acknowledgment of base ball's susceptibility to failure in this venture. "There could not be too much cricket to suit me personally," he explained, "but when competing at cricket — playing with the cricketers of England — I am afraid we would fail lamentably."[47]

Reluctantly, Wright decided to train his club at the English game with a series of cricket matches. First he welcomed an invitation to play the St. George's club, and then accepted offers to play Boston cricket clubs. The cricketers were so pleased with these matches that they begged to play the Red Stockings after the British tour, but Wright declined because it was against club policy. In the meantime, he was pleased to find out that his ballplayers were actually quite good at cricket. This seems natural enough; the two games were terribly similar, except now instead of using a thin bat to hit a small ball, the players now swatted it with a big paddle.

On July 16, 23 ballplayers, 40 stockholders, H.S. Kempton of the *Boston Herald,* and a collection of guests arrived in Philadelphia to board the steamship *Ohio,* bound for England. Boston President Appolonio called his club members into a saloon to speak with them briefly. The honor of the Boston ballclub, he contended, was on the line. He addressed rumors that had been swirling recently that the two clubs would alternate victories throughout the trip. Fortunately, both clubs had started off well that season and an even record seemed plausible. Had one team started the season poorly and the other successfully, one can imagine the poisonous effect that this would have on tour attendance. Even scandalous talk was better than no talk, for interest was essential to promoting the trip.

Hundreds of people lined the Christian Street Wharf for a quarter-mile to see the *Ohio* off. At 5 o'clock in the evening, the players were called on board. As the whistles blew and the ship eased away from the harbor, the Philadelphians remained on the dock singing "Hail Columbia" and "Auld Lang Syne." Some followed by boat along the Delaware Bay shouting encouragement, and a salute was fired as the ship passed by League Island.

At 8:30 that evening, the ship captain announced that they had just passed Cape Henlopen, the gateway to the Atlantic. Most passengers were resting in the lower part of the ship, but several remained on the deck watching the sun slowly drift away into the night. "[The] sunset view was remarkably fine," marveled Kempton as *Clipper* correspondent,

> the sun sinking like a great red ball of fire into the waves at the horizon, and leaving the light clouds fringed with a beautiful carmine which was gradually transformed to golden and purple shades, finally changing to a leaden gray.[48]

V.

When the passengers awoke the next morning, they could see no more land. The water was all that bordered the sky, and below them waves rocked the boat enough to leave many seats vacant at the breakfast tables. The talk of the morning was the near-collision of the night before with two coasters that were traveling without lights. This was actually a fairly common incident on the seas.

Most of the next day was spent quietly, while the passengers tried to figure out how to spend their time. Wright recruited as many players as he could into the cramped quarters of the *Ohio* to explain the finer points of cricket. Those who had the heart to show they were disinterested spent the days playing shuffleboard, chess, pitching quoits (iron disks), or playing ring toss. Some industrious steerage passengers even put together a newspaper called the *Ohio Daily Graphic*. The news was handwritten in ink on letter paper, and six copies were sold to net the passengers $2.

On Sunday, passengers observed the Sabbath. No clergymen were on board, so the players spent their time in the forward part of the ship, or Fourth Ward, looking for flying fish. Nothing exciting occurred until early Tuesday morning when they spied a group of icebergs, some as large as half-a-mile long and 200–300 feet tall. The icebergs did not do any damage, but on Friday the *Ohio* got its first taste of stormy weather during the afternoon. As the seas calmed during the evening, Philadelphia's Sensenderfer and Gedney took to the piano while Leonard and Hall sang a number of ballads.

On the second Sunday, the passengers settled on Boston B.B.C. director C.H. Porter as preacher of an Episcopal service. Most of the cabin passengers and quite a few from steerage came onto the deck at 10:30 for a reading from the Bible and a number of hymns. At about three o'clock that afternoon a few passengers thought that they saw a small mound at the end of the water. It looked to be the same color as the sky, so some dismissed it as a cloud. But the officer on deck confirmed that it was land, in fact a mountain range off Cape Clear, towards Cork, Ireland. The mountains grew large as they closed in to see the rocky islands of Bull, Cow, and Calf, the latter of which had a light tower. At 5:30 the ship passed by Brow Head and the captain signaled to land. The *Ohio* anchored in Queenstown at 11 o'clock at night to drop off a number of passengers and pick up a mailbag, including a copy of the *Cork Examiner*. A group gathered around in the saloon to read the paper. Only one American dispatch appeared in the *Examiner*:

THE UNITED STATES—THE INDIAN OUTRAGES

New York, Friday evening. The Indian outrages are increasing, and more troops are required.[49]

Apparently, a company of troops had been ambushed in the Western forestry.

From there, the *Ohio* traveled up the Irish Sea toward England. At 8:30 the next night, the ship arrived in Liverpool. George Wright later recounted his brother's reaction to reaching the English land:

The trip was a fortunate one as far as accidents were concerned. Nothing serious occurred except on our arrival at Liverpool, where we were taken from the steamer Ohio in a small tugboat, when upon nearing our deck, Captain Harry being anxious in each to be the first to land in old England, made a jump from the tug to the dock, with a satchel in each hand, striking fair upon his feet, but both slipped from under him, as the boards were wet from rain, and he landed in England solid.[50]

The reception in Liverpool was not what the Americans had anticipated. Instead of a crowd the size of the sendoff in Philadelphia, two Brits who had recently emigrated from Philadelphia met them there and escorted the ballclubs to the Washington Hotel. They spent the first couple days there getting adjusted, but nobody seemed to notice them.

At times, the British were blatantly rude to the Americans. Towards the end of the trip, the players ate a nondescript meal in Manchester with their hosts, and afterwards were told to pay three shillings per player for it. The next day, the Manchester Cricket Club ate lunch while the hungry Americans watched on.

A set of more accommodating British hosts showed the players around for some sight-seeing. The players, out of youth or retaliation, showed all the snobbery that they complained about in their counterparts. While riding in trains that they scoffed at in comparison to Pullmans, the young men spoke mockingly of the "Juke" and ignored the many cultural landmarks. When traveling through Wales on a Dublin route, the train passed several old castles, "many of which are doubtless remembered in history, but which a party of irreverent, fun-loving Yankees had neither means nor time to identify."[51]

After taking their two days to rest, the two clubs arrived at the grounds at 2:30 in the afternoon to find only 12 anxious spectators in the stands. By game time that figure swelled to 500 that witnessed a thrilling 14–11 Philadelphia win in ten innings. The next game, a 23–18 Boston win, attracted 200 spectators. The former figure of 500 would have been disappointing for an America game, let along the inaugural match of the British tour.

More than anything, the Brits were impressed by the Americans' defensive ability. Fielding and throwing were not stressed in cricket, and this new dimension of the game provoked incessant discussion in the press. In evaluating the game as a whole, the British acknowledged it as an intriguing game with a more exciting pace than cricket. But they were quick to dismiss base ball as a descendant of the old English game of rounders.

On August 1 the players dismounted the train at 10 o'clock in the afternoon in Manchester. They went straight to the Old Trafford Cricket Grounds to find an inspiring crowd of 3,000 spectators waiting to see the match. From there the club traveled to London, where it experienced the peak of the trip.

The train arrived in London on a Sunday night and since there was no ballplaying on the Sabbath, the players went sight-seeing for the evening. Most players spent this time shopping for clothes, or in Spalding and Jim O'Rourke's cases, hats. According to Kempton, "about the only thing I can say in favor of the various garments is their cheapness."[52] The Boston players were somewhat limited in their scenic tours by the watchful eye of Captain Wright, who would not allow them to cross the English Channel to "the Continent." The players had expected this opportunity, but a jaunt to Paris was cancelled due to insufficient playing grounds.

The clubs received a grand reception in London the next day for their game at the Lord's Cricket Grounds. A large banner was hung that read "Welcome to England," and a number of flags flapped nearby, including the American one. Whoever had arranged this particular match, Wright or Allcock, had picked an opportune time. Five thousand spectators were available to attend due to the Bank Holiday. Unfortunately, whereas all of the other three games had been well-played and competitive, especially Philadelphia's 13–12 win in Manchester, this one included many errors and home runs, not the signs of refined play that the British admired. One reason for the home runs was the large, rocky surfaces being played on. When a ball landed after being well-hit to the outfield, it tended to roll for a while on the coarse ground. The grounds were so large in England that the ball was allotted a great amount of space to roll once it hit. Wright found the grounds to be large enough to split into two fields and put the Bostons against the British on one and the Philadelphias against a separate British contingent on the other.

After introducing base ball with these opening games, the Americans participated in a number of cricket matches. The Yankee teams, which usually consisted of 18 men against 11 Brits, embarrassed their opponents by posting a 6–0–1 record. The British excused their play by noting that many of their best cricketers were on holiday and so only less qualified local boys were able to play. They especially attacked the Americans' "blind, slugging batting style."

"Decidedly the most finished bat was Harry Wright, who played good cricket," the *London Sportsman* conceded, "but this cannot be said of any of the others."[53] The American approach was, yes, unconventional, but ultimately productive. Instead of simply blocking the wicket in the defensive style of the Brits, the Yankees swung wildly at any reachable ball near the wicket. And when they hit the ball, they swatted it instead of employing the scientific method of British cricketers or teammate Harry Wright. In embarrassment, Wright tried to get the Americans to conform to the proper style, but Spalding, the heaviest slugger, simply laughed at the rustic notion.

While the *Sportsman* singled Harry out as the sole exponent of proper cricket play, O'Rourke and the other two Wright brothers—George and Sammy, who had been brought along exclusively for his cricket skill—were commonly regarded as cooperating with good form as well.

For a man who considered himself on his way out of the game, Wright was youthful in his performance that season. Back at home, when injuries to George Wright, Barnes, and outfielder Tommy Beals crippled the club, Wright took over once more in center field for a taxing 41 games. In Europe,

Wright played in all seven base ball games, scoring 75 runs to rank third in average behind brother George and Dick McBride.

After all these cricket games, the Americans found it difficult to readjust to base ball. "The fact is," Kempton wrote, "we get so tired out playing so much cricket that we are in no condition to play a good game of ball, which will in a measure account for the indifferent playing and large scores."[54]

On Friday night, August 14, the ballclubs took the 11:50 train out of London and into Sheffield. Four hours later they arrived in Sheffield and traveled to the only place where they felt "thoroughly 'at home'" along the British tour, the Black Swan Hotel. The Black Swan was a charming, old-fashioned inn usually reserved for visiting cricket and soccer clubs. Heavy, studded doors opened to a courtyard, large fireplaces sat in most rooms, and the rafters overhead were charred by smoke. The hotel reminded many of the players of a building straight out of Dickens.

The players awoke to eat breakfast at nine o'clock the next morning, less than five hours after they arrived at the Black Swan. Perhaps as a favor to Harry Wright, the native son, the players were afforded a spectacular feast to appease the hunger manifested by the long trip the night before. Shortly after breakfast the ballclub arrived at Sheffield's Bramall Lane, a surprisingly comparable grounds to the American version. It included raised seats on each of the two tiers, and was encircled by a 1/3-mile track for bicycle, racing, and running contests. This was encircled by a high brick wall to enclose the grounds, which were wet from rainfall the night before. The skies were still cloudy and the air was cold. Kempton opined that Sheffield felt closer to a spot in the mountains of Greenland than the tall hills of Sheffield, England's highest industrial city. Due to the industrial aspect of the city, Sheffield was also one of the smoggiest in the country. "Sheffield resembles Pittsburgh very much in one respect," Kempton further lamented, "smoke hanging over the town like a pall."[55]

The ugly weather served to keep attendance down to 1,000. Wright — who surprisingly sat out the game in his hometown after a tiring cricket match the prior afternoon — had high expectations for the Sheffield crowd due to its large population and general enthusiasm for sporting events. Only 500 showed up for the next game two days later, up from 100 at the cricket match's beginning two hours earlier.

While in Sheffield the ballclubs spent Sunday the 16th visiting the house of the Duke of Devonshire. Wright himself had royal blood on his mother's side, though not in Sheffield. Halsey Miller, Jr., has traced his great-grandfather's roots back to the 12th century's Henry Earl of Huntingdon, a man whom other sources — whose reliability is inconclusive —

have linked to an astonishing heritage of kings, queens, pharaohs, and various types of royalty throughout European, Middle Eastern, and African history.

The ride over to the Duke's residence in two wagonettes was once more dark and rainy. Several players were thoroughly drenched by the time they returned to the Black Swan. After the next day's game in Sheffield the ballclub traveled once more to Manchester, and then on to Dublin, Ireland, to finish up the trip.

The train departed from Manchester at 10 o'clock on Saturday morning and arrived in Holyhead six hours later. From there the ballclubs took a trip through Wales and across the channel to Dublin for 10 o'clock that evening. The next day, the Sabbath (and therefore sight-seeing day), the players went out to Phoenix Park for the day and returned at night as they had been ordered.

Accommodations in Dublin were bad. The hotel was cheap and the field was worse; most agreed it was the worst grounds of the trip. Wright had made a special point of stopping in Dublin for a couple of days, "for with all our Mc's and O.R.'s a game there would surely prove attractive and pay handsomely."[56] In fact, only 1,500 showed up over the two days, but this was not due to poor advertising; Kempton noted that it was the best advertising job he had ever seen, on the part of Dublin's James Lawrence. The problem was that it was scheduled against the Baldoyle horse races, which attracted a large following in Dublin.

The Americans arranged to put on a good show for their crowd. At three o'clock the Duke of Abercarn, Lord Lieutenant of Ireland arrived and was "inducted into the mysteries of the game" by Captain Wright. According to the *Dublin Mail*, he was a rather quick learner and His grace "struck the ball [off of McBride] with such vigor as to evoke beauty demonstrations."[57]

The Lord Lieutenant had to leave by the time the game started at five o'clock due to prior commitments. In the game, which lasted for two days, the Americans routed their Dublin opponents convincingly, in what Kempton regarded as "a very spiritless affair." Afterwards the Americans challenged Dublin to a game of base ball, but no team of Dubliners would even try them. Only six volunteered, including the Earl of Kingston. The Wright Brothers and John Kent — an amateur replacement for Boston catcher James "Deacon" White, who had stayed home for family reasons — joined the cricketers and allotted them five outs per inning, but they still lost 12–6. Afterwards, the Americans split into two teams under McMullin and Spalding, and played a game.

Early that evening, the ballclubs took the *Flying Irishman* out of Dublin and arrived at Cork at about two o'clock A.M. From there, they went to a hotel to sleep for six hours, ate breakfast, and rode a train for 12 miles to Liverpool. The players spent the day trying to get rid of their remaining English money by buying numerous souvenirs. They were also approached repeatedly by "beggars and peddlers" hoping to make their day's pay off of the wealthy Americans. The day passed slowly, and it was a welcome relief when the *Abbotsford* arrived that evening to take them home. There they were reacquainted with the same travelers that they had come across the Atlantic with on the *Ohio* over a cramped supper.

The next morning it was apparent that the rough seas that they had avoided on the way over were going to complicate their voyage home. The wind was strong and the sea was volatile. The storm continued for four days, relegating the passengers to their quarters either out of seasickness or fear of the harsh weather. On Monday, August 31, the storm graduated to a gale.

But the next day, the storm passed and the sun was out. For the next week, the sea was calm and the wind was gentle. At one point towards the end of the week a passing storm rocked the *Abbotsford* violently for four hours. Wrote Kempton,

> It was a terrible though a grand sight to look upon the great mountain waves dashed into foam and breaking high over the ship, threatening every moment to swallow her up, and it was not pleasant to contemplate how powerless we were to save ourselves. The wind howled and shrieked through our rigging, tore away our sails and bore off everything which was not firmly attached to the deck. The water swept away the deck from stern to stern....[58]

After the storm was over, a funeral service was held at six o'clock that evening. The deceased was not a member of the ballplaying corps and his death had nothing to do with the storm. The man was a steerage passenger who had died of consumption — now commonly known as tuberculosis — the night before. His body was wrapped in canvas and tucked into a crude black coffin. After a solemn reading, the coffin was slid from the hurricane deck and into the Atlantic. Unfortunately, though, the waves were still so rough that they tore the cover off the coffin, exposing the body. Then the iron weights detached, "and the unpleasant sight of a corpse floating away in a coffin was presented to the passengers."[59]

For the next few days, the players toiled in boredom, speaking of how badly they wanted to be back in America. They constantly inquired about the speed of the ship, which was at one point as slow as eight miles per hour. When it was discovered that they were close to land, many passengers sat on the deck until three A.M. to see Barnegat Light. At eight o'clock that morning, some passengers in the bowels spotted Cape May, and at 9:30 the *Abbotsford* passed Cape Henlopen. The passengers wanted immediately to get off, but the ride up the Delaware River was slow. At three o'clock the first crowds of people shouting and waving handkerchiefs became visible. When the ship docked at seven that evening the players were met by a large throng of greeters, including Deacon White. After all the passengers had disembarked, the players were led by their well-wishers to the Colonnade Hotel to rest for the night. The next day, Boston beat Philadelphia in a game so raucous that the umpire had to leave by police escort.

As the New York Express traveled along the Albany Road towards Boston, Wright had the opportunity to assess the tour he had invested so much hope in. The Americans had succeeded in making a good personal impression on the British, refuting the negative base ball player stereotype. In fact, there were no reports of drinking or carousing on the part of the players, and one writer in London was particularly impressed with their habits compared to "our beer-drinking English professional cricketers." *The Dublin Mail* regarded the ballplayers as "without a single exception, a fine set of young stalwart fellows and in excellent form for any manly contest. Wanting the goat beard and the characteristic angular features of the Yankee, they might be taken for Britishers, but for their bronzed faces."[60]

However, the Americans were unable to parlay these fine impressions into financial gain. Circumstances were so bad that the expenses of the tour had exceeded profits, and in response to this, each Boston player had to take a substantial pay cut to make up for it. All the players took the cut "perfectly," according to Wright, except Deacon White. The catcher went so far as to threaten to quit the team if his pay was not restored, which Wright dismissed as "biting your nose to spite your face."[61]

Americans were quick to scapegoat the allegedly dim-witted Brits for the financial failure. "English people," Kempton scowled,

> with their slower perceptive faculties, do not pick up the intimation of coming events so naturally as their more rapid American cousins and there is little wonder that the advance agent, who is a genial, honest Englishman but who lacks the snap and vim of a successful American business agent, should have failed to stir up public interest in the affair.[62]

Wright accepted the financial disappointment easily because he had expected it before the tour started. His objective was to plant a new game in British and European culture. Yes, he knew that base ball would not supplant cricket as the British pastime; he had admitted as much to Allcock during the spring. But he hoped that it would at least provide a popular alternative to cricket during the appropriate seasons and perhaps in English colleges. From his experiences on the tour, Wright knew that base ball would not get that far. His countrymen did not see what he saw in the game.

This was the lowest point known to have occurred in Wright's life. "We had an early frost," he wrote to William Cammeyer upon return. "I feel frosty. I am going to the sea shore today with my wife and family where the air is pure to — to — recuperate. Recuperation is needed, or — something else. What is it?"[63]

VI.

The New York Express arrived in Boston to a large reception of citizens celebrating and bands playing "Yankee Doodle Dandy," "When Johnny Comes Marching Home," and "Hail to the Chief," the latter in reference to Wright. The Bostonians had gone a long time without base ball, through a long, hot summer that called for outdoor entertainment. Wright had calculated the effect of his club being absent for the British tour, and he figured that it would be the same as going to Canada as he had the previous two years. In both cases, the Bostons were away from home during the summer playing exhibition games that did not go on the National League record. So he'd just cancel the Canadian trip and go to Britain. What was the difference?

Besides taking a tour twice as long as the Canadian one, this time the Philadelphia club was being brought along. This took away another formidable club from an eight-club league, leaving the Mutuals, the upstart Philadelphia Pearls, and the returning Chicago White Stockings as the only competitive teams left. With matchups either repetitive or abysmal, attendance plummeted. Sometimes the *Clipper* didn't even bother to send a correspondent to the games.

One other factor in the attendance drop was gambling. With the watchdog Bostons out of the country, players got more liberal in their gambling habits. On August 20, reputable umpire Billy McLean came forward with testimony that he had been offered a bribe by Johnny Radcliffe before a Philadelphia/Chicago game. Cummings, Craver, Mack, and Hicks were also implicated in the scheme. Radcliffe was eventually banned by a majority vote of club stockholders on September 1, but reinstated with the perennial Philadelphia upstart, in this case the Philadelphia Centennials.

The Red Stockings even provoked suspicion when they were shut out in an important late-season match with the White Stockings. Betting odds had been 100–20 in favor of Boston. Enthusiasts in Boston were so shocked at the telegraph report that they wired back for confirmation.

Having Chicago back in the league was not a welcome development for Boston. After a June 8, 1875, loss in Chicago, the *Tribune* reported that the White Stockings had "throttled [the Red Stockings] until they were black in the face and ready to cry 'enough' ... Harry Wright is stabbed to the heart [and the players are] kicking their red legs in agony."[64]

When Boston and Philadelphia left for Britain, the New York Mutuals were one of the strongest teams left on American soil at 17–16 on the season. During the ensuing one-and-a-half months, New York ran up its record against second-division clubs so that when the tourists returned, the Mutuals were in third place with a 27–17 record, one game behind Philadelphia and six behind Boston. Still, it seemed that the Red Stockings had the championship secured.

But on September 22 Boston was on the verge of squandering its lead against the Mutuals. Hall had been struggling badly as of late, so Wright became the regular center fielder. Inexplicably, for this game Wright took the pitcher's point instead and placed Spalding in center field. Then in the 5th, with their team up 4–3, the two reversed roles again. Spalding surrendered five runs in the 5th and 6th, but Boston tied the game up going into the 9th. Spalding gave up another run and Boston lost, 9–8.

Two days later, the two clubs played again, this time in Boston. Spalding again looked shaky and Boston lost the game by three. The Mutuals were now a serious threat, only 1½ games behind the once-untouchable Red Stockings as of September 28. They had gained five games in a matter of four weeks, a much bigger accomplishment in the 1870's National Association than modern-day Major League Baseball. After losses to the Athletics, the lowly Canaries of Baltimore, and the Atlantics, many began to count Boston out; even Chadwick affirmed, "The Reds are not likely to win the pennant this season."[65]

By the time Boston came to New York on October 9, the two clubs were 2½ games apart, even in wins but Boston five ahead in the loss column. The Red Stockings came back to create a one-run game with George Wright racing home to tie it. But he was cut down by a good relay and Boston lost the important game, its last head-to-head match of the season, to slice the division lead to 1½ games.

For the first legitimate pennant race in the NA, the finish was rather bland. Both clubs lost key games, but Boston played about three times the amount that New York did, which increased its winning percentage to .743% and its lead to 7½ over the Mutuals.

In November, Wright suggested that half of the championship fund be used to buy a medal or badge for each player, much like the championship rings now synonymous with major league titles. Each would have the club and player names, plus the year and each of the games played, including wins and losses.

That winter, Wright also pioneered the idea of long-term contracts by signing players to three-year deals. After witnessing the ever-shifting rosters of other clubs, he knew it was more logical to avoid giving the players a new contract every year. This new strategy did not work as well for the players, though, for, unlike today, management could refuse to pay for another year at any point in the contract.

Wright's ideas often overwhelmed his counterparts. At the March 2, 1875, NA convention — at which Wright was elected Treasurer — Wright introduced a number of resolutions to the committee. But "seeing that it would require an all night session to get through Harry's schedule,"[66] they hurried him along and accepted few of his ideas.

Wright was infuriated during that convention by the election of numerous Philadelphia representatives to govern the league. To him this was a premeditated coup arranged by and among Philadelphia delegates to control the league. According to Wright, "They can declare a defeat a victory and a victory a defeat, and from that decision there is no appeal. With such a committee what justice, or what protection can any club outside of Philadelphia expect to receive."[67]

The source of this alleged conspiracy came as a result of the Davy Force Case. Force's situation was far from being a rarity around the league, but it was emblematic of the revolving predicament that often distracted and discredited the NA. On November 2, Force signed with Chicago, then one month later, he also signed with the Philadelphia Athletics. However, both contracts were illegal because they were signed before Force's old contract expired on March 15. One morning at the convention, the Judiciary Committee voted to let the Chicago contract stand, but they could not present this decision until Committee elections were held that evening. In those elections, Athletics member Charles Spering was elected President, in addition to two Philadelphians already on the committee. Elections were not completed until the next morning, and when one committee member could not participate in the ruling due to a scheduling conflict, Spering inserted himself in the man's place and, as the third Philadelphian of five committee members, ruled with the majority in awarding Force to the Athletics.

Wright took this ruling very seriously. Whether to uphold the integrity of the league as its champion, as he claimed, or to prevent his chief rival from obtaining a fine shortstop, Wright tried to unite clubs against Spering and abolish the committee. In addition, he wrote several unusually angry letters to the *Clipper*, but never succeeded in his efforts.

In April, Wright announced that Boston would boycott the Athletics and encourage other eastern clubs to join him. This rage was blind. He knew full well that if the two clubs did not play against each other that season, under NA rules the record of each would be disqualified. When support from other clubs was not forthcoming, Wright held on to his fight by presenting vague excuses as to why Boston could not schedule a game with Philadelphia. Eventually he had to give in, but not before he was heartened by Hartford President Morgan Bulkeley's decision to protest his club's first game with Philadelphia.

"How long will the National Association exist," he begged of Chadwick, "if clubs composing it violate its laws with impurity whenever they conflict with their special interests? What is the use of an association if clubs refuse to abide by it or be governed by their own Constitution, By-laws and code of rules?"[68]

More than anything else, this case showed Wright the fatal weakness of the National Association. 1875 would not be an especially successful season for the League. Thirteen clubs started the season, as opposed to the all-time low of eight in 1874. Clubs sprang up in new locations such as New Haven and St. Louis, which the Red Stockings had visited only six years before. But the freshmen did not last long. In the early season, several clubs dropped out, including the Philadelphia Centennials after being Chicagoed — or shut out — by the Red Stockings.

Boston started off the season in a way that seemed to eclipse its previous three championship seasons. Without the distraction of a tour or the complications of injuries, the club was in the proper mindset to exceed past achievements and present opponents. One reason was that it knew how to win — a phrase often muddled into an empty cliché. In Boston's case, this meant that the club — primarily Harry Wright — continued to process and implement strategies to outthink and outplay the other teams. Among these strategies was the practice of platooning now being used to rotate Leonard and Harry Schafer between 3rd base and left field.

Boston got off to an 18–0 record before losing its first game on July 5 to the St. Louis Browns. The Browns had been among the teams that played the first one-and-a-half to two-and-a-half months of the season without a loss, as well as the Hartfords.

On May 17, the Hartfords played Boston in a tense matchup of two undefeated teams. Almost 9,000 rowdy Hartford spectators turned out, largely because city factories had shut down for the day in anticipation of the game. During a 1st inning rally, O'Rourke advanced from 1st to 3rd on a hit, and as he ran, umpire Al Martin quietly called time out — so quietly that he was the only one that knew about it — then shortly after he called for play to resume. O'Rourke, who had no idea that he touched second while time was out, was called out by Martin. Spalding immediately sprinted out to argue.

Spalding often took this role from Wright because their knowledge of the rule book was identically extensive. In 1873, the two collaborated on a plan to have George Wright purposely catch a fly ball in his cap. Since this play had just been declared illegal the previous winter, the ball would still be alive until returned to the pitcher. So during a game, with the bases loaded, George cradled the ball in his hat and fired to Spalding, who relayed it to first and watched it travel around the horn for a triple play. At first the umpire allowed it, but when the crowd got angry he reconsidered. Such trickery raised the spectators' suspicion whenever Spalding went out to talk with an umpire, such as an 1874 match with Philadelphia. After a long discussion between the two, a spectator flipped a sign intended for the crowd that read "Don't Dispute the Umpire" and faced it towards Spalding.

With his persuasiveness, Spalding got Martin to take out his rule book and the two studied it for about five minutes. "Read it aloud!" the crowd hollered impatiently. "Pass it around and let us all read it!" Finally, Martin told O'Rourke to go to 2nd and pretend it never happened. As the crowd booed, McVey stroked a single to put Boston up 5–0.

Hartford mounted a comeback, but lost decisively in the end. That night, both clubs boarded a train back to Boston where they were met by a German marching band and paraded with 300–400 Bostonians. Among them were 50 men holding brooms across their shoulders like rifles while "Hail to the Chief" flooded the background. Boston again beat Hartford the next day at the Union Grounds, leaving the upstarts to wonder if their run could be attributed to ability or an easy schedule, and leaving Boston to strengthen its grip on 1st place.

Boston ran with the pennant from there. In early September some thought that Philadelphia could catch up, but a 16–0 Boston defeat made it clear that the pennant race was over. The Red Stockings finished the season with an .872 winning percentage, 25 games ahead of the only other club to exceed .500, the Philadelphia Athletics. Overall, Boston outscored its opponents by a combined score of 832–344, and did not lose once in 35 games at home that season.

Ryczek described Boston's dominance — "The Boston Plan" it was called — as the National Association's "mortal blow." Unlike New York Yankee dynasties of the 20th century, Boston's success did not provoke ill-will towards the team nationwide. In fact the club was respected, and the NA was often jokingly referred to as "Harry Wright's League." But regardless of their attitudes toward the team, spectators were interested in quality championship base ball. If there was no chance of a pennant race, they simply were not going to spend money and time to see it. After Boston beat Philadelphia on September 3, clearing its path to the championship, NA crowds plummeted sometimes to less than 100 and regularly less than 1,000. They were even often outdrawn by amateur games.

The NA eased into its death starting in mid–July when the Red Stockings were in Taunton, Massachusetts, for an exhibition game against a team of amateurs. While at lunch with Wright, Cal McVey casually mentioned that he, along with Spalding, Barnes, and White were revolving to Chicago the next season. At first Wright thought he was kidding. But White confirmed it.

Wright and Appolonio were not especially angry with the decision of the revolvers, or the "Big Four" as they were called. White had often threatened to leave the club in the past two seasons and required perennial visits by Appolonio to reconsider. Barnes had never been on Wright's good side. In January 1875, Wright advised Chadwick to "lay it on thicker" when criticizing Barnes in the newspaper. "He has provoked me time and again by his careless and indifferent play where the other players were trying their best. He gives me more trouble ... than any other man we have."[69]

Above all, Wright respected the Big Four's reasons for leaving, none of which were hostile towards the Boston club specifically. The sales pitch presented by Chicago stockholder William Hulbert was geared towards a theme of Western pride. It was a perceptively ingenious strategy on Hulbert's part. He couldn't outbid Boston because they would — and did — match the offers made to the Big Four, but he could offer a return to their roots, the same attraction that lured Wright back to cricket and modern free agents such as Ken Griffey, Jr., and John Olerud to hometown clubs. Spalding and Barnes had begun with Rockford, Illinois, McVey with Indianapolis, and White in Cleveland.

Building up a western team would not only restore pride to the region but also balance out the Eastern monopoly on good ballclubs. Western interest was waning from the days of the Cincinnati Red Stockings because now the area did not have a competitive professional ballclub that would spread out the balance of power across the country and finally put a formidable NA opponent against the Bostons.

Spalding — the ambassador of the Big Four — was impressed by these big picture arguments. But he was also persuaded by the effect that this move would have on base ball's feeble management. For one thing, gambling was an ever-present evil that discredited and corrupted the NA. Spalding felt that the only way to change this was to phase in new management. Since he was being offered the opportunity to take on an executive role in Chicago along with his playing duties, this would give him the chance to personally partake in the new movement. Also, Hulbert had been offered the presidency of the White Stockings and if the Big Four joined with them it would help him to head up an influential ballclub. Spalding saw these two reasons as measures to protect the popularity of the game he loved and made his living off of.

Hulbert wanted to keep the deal a secret until after the season; otherwise it would be known that the mid-season deal had violated NA policy and therefore subjected the players to expulsion from professional base ball. But only two weeks afterwards, the details came out in a Chicago newspaper. Most people assumed it was a rumor, and the Big Four wanted to go along with that. But Spalding knew that as the leader he would be subjected to extra criticism if he denied the truth, so he decided to be upfront about it. As soon as Spalding verified the rumor, the Big Four became the target of insults by citizens and children on the streets of Boston. Their bitterness lay between matters of sorrow, distrust, and unwarranted suspicions of greed. Many feared that the ballclub would collapse, but in fact the announcement had the opposite effect. While Chicago starters slacked off knowing they'd be replaced the next season, the Big Four played harder to disprove cynical expectations.

Boston management proceeded with civility. On November 10, the club hosted a post-season banquet at the American House. Through the rings of smoke that hung over the tables after dinner, Appolonio— sitting to the left of Wright — stood to make a brief speech. He praise his men for their integrity and gentlemanly nature throughout the season, especially Wright and Spalding. He made a passing reference to the departure of some for "fresh fields and pastures new" and admonished Spalding to always work not only for his own good reputation but also for that of his associates. Appolonio closed with a compliment to Wright, who responded with a characteristically short speech. Spalding then spoke up to answer his colleagues that his decision was based on seeking his own happiness in the west and not a reaction to unhappiness in the Northeast. He thanked all the members and proposed a toast to "the champions of 1872-3-4-5-6."

That winter there was widespread suspicion that the Big Four, along with Chicago-bound former Athletics Cap Anson and Ezra Sutton, would be expelled from the league at its March 1876 meeting. At first, Hulbert refused to believe these rumors, but eventually he was convinced that he had to do something radical to avoid the expulsions. "Spalding," he said to his young associate, "I have a new scheme. Let us anticipate the Eastern cusses and organize a new association before the March meeting and then see who will do the expelling."[70]

Hulbert drew up a list of objectives for his new league aimed at producing quality play and high revenues, two things he knew went hand-in-hand. The first step towards this was to get rid of the hapless ballclubs that dragged down the profits of contending clubs trying to fulfill their schedules. "[P]eople are getting tired of seeing these one-horse clubs play," wrote the *Boston Globe*. "The sooner the leading clubs in the country devise some means to ban these weak clubs from entering the championship arenas, the better it will be for their interests and for the game generally."[71]

To this end, Hulbert sought to enact several regulations in his new league. Now all clubs would have to be based in a city with a minimum population of 75,000 people; located outside of a 50-mile radius of the nearest club (with the exception of Hartford), apply for acceptance to the league and be denied if receiving two negatives votes; and pay a $100 entry fee instead of $10, thereby discouraging weaker clubs from joining. This money would now be used to establish a central league administration instead of buying a pennant. Additionally, gambling and mid-season negotiations were banned (though, as Ryczek noted, the latter prohibition "was not retroactive"), and umpires were required to be professionals.

Hulbert slowly revealed his plan by having Spalding casually mention it in an interview with the *Chicago Tribune*. Afterwards, Hulbert traveled to the Galt House in Louisville where he and St. Louis' Charles Fowle presented the idea to Louisville, St. Louis, and Cincinnati representatives. The westerners gave their blessing to Hulbert to negotiate with the easterners: Boston, Philadelphia, New York, and Hartford.

Boston was an easy sell because Wright was already in Hulbert's camp. One might expect him to have closed his ears to the man who had just stolen the heart of his ballclub, but this situation appealed more to Wright's rationality than his emotions. He appreciated Hulbert's hard stance on gambling and the Force Case. But most importantly, he understood as a businessman the hopelessness of the NA and the ineptitude of its infrastructure. If he planned to continue his career in base ball, he had to align with Hulbert.

Hartford's Morgan Bulkeley agreed with Wright, but the other two easterners were more difficult to convince. The Mutuals and Athletics were reluctant to give up the prestige they held in the National Association. New York's Cammeyer was eventually swayed by his personal trust in Wright, and Philadelphia came around as well.

On February 2, Hulbert called a meeting of representatives from the eastern and western clubs at the Grand Central Hotel, two blocks from Collier's Room, the symbolic saloon where the NA had been born. Hulbert wisely met individually with each club representative to formally propose the new league, so that if one delegate disagreed with him, that dissenter would not influence his colleagues. But Hulbert encountered no arguments from the representatives. The plan met with unanimous approval and unilateral commitment to commence play in April.

Hulbert and Spalding immediately drew up the Constitution, naming as its objectives "To encourage, foster, and elevate the game of base ball, to enact and enforce proper rules for the exhibition and conduct of the game; and to make base ball playing respectable and honorable."[72] The new association was named the National League of Professional Base Ball Clubs. As its title suggests, it was a league intended to first consider the interests of its clubs instead of its players. What developed was quite a dramatic antithesis of the modern base ball economy. Whereas in a five-year period from 1996 to 2001, the highest yearly player salary soared from $11 million to $25.2, the 1875 Boston payroll would not even be matched for the rest of the decade.

Harry Wright was given a significant role in the National League because Hulbert liked him personally and respected him professionally. The two split the responsibility of scheduling, Hulbert to arrange for the four western teams and Wright for the eastern four. They would present these schedules to ballclubs individually, and with permission send it to League Secretary Nick Young.

Hulbert and Wright kept in frequent correspondence throughout the former's presidency and established a friendly relationship along the way. In May 1878, Hulbert tried to amuse Wright with a postcard claiming that umpire Cross had thrown a 24–5 Boston victory over Providence to protect his brother's wagers on the Red Caps, as they were now called in deference to the reinvented Cincinnati club. "How do you like *cross*-cut umpiring?" he finished, signing the letter "B: 'Y–Z'" Soon the *Boston Herald* got a hold of it and printed the text in a small editorial. "[They] must have thought they were doing the base ball world a favor and themselves a credit," the *Globe* scowled. "Whatever effect they expected to accomplish is utterly lost." On May 29 Hulbert wrote Wright to confess that he "gave way to a foolish notion that you would accept from me, as a joke, a bit of foolishness."[73] He thought that Wright would know his handwriting and piece it together with the one initial, "B" for Bill.

VII.

It is surprising that Wright had the energy to participate in the founding of the National League. During the week of Thanksgiving he had taken ill with a sickness that confined him to bed until February. At that point he took a break to help with the pressing base ball matters before taking a four-week vacation to Florida with his family.

It was unlike Wright to be stricken by sickness. He seemed to be one of those rare people that somehow avoided all illnesses throughout his life, except for occasional headaches most likely caused by excessive study of his scorebooks. When Nick Young complained of headaches the year before, Wright advised him to "first, buy a dog and second, before meal roll a lemon till soft, cut it in two, squeeze all the juice into a glass or cup and drink it." According to Wright, he and Carrie had been doing this for the past six weeks and "we know it is good."[74]

On April 28, the *Cincinnati Enquirer* reported that Wright was dead. In a long, laudatory obituary, the *Enquirer* disclosed that he had passed away from consumption the previous afternoon in Boston after being sick for the past month. The news quickly spread over the crowd at the new Cincinnati ballclub's game, prompting a wave of nostalgic discussion of their old leader's glory days of only six years before.

Harry Wright found out that he had died while talking to Morgan Bulkeley on the Hartford grounds. He was rather surprised. A journalist read to Wright the error-laden article which also listed his birth year as 1832, his first season with Cincinnati as 1868, and failed to realize that he had been managing a game in Providence on April 27, not dying in Boston. "There was really no need of his correcting the rumor," noted the *Louisville Ledger*, "for he indeed looked the picture of health and strength, commenting upon the various obituary notices he had received without the least concern."[75] He was embarrassed by the *Enquirer*'s flattery but also found it humorous. In the spring of 1877, when asked by a reporter about his weight, Wright responded that "You may tell them I weigh 170 pounds. A year ago, when I was in Florida, practising [sic] for my obituary, my weight was only 150."[76]

"Well, if Harry ain't dead, he ought to be," one paper concluded, "so that he could fully enjoy the nice things that have been said about him, otherwise they are wasted. After a man's obituary is published in the *Enquirer*, it is time he ceased to live if he knows anything about the proprieties."[77]

One would expect 1876 to have been a banner year for base ball. It was the first year of the new league, the 30-year anniversary of the first ballgame at Elysian Fields, and the Centennial birthday of the nation. But in fact it was regarded at the time as just another season. Reporters speculated cynically that one-third of the league would not last until November, especially in new league locales such as Louisville and Cincinnati. The Cincinnati Red Stockings, managed by the returning Charley Gould, turned out to be the worst club in the league, but Wright was optimistic about them early in the season. To old teammate Oak Taylor he wrote, "I am glad to hear that Cincinnati is re-kindling her zeal in the Noble Game, and hope we shall have some of the old-time enthusiasm to enliven us when we visit [Cincinnati] this season."[78]

Wright's optimism did not infect the Boston press. In early April the *Boston Herald* lamented that "there is too much of the old stock left in this nine to call it an experimental one.... We [do not] think that the Boston public expect too much from it."[79] The Red Stockings were critically inexperienced. Wright had replaced the Big Four with a set of inadequate amateurs: pitcher Borden, catcher Brown, left fielder Whitney, and 1st baseman (later acclaimed sportswriter) Tim Murnane.

The largest hole was in the pitching, where Spalding was sorely missed. Joe Borden started off well by winning the first National League game and two months later throwing its first no-hitter, against Chicago. But he soon went down with a sore arm and was done for the season. Wright refused to allow Borden to receive a salary for doing nothing, so he made him into a groundskeeper, a decision that Borden actually took without complaint.

Once Borden was dropped, backup Foley broke his contract, so Wright had to fill in until he found a replacement. According to one writer, "The pitching of Harry Wright was so puzzling to the boys that they did very little with it."[80] But he had no desire for the starting role and he turned to Tommy Bond, who had just left Hartford. This could have been a problem with the Hartford management, but Bond hadn't gotten along with Captain Ferguson and they were happy just to see him go.

Despite the club's difficulties, Wright was lauded for his handling of the young club. This was probably attributable to the nearly paternal relationship he often forged with his players, his "boys." He wore eyes of ice on the bench — "He studies his man well and during the whole game seems to be deep in thought"[81] — but he spoke with a calm reassurance that kept the boys at ease. "You need a little more ginger!" he'd yell in his grandfatherly way, and when overly excited he cried "Sit still, my heart, sit still!"

In making managerial decisions, Wright had an essential ability to "sift the chaff from the wheat."[82] The *New York Clipper* regarded him as "admittedly the best captain that ever took a base ball organization in hand,"[83] and at another point "unapproachable in his good generalship and management."[84] In 1886 one paper noted, "It is true that Mr. Wright is not infallible, and he is apt to err, just as any other person in his particular business profession will blunder, but Mr. Wright will make forty-nine good moves to every bad one."[85]

According to Wright, his basic strategy was to produce a hard-fought game of integrity:

> I try to impress upon my players the fact that people who care to see them play, whether it be at home or abroad, want to see base ball. If they cannot win, let them never cease trying until the last man is out.... The men should work just as hard when they are ten, fifteen, or twenty runs behind as when the score is a tie. Then if the game is ultimately lost no fault can be found with them on the score of indifference.
>
> If the players always work on this principle they will overcome many obstacles which for the time being might seem insurmountable.[86]

Keeping these principles fresh in the boys' minds was a challenge in 1876. In July, Wright reported "The boys are getting along a good deal better than I expected.... The amateurs I filled in with are improving fast."[87] This was a positive spin on what was a bleak contrast to the previous season's club. Boston had begun the month 15–15 and remained at .500 by the time they reached October, 24–24 with four games left to play. The team had just won its season series against Cincinnati in its 10th match of the season; the Red Stockings had won only five games that year.

By that time, Chicago was well ahead of Boston and the rest of the pack, namely St. Louis and Hartford. Wright had not expected Chicago to make such a good showing that season, remarking that all good clubs needed at least three years to gel. "The fact is you can't take a new nine even of first-class players and make them play their best the first year," but then hastened to contradict this in the spirit of politeness by saying "I don't see any reason why [the championship] shouldn't come to Chicago."[88]

When Boston and Chicago played on May 30 that season, it was considered the first big matchup of the National League. 5,000 extra seats were erected at the Union Grounds, but it still was not enough. At two o'clock, 80 minutes before the game was supposed to begin tickets sales were stopped so that the field wouldn't get overcrowded. Still hundreds of people hopped the fence and inched onto the grass, requiring police to clear the field for 20 minutes. Despite the enthusiasm among the cranks, it was a largely pessimistic crowd. They were convinced that Boston would lose on account of its fielding, but in fact the club lost it on bad baserunning.

By the end of the season it was clear that the National League had the authority that the NA lacked. At the League meeting in December, newly

elected President Hulbert moved that the New York and Philadelphia franchises be expelled for refusing to complete their schedules out west because
they hadn't felt the trip would be profitable. The Philadelphia representative broke down to plead for a second chance. Wright was so affected by
the pathetic scene that he begged on his behalf for mercy, for they had
"repented and ... 'put on clean linens.'"[89]

Hulbert showed no sympathy. He immediately proceeded in presenting the charges and demanded a unanimous vote for dismissal. The other
six clubs complied. The National League had just made a loud statement
by doing something that the NA never had nor would have done: sacrifice
money for integrity. New York City and Philadelphia were the two largest
cities in the NL, and now there would not be another franchise in either
city until 1883. The money was largely made up by the players, who now
had to pay $30 for their uniforms and would no longer receive 50 cents a
day in expense money while on the road.

In response to New York and Philadelphia's negligence, Hulbert and
Wright developed the first uniform playing schedule, as mentioned earlier.
The ballclubs did not appreciate being told when to play where, but it helped
them in attendance since the cranks now knew well ahead of time when
their team would be home or away.

The NL's expulsion of New York and Philadelphia had the indirect effect
of encouraging entrepreneurs to establish new leagues with franchises in
those cities. In order to block this competition — and therefore, many
claimed, establish a monopoly — the National League set up the League
alliance after the 1877 season.

Under the Alliance, all clubs were accepted as long as they regarded
themselves as a minor league club. This way, the NL could be considered
the only major league around. In return, territory and player rights were
respected, blackball lists were honored, and the other leagues did not have
to face the wrath of the National League. One league that did not comply
was the International League, and so after the 1878 season the NL passed
"intercourse legislation" to keep all clubs within the League Alliance —
which included virtually every other form of competition besides the amateur ranks — from playing IL clubs or playing on IL grounds.

The move against the IL was immediately denounced by writers and
cranks for the heavy-handed tactic that would certainly crush the upstart's
economy. Wright defended the move with a seemingly disingenuous claim
that it was to protect Alliance clubs from playing lower teams that would
hurt their profits. Matches with NL clubs produced an average of $295 in
profits, he argued, while outside clubs garnered only $53.

The League's muscle was also flexed after the 1877 season in the wake of the Louisville scandal. The pennant race that year was shaping up to be the best of the decade. Boston had bolted out ahead, but Louisville surged in July to overtake the sinking Red Caps. Writers and cranks alike were excited to see a good, clean race, "an exceptional one in the integrity of play exhibited by all the contending clubs in the League arena, and it is to be hoped that nothing will occur to mar the record in this important respect."[90]

Indeed, Wright stated on May 3 of that year,

> I think the public have confidence in the integrity of the different clubs and the individual players than they used to have. The clubs now play to win, and when the public know that they will take an interest in the game and attend the contest. When the people get to thinking that either nine are not doing the best they can, they become disgusted with the game and will cease to patronize it.[91]

The level of security necessary to make such comments suggests an unguarded obliviousness to the factor and personalities present in the league for a scandal as shocking in its time as the 1919 Black Sox. However, it had been clear since the beginning of the season that there was sufficient discontent among the Louisville Greys to provoke some kind of backlash. It existed primarily among four members of the team, Jim Devlin, George Hall, Al Nichols, and Bill Craver, a mischievous clique that delighted in antagonizing manager John C. Chapman. At the December 1876 League meeting Devlin had formally requested his release from the Louisville club for "fail[ing] to comply with the conditions of his contract." This was part of the general acrimony that had grown between the players and management. The pay cuts, unbalanced power between the two, and tremendous disrespect had frustrated the players to desperation. At one point, Hulbert publicly threatened to tell Paul Hines' father if his son's poor play didn't pick up.

In mid–August, Louisville seemed on the verge of sealing the pennant race early. All it had to do was play .500 ball for the rest of the season, while Boston needed to win nearly all of its remaining games. Seeing an opportunity to profit from Louisville's perceived invincibility, a New York pool seller named McCloud convinced Nichols to get Devlin, Hall, and Craver to throw an exhibition game. McCloud would make a nice profit and split it with the other four. Then the stakes escalated into championship games, and finally the pennant.

With the exception of Craver, it was surprising that these particular players would throw a pennant race. Just from Wright's relations with them one draws the impression that these were reputable ballplayers. Hall had played for Wright in Boston a few years earlier and, according to the *Boston Advertiser*, "play[ed] ball with all his heart." But once in Philadelphia, he was corrupted by the gambling crowd and developed a bad name. Wright had pursued Nichols only one season before when Foley broke his contract, and he also had tried to acquire Devlin before the 1877 season. "He is a first-class man," Wright said of Devlin. "I think there is no better."[92] When suspicions were aroused this time that Louisville would throw games to keep the championship out of Chicago, Wright firmly defended the Louisvilles.

Initially, the Bostons were simply given credit for an outstanding run to overcome Louisville and win the championship. But soon after the season, the *Louisville Courier-Journal* mounted evidence against the Louisville four and the scandal was revealed. In both of the National Associations, such incidents were dealt with softly and therefore ineffectively. The National League instead banned the four players for life and, unlike the NAs, did not capitulate in later years. This established the precedent for Judge Kenesaw Mountain Landis' handling of the Black Sox Scandal and A. Bartlett Giamatti's handling of the 1989 Pete Rose controversy. It required a measure of cruelty and narrow-mindedness, but ultimately that's what was necessary for the good image of the National League that no other method could have yielded.

The most pathetic case was Devlin, whose every attempt to return to base ball was stifled by Hulbert. At one point he tried to get a position on a San Francisco nine, but Hulbert found out and threatened to block the "professional chances" of all of that club's players.

On February 24, 1878, Devlin wrote a letter to Wright from Philadelphia:

> Dear Sir:
>
> As I am Deprived from Playing this year I thought I woed write you to see if you Coed do anything for me in the way of looking after your ground or anything in the way of work I Don't Know what I am to do I have tried hard to get work of any Kind But I Canot get it do you Know of anyway that you think I Coed get to play again I can assure you Harry that I was not Treated right and if Ever I Can see you to tell you the Case you will say I am not to Blame I am living from hand to mouth all winter I have not got a Stick of Clothing or has my wife and child.... I am honest Harry you need not Be afraid the Louisville People made me what I am to day a Beggar I trust you will not say any thing to any one about the Contents of this to any one.... I am Dumb Harry I don't Know how to go about it So I Trust you will answear this and do all you can for me So I

will Close by sending you and Geo and all the Boys my verry Best wishes hoping to hear from you soon I am yours Trouly

> James A. Devlin
> n. 908 Atherton St.
> Philadelphia Pa[93]

Devlin wrote again to Wright on November 14 of the next year in a manner far more formal in its diction and far more legible than Devlin's initial scribble. It seems that he had enlisted some help in order to make a better impression with his second letter. But Wright did not help Devlin, though it is not known if he truly wanted to or not. Certainly in Hall's case he was sympathetic, writing just two weeks after Devlin's second letter, "I should only be too happy to see you reinstated and the blemish that at present rests on your character removed."[94] Craver did not solicit Wright's help, but instead wrote to warm him to back off. He was seeking reinstatement in late 1878 and "I do not wish to have you intercede."[95]

The scandal may well have had a damaging effect on attendance league wide. Though Nick Young reported to Wright after the first game that "the season opened well all around," by June most teams were not drawing well. One friend wrote to Wright on the 26th of that month that "It would not surprise me to hear from you that the nine is not in very good odor at home, Mrs. W's letters, the actions of the press, and the failure of the people to turn out all point to that state of affair."[96] By the end of the season the Boston ballclub lost $1,433.31. This was part of a pattern of annual losses for the club accented by a collapsed economy.

The club's debts had no connection to its play. Boston fell behind the rebounded Cincinnatis in May, but soon sneaked into first place while other top clubs broke down. Boston once again took the championship by steady play and successful implementation of strategy. That year Wright started the practice of giving signals to runners, instead of just fielders. Once on base, the runner would look to the bench and if Wright lifted his scorebook from his lap, he would go. Also Boston had the advantage of playing against weak competition. Three of the most formidable clubs of 1877 had been replaced by the weaker Providence, Indianapolis, and Milwaukee nines.

By September, it was clear that Boston would win the championship. Interest focused on second place, where Cincinnati, sparked by young Mike "King" Kelly, beat out Providence and even threatened Boston by coming to within four games of first place at the end of the season.

Wright had now won 8 of the last 10 national championships, both official and unofficial, and his brother George 10 of the last 13. The only thing left was to pit them against each other.

4. Uncle Harry

"Uncle Harry is proud of his boys and smiles knowingly." — *The Sporting News, April 9, 1892*

I.

It was not a surprise that George Wright went to Providence after the 1878 season. In July, Appolonio wrote frankly to Harry, "Probably George thinks he could now [manage] even better than you, and I have no doubt he would succeed...." He even heard from "Mrs. Wright" — though it is unclear if this refers to Carrie, Abby, or even mother Annie — "that Geo. W. is trying to induce Morrill to follow him next season (presumably to Providence)."[1] An early September article in the *Boston Herald* confirmed that George was on his way out to captain the Providence club.

A move to Providence ensured an intensified rivalry between the two clubs already linked by close geographic proximity. Most citizens of Providence believed that Boston looked down on their city, and they already had distaste for their northern neighbors. But was there a sibling rivalry now to also factor in?

Certainly, cranks wanted to believe a sibling rivalry existed among the Wright Brothers; it would make the upcoming pennant race more interesting. For those who wanted then, and for those who want now, to find a split between the two, they can find suggestions of it in the facts. But for those who wonder what the true status was, there is probably no evidence worth taking seriously. Some have noted that George was rarely mentioned in his brother's correspondence. Perhaps it is because George used to cut practice on him frequently while with Cincinnati and Boston. Most likely,

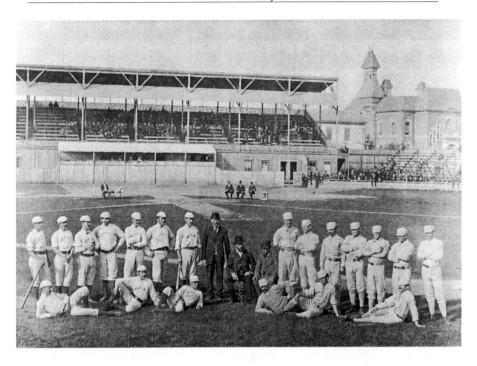

Harry Wright's Boston Red Caps pose on their home field with brother George's Providence Grays during the contentious 1879 season. Wright sits at center with cap and cane, while George is sprawled second from right. (National Baseball Hall of Fame Library, Cooperstown, N.Y.)

the omission has to do with the primary content of the correspondence, more often a collection of game arrangements than personal anecdotes and the like. It is most likely that any tension that did exist between the two came from a competitive nature and not a personal contempt.

One outlet for that competitiveness was in the sporting goods business that George had gone to Providence to be closer to. 1878 had been a banner year for Wright & Ditson; "I understand he never did so well in business as this year,"[2] wrote Appolonio. One year earlier, Harry had become a partner in opening the Wright, Howland & Mahn, Manufacturers and Retail Dealers in Base Ball, Cricket & Sporting Goods; usually, it was just called Wright & Mahn. (Howland apparently dropped out sometime early on.) Wright's function was to give the company name recognition and occasionally relay messages to Mahn. His influence was useful in getting the National League to officially adopt its baseball in 1877.

Wright's most significant contribution was the scorecard he sent in for patent rights in May 1878. He had picked up the scoring style from

Chadwick in the 1860's and developed it into his own version, continuing to modify it for the rest of his career. "[A]t first sight," admitted Chadwick, "the scoring system would appear to be a complicated alphabet to remember, but when the key is applied it will be at once seen that a boy could easily impress it on his memory in a few moments."[3]

Here is an example of the scorecard, given by Chadwick:

PLAYERS	POS'N	1	2	3
1. Master	C	SF 1		
2. Creighton	P	4A 2		
3. Pearce	SS	5B 3		
4. Pearsall	1 B		6 LD 1	
5. Oliver	2 B		7 F 2	
6. Smith	3 B		1 TD 3	
7. Russell	LF			9D 1
8. Marrott	CF			3F 2
9. Grum	RF			hrK 3
Total runs in each		0	0	9

A—1st base, B—2nd, C—3rd, H—Home plate, F—Catch on the fly, D—Catch on the bound, L—Foul balls, T—Tips, K—Struck out, R—Run out between bases. HR—home runs, LF—Foul ball on the fly, LD—Foul ball on the bound, TF—Tip on the fly, TD—Tip on the bound....

"Harry Wright's Base Ball Scorebook" became Wright & Mahn's hottest commodity, selling for $1.50–$2.50, depending on size. Plenty of room was given for instructions and statistics. Newspapers hailed its design as superior to anything else on the market. Wright attempted to sell the rights to Wright & Ditson and Spalding in 1882 and finally did so in '84.

In 1878 Wright also became one of the early recipients of endorsements when he represented a turnstile manufacturer. Though he had nothing to do with the invention, his name helped to sell the product well and establish the success of endorsements.

Times were a-changing in the Wright family in the late 1870's. Amid the rivalry of George and Harry, Sammy Wright proved to be unequal to his brothers. On May 30, 1879, Cincinnati released him after posting a dismal .198 batting average and an .886 fielding percentage the previous season. Sammy had entered the professional ranks with New Haven in 1876, and averaged a hit in each of his 30 games but also had 1.43 errors per. When the club shut down in late August, he stopped playing, unlike most of his teammates that signed elsewhere. He did appear in a game for Boston, though, on October 19 when right fielder John Morrill suffered a finger injury.

Brother Harry had long tried to keep Sammy away from professional base ball, advising him to instead to "attend to his business."[4] His "business" probably refers to his drinking problems and other bad habits. Something had to have offset Sammy's apparently outstanding talent. Harry once recalled, "When boys, Sam's fielding always pleased me better than George's. He was more earnest and persevering, and time and again I have seen him take balls that George would shirk."[5]

After his short-lived base ball career, Sammy settled in the Dorchester District of Boston. There he headed the cricket department at Wright & Ditson and frequently umpired; according to his eldest brother, he was a good one. In 1885, Sammy opened his own sporting goods shop in Jersey City, New Jersey. It did good business initially, but was hurt by erroneous reports that he had left Boston to open a saloon. Sammy never married, but lived with sister Mary and at times Brother Harry's children. He died at the Wrights' old family home at 24 Grampian Way in Boston of a cerebral hemorrhage in 1928.

Sam Wright, Sr.'s death in late 1877 added to the spinning nature of Harry Wright's life in the late 1870's. Sam had been stricken with Bright's Disease of the kidneys since early 1876, but did not realize it until the summer of 1877. By then it was too late. On Sunday, December 9, Sam was "stricken with paralysis" on the right side of his body while eating dinner. For the next week, he was virtually unconscious. Harry, George, and Sammy were at his bedside throughout the week, but, George lamented, "he has not known any of us." Sam passed away quietly at George's house on the morning of December 19. His last great pleasure had come about three weeks prior upon reading Chadwick's recollection of an old St. George's game in which he had scored several runs.

At Sam's funeral two days later, Harry was disappointed by the absence of many of his father's old friends and teammates. "[B]ut in this city [F]ather was comparatively a stranger." Though not well known in Boston, Sam had been an ardent supporter of the Bostons. However, his eldest son wrote, in New York "the mention of his name will recall to the minds of many, scenes long past, in which [F]ather was a busy actor, and cause a sigh of regret for those good old timers' ... when he was in his prime. But now, like those 'good old times,' [F]ather has passed away and lives only in memory."[6]

II.

In September, Wright had contacted Ross Barnes about replacing George in the lineup as Shortstop. Barnes declined in hopes of "follow[ing] a legitimate business this winter." But if that didn't work out, he hoped to secure the spot after all. In a spirit often perceived as a post-free agency trend, he noted "Money, money, money, that is the article I am looking after now more than anything else it is the only thing that will shape my course ('religion is nowhere'). Please keep this letter confidential...."[7]

Another confidential letter came on a piece of Springfield, Massachusetts' Haynes Hotel stationary from Davy Force. He admitted that he had already signed with Buffalo, "but between you and myself (confidential) I don't want to play alongside Mr. [Tom] Carey."[8]

Wright ended up settling for J.L. Peters, recommended by a New Yorker who signed only as "An old admirer of *the Boston B.B.C.*" Providence upgraded significantly in addition to the acquisition of George Wright. Past and future stars such as John Montgomery Ward, Joe Start, and Mike McGeary were also added to make Providence a legitimate contender.

By August 14, Providence was "just a length ahead" of Boston and Chicago. "The race for the Championship is getting red hot," Nick Young wrote, "with a fair prospect of its becoming still hotter."[9] As the race narrowed between the two New England rivals, Boston even went so far as to attend a Providence game on an off-day just to root against them. When Providence won anyway, the Boston players, according to one paper, responded with "remarkable quietness."[10]

In the final week of the season, the two rivals played a deciding three-game set in which George Wright scored the winning run for Providence. According to the *Providence Daily Journal and General Advertiser*, the Providence cranks had a celebration comparable to that held for Lee's surrender at Appomattox. "They crowed.... They shook hands.... They held a regular love feast.... It was worth while to be there, just to see the excitement. It was unthinkable to catch some of that enthusiasm."[11]

George Wright had led his team to a 54–25 record and the national title, averaging seven runs per game along the way. The rookie manager had once again been part of a championship club, the only man to do so in his sole season at the helm.

Why exactly George Wright left Providence after his first season is uncertain. Perhaps he had proved all he needed to— to himself, his brother, and the base ball society. In 1880 and in the following two years, he participated only infrequently, filling in from time to time with his brother's club when on Eastern trips that would not take him away from his business. During the last weekend in May, George played for Boston against Chicago.

Before the game, Wright had written to Providence President Henry T. Root asking that George be released to play with Boston for the day. This, Wright acknowledged, was "equivalent to a release for the season," and hastened to defend —"we simply asked for a release and it was granted." At that point, Boston Base Ball Association Treasurer Frederick E. Long interjected, "That's so. That was the spirit and the letter of the dispatch. I think that the president of the Providence club, knowing that George would strengthen our team, generously permitted him to come to our aid."[12]

Their ready defense was designed to offset the mounting criticisms from Cap Anson. Though his team had lost 11–10, Anson anxiously pointed out that he had entered a protest "before the ash was agitated or the sphere was shocked."[13] He appealed to Hulbert for action, but got none. In spite of the league's firmness in other cases, the *Boston Herald* noted, "We have little to expect from the League of Justice, because, as our readers know the League is not a body formed for the administration of Justice, but a sort of Star Chamber Court to oppress and destroy whatever stands in its haughty way."[14]

Despite George's occasional help, Boston was a disappointment for Harry Wright's last two seasons in the city. "Take notice, Boston boys," one paper warned with a sneering condescension, "safe hitting and perfect fielding win the game; even if you do not all get home runs in every game."[15] The players were also acting so lazy that one man, after speaking with Wright about the problem, volunteered to take a $300 pay cut. According to one writer, the Bostons played "in a careless, 'devil-may-care' sort of a way both at the bat and in the field."[16]

By mid–July, when speeches didn't seem to reform the players, outfielder Charley Jones was fired from the club for indifferent play and insubordination. Jones had demanded $378 in back pay owed him from his contract. When he told Wright that he would not play until he received it, Jones was fined $100 and suspended, then expelled. The heavy-handedness of Wright's actions, sanctioned by management, became the basis for controversy among base ball circles.

In fact, Wright's authority was limited. After the 1878 season, his once-strong control of the club was reduced to a "nominal" level. "The Boston club's failures since the close of the season of 1878 were not due to any falling-off in Harry's managerial ability, but to the fact that that club was simply run in the special interests of its boss."[17] Indeed, once temporarily restored to a higher level of authority by the end of the 1880 season following the Jones expulsion, the *Boston Herald* reported that "the Bostons are playing a magnificent game, both at the bat and in the field, and have been doing so for some time."[18]

But three straight losing seasons was too much for Wright to accept. The *Herald* reported, perhaps in exaggeration, "Harry Wright clawed three boards off the side of the Director's room yesterday in his agony."[19] After the 1880 season, some speculated that the Bostons would fold. Club officials assured the cranks that this was not so, but at the same time called on them to rally their support to stabilize the franchise.

Wright's business sense and his managerial ambition could not allow him to reject the offer from Providence that came after the 1881 season. Unlike Boston, the club had a detached and inefficient management that needed a stern influence like Wright to take over with what the *Herald* described as "unlimited power."

III.

As soon as Wright signed with Providence, the club's stock shot up from a "low discount" to a hot commodity, which was only a temporary spike in the Greys' fluctuating economy. Providence was not a base ball town. Even during its championship season of 1879, the Greys could only draw well when Boston or Chicago came to town, though the city was big enough to support a National League club, and so was their 6,000-seat Messer Field.

Two factors were at work in the low attendance figures. First, Providence was a working city that observed the Sabbath. Since their only off-day, Sunday, was off limits to base ball, the Greys were not able to access the working class population on a consistent basis. Secondly, Providence was strictly segregated by ethnic groups, not so much by imposed restrictions as by the tendency to stick with one's own. Each group tended to identify with its nationality instead of its city. Therefore, each reserved its allegiance for the local clubs of its kinsmen instead of the professional nine filled by men from across the country.

Despite spending only two years in Providence, Wright had some of his most innovative breakthroughs during that time. His most noteworthy was the 1883 establishment of the Providence Reserves, a secondary nine developed in the hopes of producing professional talent for when the parent club could use some. In essence, this presents the concept of a minor league for the first time. Unlike modern farm clubs, the Reserves played on the parent club's grounds when that club was on the road. Other clubs protested that this would saturate local interest in the game and ultimately injure the gates shared by Providence and visiting clubs.

However, by the end of the season the concerns of other League ownerships had been placated by the popularity of the Reserves and the effect that they had on driving down salaries. Naturally, as more professional-brand players were developed, less money was needed to attract one since supply exceeded demand. Though the practice was popular, the farm system would not catch on until fostered by the St. Louis Cardinals' Branch Rickey decades later. But, unmistakably, Harry Wright had planted the original thought; according to the *Sporting News* in 1883, he was "the father of the 'reserve club' system."[20]

Other Wright inventions failed and did not return. In 1880, he came up with the idea for a flat bat, a semicircle smoothed on the flat side to make for fewer foul balls and encourage scientific hitting. With the flat bat, Wright argued, " 'placing' the ball will be made easier, and players who have been hitherto ranked as weak hitters will develop into strong ones, and strong ones as relates to long hard hits, but in the view of making safe line hits that will advance men on bases."[21]

The latter part of Wright's explanation was included to answer the call for more offense at the time that made tools of scientific hitting undesirable. After four years of advocacy, Wright finally convinced the National League to officially adopt the flat bat at its League meeting in December 1884. To appease both offensive and defensive-minded sides, the NL offered the flat bat as an alternative to the round bat. There was little enthusiasm among the players, though — even George Wright condemned the bat's chances of success — and the idea quickly died out.

In 1882, the National League came up with its own failing innovation. Boston President Arthur Soden suggested that all clubs change their uniforms before the season to distinguish each position with a different color. In Providence's case, the lineup looked like this: pitcher Ward — light blue; catcher Gilligan — scarlet; first baseman Start — scarlet and white; second baseman Farrell — orange and black; third baseman Denny — blue and white; shortstop Manning — maroon; left fielder York — white; center fielder Hines — red and black; right fielder Radbourne — gray. Each player wore blue stockings, white pants, a brown undershirt, and a tie. Besides looking ridiculous, this new practice was impractical. In the heat of a pick-off play, would the pitcher throw to his 1st baseman or the runner who wears scarlet and white for the opposing team? What if the manager wanted to switch the positions of two of his players who wore different uniform sizes? Would they have to change clothes first? The idea was dropped quickly.

Providence was an exciting team that season, hampered by weak fielding and driven by strong pitching. The best evidence of the latter was an 18-inning 1–0 win over Detroit on August 17. Naturally, scoring opportunities had presented themselves during regulation play, but good defense on the part of Providence prevented them from coming through. In the 15th, Providence nearly scored when George Wright — a .162 batter that season, disillusioned by the breaking pitch — tripled off of Ward's pitching opponent, "Stump" Weldman, with a "corking hit" to left that went through the carriage gates and settled outside the grounds among the "street urchins." The ball was recovered and relayed home in time to nail George as he tried to score. Harry argued vehemently that the ball should be declared a home run since it was handled by an outside party. Unlike many umpires who automatically deferred to Wright, this one refused, and the game continued.

All along, the 1,200 cranks watched the game anxiously "as though awaiting the outcome of a presidential election."[22] Finally, in the 18th, Radbourne led off with a home run that easily cleared the fence and provided for no argument. The 18-inning game had lasted only 2 hours and 40 minutes.

In the middle of the next month, September, Providence played Chicago in a crucial three-game series. Providence had taken an early lead in the pennant race that season, but Chicago won a three-game series in June and soon eased into contention. By the time that the two played in Chicago on September 12–14, Providence had forged a 3½-game lead. The series that followed, King Kelly remembered, consisted of "the three most exciting games I ever played in."[23]

The first game was tied at 4–4 going into the final inning. With Kelly on first base, Burns slapped a hit to George Wright at shortstop that set up a potentially devastating double play. But instead of taking the conventional route, George tried to tag 2nd base and throw to 1st. Kelly sprinted towards 2nd to barely beat George and then throw his arm up into George's shoulder just as he was about to release. The throw tailed into the grandstand and scored both Kelly and Burns with the winning runs.

Afterwards, Harry Wright was livid. Indignantly, he blamed the loss on "Kelly's infernal tricks." Kelly — who met Wright before the series to unsuccessfully suggest a wager of a new hat for the winner — approached the opposing manager afterwards to plead his case. "Harry, when I saw George raise his arms, I knew that if something didn't occur we would be defeated. I didn't think of George or myself, only of the Chicago club."[24]

Wright forgave the aggressive play, but insisted that "if not for Kelly, the Providence club would have won the series and the championship."[25] Instead they lost the next two games and fell behind Chicago two days later. Though the Greys rallied to tie the White Stockings, they ultimately lost the race at the end of the month. Wright was still upset about Kelly's play, as well as a late-season series in which the Buffalo club surrendered a home series to play in Chicago for the White Stockings' convenience. Partly in response to Wright's complaints, the League sanctioned a post-season exhibition match between Providence and Chicago, a precursor to the official championship series of two years later and the World Series play that began in 1903. Instead of taking the games seriously, the Providence players caroused until sunrise at times and did not look sharp for the series. According to some, Chicago purposely allowed the series to extend to the maximum nine games in order to pick up more gate receipts.

The year of 1883 was another good year for Providence. In the most profitable National League season to that point, Providence ran neck-and-neck with the top of the division, ending up with a 58–40 record. Though this only earned a 3rd place finish, it put the Greys 41 games up on the pathetic new Philadelphia club. It was hard to believe two paths so distant would be bridged by Harry Wright.

IV.

It was speculated as early as September that Wright would resign from Providence at the end of the season, though initially it was believed that he would sign with New York. Instead Wright left Providence — the imminent pennant winner — for the last-place Philadelphias.

Philadelphia did have the excuse of being what would be called today an "expansion club." It had organized in the fall of 1881 and was officially adopted by the National League a year later. Director Al Reach wanted to name the club the Athletics, but Hulbert would only allow them to be known as the Philadelphias. Ironically, New York also re-entered the league that season, to help replace the Troy and Worcester clubs. Knowing that they had no chance to contend, the Philadelphias declared 1883 "the experimental season." 50 cent admission fees were charged, but this hurt attendance badly. When the rate was cut to 25 cents, attendance picked up even though the wins did not. In turn, the local cranks demanded a significant improvement, and it seemed to management that the only answer was to sign Harry Wright.

The Philadelphias' main competition was not the National League opponents but the crosstown rivals of the American Association, the Athletics. The National Alliance counterpart had championship talent and a 25 cent admission fee from the start, making it instantly successful. The two clubs frequently played in intra-city matchups that drew evenly-split massive crowds of up to 12,000 cranks. The games were competitive and hard-fought. In one game in April 1884, Wright delayed the game for a half-hour with a "kick" over the Athletics' choice of an umpire.

That season, despite the Athletics' competition, the Philadelphias made a significant profit. $39,582.84 was brought in against $33,554.05 in expenses, for a margin of $6,028.79. Three-quarters of this money was distributed to stockholders, while the last quarter was given to Wright. The same method of distribution was employed one year later when profits were doubled to $13,106.68. It is unknown whether this was one of Wright's contractual stipulations or spontaneous generosity in gratitude for his unexpected success in bringing the Philadelphias up to 6th place (40–72) and 3rd place (56–54), in 1884 and '85, respectively.

Wright's managerial achievements stirred speculation that he would accept a more lucrative deal with the Athletics, but he instead signed a three-year extension with the Philadelphias in October 1885. Wright felt more appreciated in Philadelphia than he had elsewhere. In 1888 he noted, "I won the championship six times [with Boston] and the most we ever got was an oyster supper. Now the whole town turns out to meet the boys when they return from a fairly successful trip."[26]

However, Wright was not given the same financial assistance in acquiring players as he consistently received in Boston. In 1884, the *Police Gazette* reported jokingly that "Harry Wright was seen down at the Battery the other day among a ship load of emigrants, looking for new pitchers and catchers. He has already tried all in this country and is now on a quest of foreign talent."[27]

In 1886, the Philadelphias had a lineup consisting of eight new players. "We will show improved play," Wright insisted, "and make it very interesting for the two clubs to maintain their lead that finished the season ahead of us last year. The contest for first position promises to be close and exciting, and the Philadelphia Club will be the leader."[28] One writer dismissed this optimism as a mask of encouragement for his players. Instead, "Mr. Wright is cognizant of the fact that it would be too much to hope to win the pennant this year."[29] Therefore Wright knew the club needed extra training before the season began. His concept was what today is called spring training.

The 1886 "Southern trip" — as it was then called — was taken by Philadelphia to Charleston, South Carolina, from March 15 to 27. They were followed South by the Pittsburgh and Detroit clubs, who went to Nashville, Tennessee, and Savannah, Georgia, respectively. While there, Philadelphia played a number of games against local clubs and stopped to play in Baltimore on the route back.

Wright was enthralled with the results and sought to return South in 1887 if grounds proprietors down there were willing to oblige. On January 22, he was uncertain whether Philadelphia management would allow the expenditures of another trip. He met with Reach the next week to discuss general club matters, and at one point mentioned the Southern Trip. Wright's case was convincing to a team that wanted to win. "I tell you, there's nothing like it," he once said. "Besides getting in good training, the men all learn each other's play — get into each other, as it were. In this way they don't lose the first six weeks of the regular season, as in the case with the team which began the circuit with 'raw' men."[30] At another point, he contended that as a result of the Southern Trip, "They were in perfect training and stood the best chance of any of the teams for winning the pennant."[31]

Apparently persuaded by these arguments, Reach offered no commitment publicly, but stated vaguely that Wright would probably do whatever his good judgment advised. With that, Wright set up a tentative schedule to leave Philadelphia on March 1, stay for a month, and return in April for the nine-game intra-city matchups. The trip to Savannah — out of uneasiness, he had rejected an offer to go farther south to Florida — was not unusual in its uncertain arrangements. On most of these trips, Wright would line up a number of cities to reach and aim to visit them around a set time.

Also in the area of the players' attendance, the standards were looser than they are today. Before leaving, Wright would send a letter soliciting the players to come, and in return they would send back a letter indicating their intentions. Most did this, but some refused. Notably, in 1887, four players — Ferguson, Casey, McGuire, and Bastian — did not come along due to salary disputes. Wright tried to talk to them about their gripes, especially Charley Ferguson, who quibbled over a $300 difference. Two years later, another four didn't show up. Decker and Wood had tickets waiting for them, so they were supposed to be there. Decker sent a telegraph anxiously notifying Wright that he would take a rail out of Chicago, and Wood promised to be there when camp started on March 15. Thompson and Sanders sent no indications, though, and Wright wrote them sharply to say that he expected them at the club's base in Jacksonville, Florida, when the train arrived.

The reluctance on the part of some players may have been due to the long, hard days of Harry Wright's Southern Trip. The typical routine can be shown by a day at the 1888 site in Cape May, New Jersey. At 6 o'clock A.M., the players awoke to a salt water bath and were rubbed vigorously with coarse towels. At 6:30 a brisk three-mile half-hour walk was taken across the beach to the Government Life Station. As the sun drew up behind them, the men returned to the hotel for a hearty breakfast. From there, they exercised with Indian clubs and dumbbells until lunch, took an hour-long walk and spent time working on grounders and line drives at a large indoor hall. After supper, the men sat around playing checkers and "swapping lies," according to Wright, until bedtime at 10 o'clock. Throughout every Southern Trip, the club practiced daily, except for Sundays, and played a minimum of five games a week, often two per day.

The trip to Cape May in 1888 was an attempt by Wright to get the springtime results for less travel costs. The club stayed at the Sawyer's Chalfont, a stylish hotel only a few minutes' walk from the Cape May Athletic Club. Wright had tried to get permission to conduct practice on the lawn of the Stockton Hotel, but either weather or proprietors' restrictions precluded this attempt.

As a site for pre-season training, Cape May was a bust. So in 1889 Philadelphia followed Washington's lead of the season before and traveled to Florida. It is surprising that the club didn't go there from the start, given Wright affection already held for the state. "I'm glad to get back here," he said. "It does me good to get back into the sunshine. And the men are delighted. Some of them have never been South before and they are charmed with their first experiences here."[32]

The 1889 trip to Jacksonville was a success. Despite occasional rain that slicked the fields and brought on numerous errors, there was generally good weather, as well as good crowds. The fields were plowed and conditioned well, and the spot turned out to be an ideal location for training. One paper noted that Jacksonville was the "headquarters for winter base ball."[33]

Wright knew the financial implications of linking his club with Jacksonville, much like George Steinbrenner has realized the profitability of linking the New York Yankees with Tampa, Florida. In 1889, Wright announced,

> I want the people [of Jacksonville] to understand that the Philadelphias are here to identify themselves with Jacksonville.... For the present,

though, my team is practically a Jacksonville club. It is going to stick to Jacksonville, is prepared to "play ball" for her.... So we don't care how loud Jacksonville shouts for us. We shall take just as deep an interest in every game we play as if the pennant were at stake and as if all Philadelphia were looking at us and expecting us to do our prettiest.[34]

By 1892, the Philadelphias were splitting time between Jacksonville and Gainesville. When asked why Florida was such a popular training site, Wright answered, "In former years it was rather expensive, but now the twelve-club Southern League will offer good guarantees to the league teams, and I think the trips will be taken by most of the teams."[35]

In 1890, Wright said "I'm satisfied that by another year all the League clubs will play a six or eight weeks' Florida season in February and March."[36] He was nearly right. In the summer of 1890, Chicago, New York, Brooklyn, and the Philadelphia Brotherhood club all came to Florida. Even the players of clubs that did not go South often played there anyway, such as King Kelly, Arlie Latham, and future championship manager George Stallings. The Southern Trip had become an institution.

Given the success of the 1887 trip, the Philadelphia, Chicago, New York, and St. Louis management got greedy and sent its players for a post-season trip to Los Angeles and San Francisco that winter. Wright opposed the idea from the start because, unlike the Southern Trip, this had nothing to do with training the players. Instead of preparing them for the next season, it would only tire them out and hurt their chances for 1888. Players just getting used to the extra labor of the Southern Trip were now also trying to condition themselves for an extra two months after the season as well. Ferguson came away with a lame arm, and others deserted their clubs because they had fallen in love with California.

The players arrived in Los Angeles in early November and began play on the 6th with a 21–5 defeat of L.A. before an encouraging 2,000 cranks. New York and St. Louis arrived two weeks late. By mid–December, Philadelphia was playing against St. Louis and Chicago frequently, as well as the L.A. contingents. On Christmas Day, they were tied by Los Angeles before a crowd of 3,000. California papers harshly criticized the easterners for their subpar play, and contributed to the growing consensus that the Western trip lacked the sensibility of the Southern one. The clubs did not return the next fall.

Wright knew the importance of the Southern Trip was as a means, not as an end. The training was to prepare his men for the championship season. Though he knew the spring games meant "nothing," he agreed to cover Philadelphia's progress in 1887 on a free-lance basis for the *Philadel-*

phia Record in exchange for $3 a day. "The score of each fine winning prac-
tice game," he said in finding the good in this seemingly meaningless coverage, "will be greedily scanned by the enthusiasts [in Philadelphia]."[37]

It's rather surprising that Wright kept getting offers to write for newspapers considering his insistent criticism of his own writing skills described
earlier. In addition to the *Record*'s offer, he also accepted an offer to cover
League games for the *Cincinnati Enquirer* in 1877. And in May 1875, he
was approached by the proprietor of "Forest and Stream" magazine about
becoming its base ball editor. Wright couldn't believe the offer. Nervously,
he consulted Hulbert and other colleagues confidentially. They advised
him to talk to the proprietor in New York and bring Al Spalding with him.
That's just what he did.

Time and reality convinced Wright to stick with his day job. After
returning from the Southern Trip in Charleston, the Philadelphias got off
to what Chadwick deemed a "good start." After a summer swoon that had
Wright "phillied with grief," according to the *Detroit Free Press*, the team
pulled off a late-season surge typical of Wright's squad. With graceful
fielding and reliable pitching on the part of Ferguson, the Philadelphias
improved their record to a 4th place 71–43.

In 1887, the Philadelphias advanced to 2nd place with a slightly lower
winning percentage than the year before. The remarkable aspect of the
feat was that the club had very little talent, and in fact they had been count-
ing all along on their revamped Philadelphia Ball Grounds to keep attract-
ing cranks when the team was sinking. Yet "From nothing," wrote the
Sporting News, "[Wright] has slowly but surely built ... a team that will
yet do him credit."[38] Chadwick added, "I don't want to flatter the 'old man,'
or dose him with 'taffy,' but I must say that I regard him as the most thorough, efficient and successful professional club manager there is in the
country, and I consider that the Philadelphia Club is very fortunate in securing his valuable services as manager...."[39]

However, Wright was beginning to conflict with some of his players.
In late 1886, this fact came out in a pair of incidents involving shortstop/
captain Arthur Irwin and then Ferguson.

On August 28, Philadelphia was up by two on Chicago in the 3rd
inning when the White Stockings rallied for four runs. With Clarkson at
bat and Burns on second, pitcher Casey threw a wild pitch up in the zone.
Catcher McGuire lunged for the ball but only caught enough of it to injure
the forefinger of his right hand. As Burns held up at third, McGuire called
a timeout to request that he be taken out of the game. Immediately, Chicago manager Cap Anson rushed out behind the plate. "Let me look at the
finger," he ordered McGuire. "That is nothing. You can catch with that."[40]

Wright did not trust Anson's opinion. "Can you catch it out?" he asked McGuire.

"Yes, I guess so."

"Well, he won't play it out," interjected Irwin. As Philadelphia Captain, he had a superior authority over in-game decisions.

"Won't he?" umpire Powers asked, rhetorically. "Well, he will play. His hands were sore when he came in, maybe, but that ball never hurt him. He'll have to play it out."[41]

Wright accepted the decision while Irwin continued to fume. "Well, Mac," said Wright, "if Powers insists on you catching, you will have to do the best you can."[42] With that, he returned to the bench, where he was soon accompanied by Chicago executive Al Spalding. The two argued that, whereas Irwin had encouraged McGuire to play back and catch the ball on the bound after surrendering four runs playing at normal depth, the catcher should instead inch forward. Wright called for McGuire to do so, and the catcher obliged. "Hold on then!" Irwin shouted to McGuire. "You go back where I told you to play. And you—" wheeling around with a finger extended towards Wright—"go back and sit down! I'm running these players."[43] Wright obediently sat down without an argument.

McGuire again complied with his instructions. But, stubbornly, Wright insisted on moving him closer to the plate. This went on for a few minutes as the crowd became restless. Finally, Spalding once more came out of the stands, this time to speak with Anson and then Wright. "We'll withdraw our point," he announced. "Put in your other catcher, and we will play the game out under protest." With new venom, he turned to Irwin. "We'll take good care to see that you play ball, too, Mr. Irwin. We'll have you disciplined for your tactics."[44]

By the time backup Clements put on his equipment and stepped behind the batters' box, over half an hour had elapsed since Casey's wild pitch. The cranks had lost interest, and many had left in frustration. Most were relieved when Powers called the game off after the 8th inning.

Charges were subsequently brought against Irwin by both Powers and Spalding for violation of Section 42 of the League Constitution. This charge protected against prejudicial acts used to delay or complicate a game, and could have potentially resulted in expulsion. Irwin dodged that fate, and also issued an apology to Wright, who didn't fully realize until speaking with observers how disrespectfully he had been treated.

Two weeks later, Ferguson crossed the line when he blamed his teammates for the loss in a game that he pitched. In turn, the players blamed Ferguson for the loss. When Wright sided with them instead of him, Ferguson packed his bags and left for Philadelphia.

Afterwards, one of the players sidled up to Wright to ask what he planned to do. "Do?" Wright asked, his eyes cold and spontaneously fierce. "Why I shall simply suspend him for the balance of the season and fine him $200. If upon our return he fails to report at practice hours and perform any duty he is called upon to fulfill in the line of base ball, then I shall see that he is blacklisted. He certainly deserves even that punishment."[45] The players fully supported this position.

When asked about the situation publicly, Wright insisted that Ferguson had fallen ill in Chicago and had to go home. Though this was not actually the reason that he left, there was some truth to the story. In fact, Ferguson was so sick that he spent ten days at home in bed, but was back by October. By that time, he figured that the club had let the issue die, but in fact they subtracted the $200 fine from his season's pay. Ferguson was so mad that he signed on to coach the Princeton College club for the 1887 season. By mid–March, he gave up the job, though, and returned to Philadelphia.

These problems with players drew complaints from Philadelphia executive Col. John I. Rogers that Wright was not enough of a disciplinarian. In fact, that's just what he was known as, even before these charges came to encourage a defense. "[Wright] is a thorough disciplinarian, and can reflect that he has always been a leader of a corps of gentlemen against whom no word of suspicion can be uttered."[46]

Besides the Ferguson case, several incidents in Wright's Philadelphia tenure bear the latter opinion out. For instance, one time outfielder Jimmy Fogarty didn't want to play in a game, so he climbed up a tall brick wall to watch it from there. When Wright found out about this, he marched up to the top of that wall and yanked Fogarty down by the ear, according to the *Philadelphia Herald*. After being threatened with a fine, Fogarty was easily convinced that he'd be better off playing.

While not eager to criticize his ballplayers, Wright was not afraid to. He was often frank about a player's failings, whether in speaking to another or to the man himself. In an 1875 letter he wrote of Jim O'Rourke, "A first baseman shouldn't stand on one leg with his arms folded thinking of 'the girl I left behind me,' when the ball is being delivered to the bat, as he did frequently."[47]

In addition to firm stances taken with individual players, Wright instituted team policies to ensure hard play on the field. In 1885, pitchers were fined $1 for not covering 1st base, and in 1893 batters that did not run out ground balls were charged $10.

However, Rogers insisted that Wright's methods were not strict enough. At one point in Wright's managerial tenure, the club lost two games in a row. In reaction, Rogers requested that the manager give his men a "very positive talk" once a week and hold a clubhouse meeting after every game to review all of the mistakes that had been made and how the team's play could be improved. In addition, Wright was to stop them from eating big lunches on game days and encourage the players to spend their mornings resting or taking brief rides as opposed to billiards and sight-seeing.

Rogers' micromanagement from the top was emblematic of a trend that had begun among many major league clubs. Increasingly, decisions and authorities were being taken away from managers and given to the executives. This alienated such prominent managers as St. Louis' Charles Comiskey and Chicago's Anson, prompting the latter to leave for what was ultimately a three-week stint with the Giants after two decades with the White Stockings.

Colonel Rogers had a reputation for running his club like a military unit. He had been the colonel of Pennsylvania's Governor Pattison's staff and served as Judge Advocate General of Pennsylvania. His involvement with base ball started most notably with the development of the obscure Bachelor Base Ball Club into the Philadelphia Athletics in 1871. Reportedly, he "became disgusted" with base ball in the early 1870's and went on with his political ambitions and his business as a lawyer. In 1882, Reach convinced him to join in the Philadelphia venture and serve on the league's legislature, where he became known as the "lawyer of the league." While this title suggests that Rogers was rather successful in getting his way, he could be infantile when he did not. One instance of his temper was shown at the 1893 League meeting when he had to be dragged out of the room by Wright and Reach while thundering through a caustic verbal tirade against advocates of 50 cent gate fees.

Wright's relationship with Reach is not as easy to understand as with Rogers because it was usually the latter that spoke for the team in the press. The one tenuous incident that can be found between the two is in a February 1882 letter from when Wright was with Providence. In arranging a game, Reach broke an earlier agreement by insisting on giving Providence only 45% of the gate fees, with no money guarantees, and no agreement to a return match. This was very disagreeable to Wright's standards, and he accosted Reach for these maneuvers in a subsequent letter.

Though his reaction is unrecorded, it is reasonable to believe that Wright was irritated by Reach's policy on ball maintenance. During the 1880's, while finances were sagging, Wright was charged to keep a meticulous record of the number and condition of all baseballs owned by the Philadelphias. This would not have been such a difficult job if Reach had not insisted on using his company's "rocket" balls during practice because they were cheaper. Often Wright or one of his players would have to leave the park to persuade a young "street urchin" to give up the ball in exchange for a ticket to that day's game.

Beyond the annoyances, Wright was upset by the lack of power that he had, the very reason that he had left Boston early in the decade. At one point, Reach denied the existence of this problem. "[There] is not now, nor has there been in the past, this year or any other year, any trouble between Messrs. Wright, Rogers, or myself. Mr. Wright … has had full and absolute control of his players."[48] Wright was not convinced.

In the spring of 1886, Philadelphia Athletics manager Al Sharsig offered Wright a lucrative $7,000 contract and part ownership of the club. Wright rejected this offer but began to wonder why he should not have the same opportunity with the Philadelphias. He approached Reach with the idea, but was hastily rebuffed. This nearly broke the camel's back. Wright was sick of management and sick of being used as a scapegoat for any problems that came up on the team. With his contract up at the end of the 1888 season, the *New York Times* noted that "very liberal concessions will have to be made to him to induce him to sign with the club in 1889."[49]

Instead Wright gave in. His only resignation was his own to an unsatisfying and frustrating position which he could have easily escaped of by signing with other anxious teams. Why he stuck around is not known. What is known of the effects of this, however, is dramatic for Harry Wright. His frustrations ultimately turned him bitter towards base ball. This came out in his fervent discouragement of his sons Willy and Harry, Jr., in regards to pursuing base ball careers.

Willy had been a bank clerk for all of his young career until 1887, when he resolved that he "could not stand the pressure." His new ambition was to make it as a professional base ball player, but he was determined to get there on his own instead of by his father's connections. After playing in a Fast Day game on a picked nine with his Uncle George, he signed with the St. Albans, Vermont, club for $100 per month. Willy stood out among his peers as a superior pitcher and all-around player capable of realizing his major league aspirations.

Harry, Jr., joined the professional ranks even earlier, in August 1886 with the St. Johns of Quincy, Illinois. It appears that he turned in a rather satisfactory performance in the role of Pitcher, and went on to play for the Tippecanoe Club of Philadelphia as of July 24, 1888.

Only three weeks after that date, amid the success of his other sons, Wright lost his second youngest son when 13-year-old Albert died of typhoid fever at the family's residence on Twenty-Second Street in Philadelphia. The family was not quite prepared for this transpiration. The formerly healthy and vibrant young man had contracted this illness only recently, and it was not believed to be very serious. This would not be the only son Wright would have to bury in his life, either. As a result of circumstances now unknown, it is believed that Willy also died before his father's demise in 1895.

These losses only intensified the difficulty of dealing with Annie Wright's death while Harry was away on the Southern Trip on March 24, 1887. She had also died unexpectedly of heart trouble at her home in Roxbury, a suburb of Boston.

Just as transition had been a theme for Wright in the late 1870's, death was a constant haunting in the late 1880's; it even trailed him into the realm of base ball when Charley Ferguson died suddenly on April 29, 1888.

After wrestling with the decision for two years, Wright had finally decided to play Ferguson at 2nd base. Ferguson had been a steady pitcher with an angled, almost side-arm, motion, but since 1887 he had wanted to become a second baseman. That August, he severely strained tendons in his right foot due to adjustments to the more stringent pitching rules of '87, according to doctors. It seemed that his pitching career was over. But Wright refused to concede Ferguson's steady pitching, and he plugged him back into the role after his return. The reversal in the spring of 1888 surely heartened Ferguson, but he was taken ill the day prior to Opening Day. Many who had witnessed his suspension in 1886, lame arm in L.A., and the opportune injury of the season before, shrugged off the illness cynically. But as it turned out, Ferguson passed away on his tenth day in bed from typhoid fever, the same thing that killed Albert Wright.

The flags flew at half-staff in Philadelphia above the uniformed Philadelphias with a haunting black armband on their sleeves. Besides the emotional impact of the loss of a 25-year-old teammate, they effectively lost the season there as well. Instead of the late-season surge of the year before, Philadelphia began to lose game after game by merely a run or two.

Shortly after Ferguson's death, the Philadelphias plummeted to last place. Charlie Bastian was not working at 2nd base and Wright began to look frantically for a replacement. His best reports were on a young man named Ed Delahanty. A scout sent to watch him play in West Virginia came back with a report so complimentary that Reach himself went down to witness a game. He immediately offered $2,000, a record contract for a minor leaguer.

Del instantly became the club's star, and with that status came forth a self-sufficient and self-serving flamboyance. At one time he was sent to the plate with orders from Wright to bunt. But after spotting a good pitch, Delahanty instinctively swung for a home run. As he returned to the bench — much like in the Ed Andrews story found in Part I — he found his smile met by a hard look on Wright's face. "That will cost you twenty-five dollars," the manager said without emotion.

"What for?"

"For not bunting."[50]

Though Wright's disciplinary tactics were strong, he was ultimately the best influence on Delahanty. One could consider him a father figure to the young ballplayer. "Be less impetuous, Edward," he would say softly. "Calm yourself. Modify your speech. It doesn't do you a bit of good to be too strong in big words. It won't help make you a better ballplayer."[51]

Like any father-son sort of relationship, there were constant struggles between the principles of independence and obedience. Perhaps the most famous incident of conflict between Wright and Delahanty came on Monday, May 18, 1891, when Del wanted to take a kid on the bus from the club hotel to the ballgrounds in Pittsburgh. Wright steadfastly refused, prompting a heated argument between the two. Eventually, Delahanty "went in a huff" to his hotel room where he threw off his uniform, put on his civilian clothes, and announced that he would not play. He was fined $100 and suspended indefinitely.

While incidents like this served as a temporary wedge between the two, in the end it drove a relationship of reverence for one, dutiful care for the other, and mutually a flow of respect. Upon his mentor's death, Delahanty told a reporter that "God breathed pure Hibernian oxygen into the heart of Harry Wright.... Even if he was of English descent."[52]

V.

Between the insurgence of Delahanty and the steady guidance of Wright, the Philadelphias finished in 3rd place in 1888, but dipped below .500 to 4th place in '89. An injury to Delahanty in early June left Philadelphia fighting with New York for 2nd place. At one point, the Philadelphias even literally fought, on September 6, 1889, against the White Stockings. As police took to the field and made arrests, Wright stood in the middle trying to calm his men down.

Harry Wright, Jr., once recalled an instance when his father was managing and "a catcher lost his head and raised his hands to Father. Father, always cool and even-tempered, sparred with him only to quiet him down. The player must have had a lot of respect for Father's athletic ability because he finally gave up, saying, 'So you can do that well, too,' paying tribute to Father's boxing ability."[53]

In the winter of 1889–90, it was an inner division that split the Philadelphias and the National League as a whole. That season, the Brotherhood — a fraternity of rebellious players that represented an early form of a base ball union — officially broke away to form the Players League. The actions of the Brotherhood had been imminent from the Philadelphia perspective since 1886 when Arthur Irwin acknowledged that he was one of seven club members to join the fraternity. At the time, Wright said that he only knew what he read in the papers; otherwise he was oblivious. And the players tried to keep it that way.

The Players League's Cleveland President, Al Johnson, remembered an incident in 1889 when Philadelphia was playing in Cleveland. One night Smith was discussing some private Brotherhood information with Philadelphia's Fogarty, Farrar, and Clements. As the four conversed, Wright suddenly walked by with an associate. Fogarty changed subjects smoothly, talking about a prizefight he had attended, and Clements "helped him out."

It was from experience that the players knew to keep such information from Wright. He was likely to report any kind of insurrection and punish the players for it, a mentality that the PL was designed to allow escape from. The players knew that his policy was conceived out of duty, not contempt. His public regard for the Players League — as a league, remember, not as a labor force — was diplomatic, hastened to include a firm respect for the players' rights to secede if necessary. After all, "I don't want any players on my team who is not with me heart and soul."[54]

Though Wright recognized the players' ability to make this decision, he was one of the most coherent naysayers among the passionate denunciations from the National League. "It is all very well for any set of men to believe that there is naturally a bonanza in base ball," he conceded, "especially if the players be stars or champions. [But] I wonder if it even occurs to them the losses they are liable to sustain? It is just as easy to drop many thousand as it is to make them."[55]

To Wright's disgust, the *New York Clipper* suggested electing him as Secretary of the Players League, and, while they were at it, combine Secretary with President and Treasurer and assign the office to Wright. "The election of Harry Wright would be enthusiastically endorsed by every newspaperman throughout this country for all would be treated alike."[56]

Wright never even thought seriously about leaving for the Players League. In fact, he was quite upset that his name was suggested without his authorization. Above all factors in his thought process, he believed that the PL had no chance. His prediction was perceptively accurate, in hindsight. "I am of the belief that one season will suffice to prove which organization is here to stay.... The public, of course, has a natural tendency to support the old favorite players, whether in or out of the league, and it will probably bestow its patronage in that direction on the start."[57]

Perhaps the most remarkable development found in studying the intersection of Wright's story with the Players League controversy of 1890 is the degree of reverence with which members of the Brotherhood regarded him even after he condemned the viability of their league.

> Notwithstanding the fact that Harry Wright did not join the Brotherhood last winter when he was urgently requested to do so, he is still idolized by the players in the new league, who will make almost any sacrifice for him, and they have often assured him that any time he wants to join forces with them he can have anything he asks for.[58]

The fact that Wright stayed in the National League, and Cap Anson for that matter as well, helped tremendously in upholding the prestige and tradition of the establishment. However, the Philadelphias had been reluctant to reserve him, in spite of the well-known interest of the Players League. It was later discovered that the club had approached St. Louis' Charlie Comiskey about taking over (to his angry refusal), and engaged Toronto ballclub manager Cushman to sign new players. Yet Wright was promised in negotiations that he would have total control over his players and all signings of players. Wright had also sought a three-year contract, but was countered with two due to the uncertainty of circumstances, given the new presence of the Players League.

On the whole, Philadelphia suffered few losses to the insurgent league. In fact, it fared the best among National League teams. The toughest loss was Ed Delahanty, who switched to Al Johnson's Cleveland franchise. Philadelphia was at a stop in Charleston on its way back from Florida when Delahanty received a package from Johnson containing a $3,500 contract — including $1,000 in advance payment — and some "sandwich money" for the rest of the train ride. Del was easily swayed by the opportunity to make such money and play closer to his roots. He rushed to pack his suitcase and headed off to the train station, but he was intercepted there by Wright, who tried desperately to convince him of the "unmanliness" of his desertion. Delahanty was not receptive, and he brushed by to take the train.

Though his losses were comparatively small, Reach was indignant and "positive that the Brotherhood League will be short-lived. [They] are a symbol of management of arrogance," he said. "The light they are changing is an imaginary one."[59]

Philadelphia's Brotherhood President, H.M. Love, obviously disagreed. Love was convinced of his club's viability, citing 282,000 in Philadelphia's home attendance the previous season. "Oh, yes," he assured, "we are in the business to stay, as Mr. Reach will find to his sorrow."[60]

Wright understood the implications of the new rivalry. With friends and associates on both sides—even George Wright as part-owner of the Boston Brotherhood club—he recognized soberly, "Sentiment will have to be banished and base ball again put on a business basis."[61]

VI.

From the beginning, the battleground was on paper. The National League v. Players League rivalry was quickly presumed to be "won" by the side that accumulated the highest attendance figures. Naturally, a system this subjective encouraged desperate owners to submit dubious figures that could be inaccurate, but not proven to be so.

The National League was the aggressor in exercising this tactic, though certainly it was not the only one using it. The first strategy was to wait until the Brotherhood released its schedule to release the National League's. That way, the NL could schedule in the same places on the same day with comparable matchups and calculated gimmicks.

The gimmick was key. Since the issue was attendance itself and not who made the highest profits, the National League held several special events such as Ladies' Day or Actors' Day — Spalding's idea — where each fan that qualified received free admission. In the end, Spalding admitted to using such tactics and even altering publicly released attendance figures in hopes of creating a bandwagon effect. He claimed to keep an accurate total behind the scenes.

Despite Spalding's efforts, the Players League appeared to have won the attendance fight. But that result had all the significance of an old-fashioned Texas election: everyone knows that the numbers are wrong, but both sides cheated, so what's the difference? By the most accurate figures available, the Brotherhood had a higher overall total — 980,887 to 813,678 — in 48 more games. However, the average attendance still favored the Brotherhood, 1,843 to 1,506.

In Philadelphia, the PL also won with an average attendance just 175 fans higher per game. The Philadelphia Brotherhood had not been expected to compete with the Philadelphias, and in fact they were expected to be the first casualty of the league war. They were up against a strong young team that was only getting stronger and had the respected Harry Wright at the helm. In July, the club nearly did fulfill its bleak prophecy, but a wealthy pair of brothers named the Wagners came in to rescue it. On the other hand, the Philadelphias made a $30,000 profit, the median between the most successful, Brooklyn at $50,000, and least successful, Buffalo at $10,000. But it should be noted that all National League clubs made a profit in 1890.

Though the Philadelphias lost to their PL counterpart in attendance, they made for a much better ballclub, finishing in 3rd place with a .595 winning percentage as opposed to the Brotherhood club's .519, 5th behind George Wright's Bostons. (Harry happily noted that if all Brotherhood clubs were run as efficiently as George's, the league would have survived.)

The Philadelphias had started the season with immense promise. By early May the club was in 1st place with a .714 winning percentage and a pack of mediocre ballclubs trailing behind them, with one or two exceptions. After taking three of four from New York, manager Jim Mutrie said that "If anybody thinks Harry Wright hasn't a clever team let him present a set of men that can beat them."[62]

Then in late May — the 21st or the 22nd, it is not exactly certain — Wright was stricken by blindness. He had caught a cold several weeks before that had finally settled in his eyes, giving him a serious inflammation that confined him to a dark room with intense pain affecting the entire nervous system. Doctors diagnosed it as catarrh of the eyeballs. "His sufferings have been great," wrote Carrie, "for the inflammation has been so severe that it is almost chronic. All that can be done we are doing."[63]

An oculist stopped by twice a day to administer eye treatments, and in the meantime he was attended to by Hattie and Stella, one by day, the other by night. "Harry is blessed with a devoted wife and loving daughters," wrote a somber Henry Chadwick, "and their nursing and his own characteristic pluck and endurance will, I hope, soon bring about his recovery."[64]

Unfortunately, Carrie was not able to take care of her husband, though eventually by July she came to stay in his room to read to and talk with him. In the immediate aftermath of Harry's illness, Carrie had a breakdown and was "also confined to her bed." Throughout the first week of his recovery, Harry had to walk with assistance to the adjacent bedroom to see Carrie. The sick twist of the situation made it all the more painful. Carrie wrote, "It has been great a trial to Harry as well as myself not to be able to attend to him myself."[65]

As of May 27, the doctors said "that the present is the crisis of his disease."[66] He was being attended to by three doctors, including two oculists, who insisted that he would "pull through all right" due to the vibrancy of the patient and the care of his daughters. Despite the doctors' assurances, the family believed that they were only holding back the true extent of Wright's condition.

The public was even less informed of Wright's condition in the immediate aftermath, except for a May 30 assurance to Reach and Rogers by the
physicians that he'd recover his sight. Players from the Philadelphia NL
and PL clubs, as well as various visiting clubs, stopped in on a daily basis
to check on Wright. But the family would not allow anyone to see him, so
they stopped coming. Still, numerous telegrams of sympathy arrived from
across the U.S., Canada, and England. Benefit games were also played for
Wright in Philadelphia, though no one knew if he approved of such ges-
tures since he was kept in seclusion.

Initially, Wright's recovery was slow, which was natural due to his age
of 55. The doctors began speaking about a recovery in terms of months.
He insisted on weeks, and on managing right after that. As of June 3, he
could tell daylight from darkness. Then in late June, Wright returned to
a state of total blindness. He suffered from aches and pains, and ran a high
fever. On the evening of July 7, one physician told 19-year-old Harry, Jr.,
rather optimistically, "Your father will be able to see, but how much I cannot say as yet."[67]

That month, Jimmy Fogarty told the newspapers that friends of
Wright's believed that he would be permanently blind. Yet in the middle
of July he appeared at a game to a rousing ovation, and late in the month
he accompanied the club on a western trip. By the middle of August he
was regularly sitting on the Philadelphia bench. He "couldn't quite follow
the game," but at least he was improving.

In the time since his absence began, the Philadelphia club had fallen
out of first place and stumbled through June. In July, the club recovered
with a double-digit winning streak, but the momentum soon dissipated
and the Philadelphias, as mentioned earlier, ended up in 3rd place. Any
success achieved in that time was attributed not to the tutelage of interim
manager Al Reach, but the residue of Harry Wright's teaching.

When Wright took back the reins toward the end of the year, he was
obviously limited in his capacity to manage. He would stand by the bench
the entire game and give each batter his instructions before he walked to
the plate. This and his yelling from the bench irritated some, but they
accepted it from the old whiskered man so pitiful with his field glasses
pressed to his face. He looked so much more feeble than his colleagues
were used to. According to Chadwick, "Harry Wright ... was a sight to
bring tears.... He wore a passe straw hat, and the fierce ... wind from the
North gurgled and moaned through the hair on his face like the sound of
a lyre in a gale."[68]

At one point in late September, when Philadelphia stopped in Cincinnati for a series, the *Enquirer* noted nostalgically,

There has been a great change in the Captain. The years that have rolled around since he wore the red stockings of the Queen City teams have left their mark. Instead of a strong, muscular athlete, in the full prime of his manhood, as Harry was in 1869, [the fans now] see a sedate-looking individual in quiet attire, whose hair and whiskers are plentifully sprinkled with gray.[69]

An operation on Wright's left eye in December did not go well and in fact hindered his progression towards a full recovery. Plans for an operation on the right eye were immediately stopped. At that point, he could still barely recognize good friends, but by January 10 he was reportedly "nearly himself again." In March, his eyesight was fully restored.

Wright is seen here managing from the bench late in his career with Philadelphia. Note the trademark straw boater upon his head and meticulously-kept scorebook in hand. (National Baseball Hall of Fame Library, Cooperstown, N.Y.)

Wright's managerial career was still in question. In late 1890 it was speculated that he would require an assistant manager in the coming season to relay messages and follow the game better than he could. Then in late February 1891, the *Sporting News* anticipated that he would announce his retirement, as much for his failing eyesight as his troubles with management. Instead Wright continued as manager and even went so far as to confide to close friends that he believed that his club would win the pennant.

Those close friends ended up letting the press know about Wright's instinct just before a game against Chicago. The Philadelphias were one-hit by pitcher Donaghue, almost no-hit if not for a late-inning spoiler. After the game, Leonard Washburne, rather amused by Wright's prediction, reported that "Last night people in the hotel where the Pennsylvania club exists, were awakening throughout the long still hours, by a rumbling noise like an overloaded cab rolling down a deserted street.

"It was Harry Wright changing his mind."[70]

Surprisingly, Wright was known to make such bold predictions from time to time. In 1889, when the Philadelphias finished below .500 for the first time in five years, Wright had excitedly boasted to a reporter in March, "I have not in all my long experience had such a strong set of players to begin the season with...."

"Do you think the Phillies are pennant winners?" the reporter nudged.

Wright laughed amusedly, but quickly responded. "I do. I am not in the habit of bragging ... but I have such a splendid set of men this year that I do not believe there is a club in the League that can beat us out."[71]

Perhaps Wright's enthusiasm in early 1891 was sparked by the relief over the end of the League War. For a time in late summer 1890, it appeared that the Brotherhood was on a course to establish success. After buying out the National League's Cincinnati franchise, the executives proposed a truce with the NL if they would recognize the circuit as a major league. Presumptively in this vein, the NL invited the Brotherhood to its October meeting. The meeting was actually an opportunity for the NL to buy a few clubs out and destroy the resolve of the Players League. When Brotherhood leader John Montgomery Ward found out about this plan he begged the owners not to sell; but it was too late. One PL owner admitted that he had sold out to the NL because he could not stand his "ungrateful players."

There were some last-ditch efforts to resuscitate the Players League, but finally Ward grunted with reluctance that the League was dead. Spalding acted graciously, at least on the surface, in accepting Ward and other players back to the NL, but no significant changes were made to the reserve clause, the issue that had driven the entire rebellion.

With the League War over, there was a great deal of excitement for the 1891 season. The total number of fans that had supported the two leagues in 1890 had easily exceeded the number that had attended National League games in 1889, and those remaining fans now had to support the one league once again. While Players League fans may have held grudges towards the National League, nearly all the stars of the Brotherhood had returned there for them to see. In Philadelphia, Delahanty returned with a new disposition. He was determined to be a more disciplined ballplayer and character. Wright helped him to control his temper and even give up drinking, a temporary success that he would ultimately capitulate on. (It would be a fatal choice for Delahanty. It was on a train ride while with Washington on July 2, 1903, that he was thrown off for drunkenness and next seen washed ashore in the Niagara Falls days later, dead at age 35.)

Despite the returns of both Delahanty and Wright, the Philadelphias finished at a disappointing 68–69, 4th place among a field of six. The club had actually started off in 2nd place but then plummeted to 6th and seesawed the rest of the way. In September it looked as if they could slide through the top tier, but then a rash of injuries hit and the season was effectively over.

The 1892 season was quite dissimilar. In this case, the Philadelphias started off 4–7 behind the 10–1 Bostons, leaving them in a pretty hopeless situation. But after the western tour ended in mid–May, they were in 3rd place and on the way to a 72–57 record, only good enough for 4th place. Wright had been uncharacteristically unsuccessful in instilling a steady defense to back the club's star pitcher, Tim Keefe. Keefe, an eventual Hall of Famer, had been released by New York in mid-1891 and picked up by Philadelphia, for whom he went 19–16 in 1892, with a 2.36 earned run average.

Before the season, Wright received an insulting $2,000 contract for both 1892 and '93. He accepted it. But the difficulties of managing were too much to handle, and as Chadwick put it, he was on the verge of being "unable to fulfill his duties or bear longer the fatigue of club management."[72] One of the biggest reasons was the death of his wife Carrie on February 5, 1892.

It had taken only a short period of time for Carrie's health to deteriorate. In 1890 she had accompanied her husband on the Southern Trip to Jacksonville. But by the end of the year, after all that she had been through with Harry, she was described as an invalid, and was not expected to get better. On February 2, 1892, doctors determined that her only choice to keep living was a complicated surgery that would have to be performed the next day. The risks were there either way, so Carrie and Harry consented. But Carrie was in so fragile a state to begin with that she couldn't make it through the whole operation and she hung on barely until the morning of Friday, February 5. Before passing away, she gave Harry an "affectionate goodbye."

Wright was so sorrowful that his family feared that he was slipping into a depression. But by July 1893 he was engaged to a woman believed to be Mary Fraser's sister Isabelle. (This is according to the *Dictionary of American Biography*, which also incorrectly listed George Wright's mother as Mary Love.) Wright was asked one day in July if congratulations were in order. "The contract's not yet signed," he responded with a smirk.

"But the engagement is on," the reporter dug, "isn't it?"

Reluctantly, Wright answered "Yes."[73]

The wedding date was set for a few months later, and actually carried out in January 1895, as reported in the 27th's edition of the *Sporting News*.

Isabelle was a special education teacher from Harlem of whom very little other information is known. Halsey Miller, Jr., remembers often hearing his aunts Hattie and Carrie refer to a "MEAN stepmother," but never address her by name. As Halsey noted, "The Wright family is extremely close mouthed, and did not readily give out information. For example, my mother, Caroline Mulford Borden [Miller] claimed not to know the name of her grandmother, Carrie C. Mulford. Ann Tone was never mentioned either."[74] The latter, he suspects, was due to her Irish heritage.

There are two likely reasons why the children and their stepmother didn't get along. First, at the time of the marriage, all of Harry's children from his 2nd marriage were over 20 years old — with the exception of William at nearly 18 — and still living at home. In Hattie's case, she had never married and spent much of her time attending ballgames with her father and taking notes on the contest, especially during a temporary relapse of his blindness in 1892.

Secondly, if she was the sister of Mary Fraser, it is likely that some of Mary's children's resentment for their half-brothers and half-sisters rubbed off on her.

While 1892 and '93 were difficult years personally for Wright, they were better for his Philadelphia ballclub. In 1893, the National League was returning to prosperity after two years of paying off its old League War debts. Philadelphia led all clubs with a $50,000 profit margin despite being the worst road attraction in the league. The key to this seeming contradiction was that Philadelphia had resolved to keep its salaries in check. No more three-year or $3,000 contracts were to be given out. Before the 1894 season, Wright was handed a note from the club management decreeing that "There will be no extra agreements with anybody next year. Maximum salary will be 1800 for '94."[75]

On the ballfield, Philadelphia started off well. Boston had expected to win the pennant as easily as it did two decades before in "Harry Wright's League." But instead it stumbled out of the gate, leading some to suspect it of hippodroming, or throwing games. On Tuesday, June 20, the Philadelphias beat Baltimore for its 6th consecutive win, and on the next day they found themselves tied with Brooklyn for 1st place. Wright was astounded by the crowd support. Fans got so loud at one point that play had to be stopped in order to hear what the umpire was saying. The city immediately began talking wildly of a pennant, and for the first few months attendance was so good that Washington switched a number of its home dates to Philadelphia.

As of June 24, the Philadelphias were tied atop the National League with the resurgent Bostons, trailed closely by the Brooklyns. Two weeks later, the club was two games ahead of Boston and well ahead of Brooklyn, but that changed shortly after when Boston came into Philadelphia and knocked them out of the pennant race for good. By July 28, the Philadelphias were 2½ behind Boston. After a couple days they were passed by Pittsburgh and then Cleveland. At one point in late July, the players joked that it was Isabelle's fault. She had come to a game with Brooklyn just after the announcement of her engagement only to see her fiancée's club lose. Afterwards, the players jokingly called her a "hoo-doo," or a curse.

The Philadelphias ended up in 4th place with a surprisingly fine record of 72–57. They were just 1½ behind Cleveland and well back of Boston and Pittsburgh. Such a late season drop-off was uncharacteristic of a Wright ballclub. Usually it would get hot down the stretch and play tough until the last game. But this time, it did not happen, despite nationwide support, especially in St. Louis, where fans rooted heartily for Philadelphia as soon as their club was plainly out of contention.

In mid–October, Col. Rogers wrote to Wright to express his disappointment in his manager and to tell him straight out that he was going to be held personally responsible for the poor finish of the club. In the postscript, Rogers added bitterly, "We should have finished first."[76]

Of course, this chastisement was nothing new for Wright, but it may never have been so straightforward as in that letter. At the end of the 1892 season, Rogers had been asked if he intended to fire Wright. "No," he answered. "Harry Wright's services have been entirely satisfactory to the officers of the club, and as long as we are in business and he is physically able to perform the duties of a manager, he will have charge of the team."[77]

But Wright knew that he was at risk, no matter Rogers' pledges. According to Wright, "when I bade good-bye to the players at the close of the season I told them that it would be no surprise to me if I was not manager of the club next year."[78] Yet as the off-season began, there were indications that he might stay when Reach and Rogers allowed him to continue making moves to set up a team for 1894. In hindsight, the only indication that gives is that the two executives took a while to make their decision.

In mid–November Rogers called Arthur Irwin to his office for a long interview. It had been rumored for years that Irwin would take over for Wright as manager. In 1888, Irwin had refuted the notion by insisting, "I want to see Mr. Wright just where he is in 1889. He is the most competent man for the position. I never played under a better man."[79]

Days after Irwin's interview, Wright was let go by Philadelphia. Since his contract was up, it was more of a non-renewal than it was a release or a firing. According to Reach and Rogers, it was because in ten seasons with Philadelphia he had never won a pennant. Wright believed that this failure was a result of injuries, but it did not matter. The argument was the most logical one put forth by the executives. After seeing the unprecedented reaction of the Philadelphia fans, the club was desperate to replicate it and this time follow through on it with a pennant. Since Wright had not shown the ability in his decade with the club to engineer and *sustain* such success, then the only recourse was to let him go and do it while there was still momentum left in the club's system.

Wright was surprised by the abruptness of the decision. He knew the axe would come at some point, but he had already been entrusted with power in the off-season and therefore had no direct indication that he was about to be let go. But he was conscious of the proprieties of receiving the news with graciousness. He respected management's right to make such a decision and expressed his regret at having to say goodbye to so many friends.

After hearing the news, the public was not willing to let Reach and Rogers, especially the latter, off the hook. This was complicated by a couple revelations that followed. First it came out that in 1889 Rogers had telegraphed Charlie Comiskey about jumping to Philadelphia for a large salary and replacing Wright after he was fired. Comiskey regarded this as deceitful and wrong. He not only refused, but showed the telegram to Browns owner Chris Von der Ahe, Secretary George Munson, and a local sportswriter. When Rogers found out about Comiskey's reaction, he begged all who knew about it not to say anything. And it worked for the four years until Wright was actually let go.

Also before getting rid of Wright, Rogers contacted Cap Anson to offer him the job. Anson refused and advised him that letting go of Wright was a mistake. But Rogers ignored this advice and turned to Irwin, who got the job.

Many fans were so excited by the treatment of Wright that they threatened to boycott Philadelphia games. Rogers immediately defended his and Reach's decision; but instead of sticking with the more logical reason expressed before, he emphasized that Wright was failing in health and "entirely too easy with his men."[80] According to Rogers, Wright had never imposed a fine on a player in all his time with Philadelphia.

Surely Rogers avoided the reason that Wright had failed to win a pennant because it could not stand against arguments that it wasn't his fault, that injuries got in the way. The two excuses he used in its place, however, were false. Wright's health, in fact, was representative of a phenomenal recovery. He was bicycling now more than ever, a practice that he had started as early as 1889 by riding to and from each Philadelphia home game. The statement that he had never imposed a fine on a Philadelphia player was the most blatantly false reason. One may recall the various fines handed out for lagging players and the heavy fine on Delahanty. That was an instance in which he not only imposed the penalty, but made it stick. The Philadelphias were known as a disciplined club as a result of such policies, as was customary of Wright's ballclubs. During the 1892 season, New York's Roger Connor had noted that Philadelphia had no alcoholism on its club, but instead the players were all at least relatively well-behaved men who respected Wright and listened to him obediently.

Rumors immediately began circulating that Wright would manage elsewhere, most likely Brooklyn or St. Louis. The latter possibility actually was close to coming through. Wright had been in correspondence with President Von der Ahe and prospects looked good. In early January 1894, Von der Ahe was asked if he thought Wright would end up managing the Browns. "Yes," he answered confidently, "I think so.... [Chances] are we will conclude the negotiations going on, and I will give him full control of the team."[81] Realistically, it is doubtful that negotiations came that close; Von der Ahe was known as a rather flamboyant owner whose words had to be taken with a grain of salt.

The Browns deal broke down just before the National League meeting in March. At that point, James A. Hart brought up an idea first suggested in the *Public Ledger* and supported by the *Sporting News* on January 30, 1893. The idea was to appoint Wright as Chief of Umpires, an admittedly honorary position to observe umpires and submit reports to the National League office. As soon as Hart proposed this, Col. Rogers seconded the motion. Wright, who was present at the meeting, was overwhelmed by the offer and he gratefully accepted. He was quickly surrounded by players, magnates, and fans anxious to express their congratulations. He was asked to make a speech, and obliged with a toast to the National League and base ball itself. For this he received three cheers.

Chief of Umpires was the perfect role to fulfill the National League's obligations. The executives felt badly for Wright, who they knew was close to death and quite incapable of taking on a new job of any significant strain. The position was a new one that did not even have to be renewed upon his death. In fact, it was not resumed until five years after his death by John B. Day, who was given enough new authority to make the job an important one. Wright's position, on the other hand, had very little authority. One owner suggested that in order to make him really earn his $2,000 per year contract, he ought to serve as an arbitrator between players and management, a concept that is familiar today.

The position also placed him in an area in which he had credibility. Of course, he was a player and a manager, so he understood their side of matters. But Wright was also unusually sympathetic to umpires. One writer observed that "You never find Harry Wright kicking [or arguing hotly with umpires], and in this respect he is the superior of all the rest."[82] According to Nick Young, Wright was so deferential to umpires because he "recognized the fact that the [umpire] occupied the most thankless position in the ballpark." When controversial plays hurt his club, Young said, Wright would tell his upset players, "If you had played your position properly my boy, it would not have been possible for the umpire to give an opinion against you. Always keep in mind that the umpire is trying to perform his duty impartially, and to render decisions upon players as he sees them. His word is the law of base ball."[83]

The modern observer must understand that umpiring was a much more dangerous job in those days than it is today. The now humorous line of "Kill the umpire!" originated with cranks who had serious inclinations to follow through, as can be seen by newspaper clippings of the 1880's and '90's that are filled with instances of murder on the ballfield, often perpetrated by or against an umpire. Under the headline "An Umpire Kills a Player," one writer reported from Louisville:

> Ben Bates, while umpiring a ball game near Owensboro for two clubs of boys Sunday afternoon last, made a decision in the sixth inning to which Frank Morris, at the bat objected. A bitter quarrel ensued and a fight followed, resulting in Bates fatally stabbing Morris with a pocket knife. He was arrested and Morris soon died. Bates is but sixteen years old.[84]

Even Wright was put in the line of fire at some points in his tenure. On Tuesday, August 7, Wright was in attendance at a game in Philadelphia. It was a beautiful day for base ball, and the stands were packed accordingly. Three Philadelphia ballplayers were on the field practicing as usual before the game, while the rest lingered in the locker room. One fan allegedly saw a couple of kids smoking cigarettes in right field and soon after a few flames caught on to the wooden grandstands and spread into great waves of flames. Pitcher George Haddock raced out of the grounds and pulled the fire alarm.

As soon as Wright heard the alarm, he raced on his bike from the pavilion to the field, where he figured to be safest. However, a heavy northeast wind blew the fire across the park and it began to envelope the field. "The flames spread with a rapidity that I never saw before," Wright marveled. "They appeared to keep up ... and finally formed into one great blaze." It was so hot on the field that it "scorched" his face and "left a burning sensation."[85] Eventually, the fire was put out by a crew of brave Philadelphia firefighters, but not before it caught on to a house, a business,

and a local stable. This was one of a number of fires that took place in the
National League that year, on the wooden grandstands in Boston, Chicago,
and Baltimore.

One of the perks of Wright's job was that he rarely had to leave Philadelphia. One writer stated that he did not leave the city on business until
July. Apparently, he had traveled elsewhere beforehand simply as a fan,
though there seems to have been little difference between attending as a
fan or Chief of Umpires. For example, in May he was on hand for the
opening day between Boston and Cincinnati. While there he answered
rumors that he was leaving for another job. There had been rumors that
he was going to head up the creation of a league to rival the NL. Wright
refuted it firmly. "I know nothing of any such scheme except the stories
that I have read. They are absurd. As far as I am concerned, I am with the
old league. It is good enough for me." (By the way, would Wright have
approved of the new American League seven years later? In this interview,
he stated, "I'd like to see two associations working in harmony and I think
there is room for two....")[86]

Wright spent the year of 1894 in rather good health and considerable
activity. But his condition was about to take a downturn. In late October
1894, Wright was seriously ill with arthritis in his swollen hands and feet.
The pain was so bad that he was hardly able to sleep at night. Wright hoped
that a change of scenery from his confinement at home in Philadelphia
would help, so the family went to Atlantic City, New Jersey, for a week.
Along with Florida, this had become a favorite vacation spot for the
Wrights. They had vacationed in Atlantic City for a couple of weeks after
the 1889 season and several other times, and it seemed to be helpful in making Harry feel better.

Reports of his health were infrequent, so it is difficult to tell how he
did in the fall and winter. But by late May 1895, he was in a great deal of
pain and again on the verge of blindness. However, it appears that shortly
after that, he recovered once again and, according to Chadwick, was grateful to have his sight back and excited to go bicycling.

In mid–August Wright was confined to bed with bronchitis. It took
until early the next month for him to see a doctor in Philadelphia. Dr.
John A. Boger advised him to go to Atlantic City by the fresh salt air and
visit Dr. Francis W. Bennett. Wright arrived in the city on September 18
and immediately felt better, so he didn't bother to see Dr. Bennett. On Saturday, September 21, he finally realized that it was time to give in and see
the doctor.

A quick check-up showed how bad of a state Wright was actually in.
He was immediately sent to a sanitarium where Drs. Boger, Bennett, and

William Pepper observed him with the "gravest fears." They soon found that he had catarrhal pneumonia, the eye problem that had plagued him for five years. But, even more seriously, he had suffered a rupture of the pleura, also known as pneumo-thorax. The second condition was most disconcerting, something Dr. Bennett described as a "rare and exceedingly grave affliction in one at his age."[87]

The doctors gave Wright a good chance of surviving because of his strong will and determination to overcome the illness. Despite excruciating pain, the doctors noted that he was handling himself "heroically." Dr. Bennett helped this by giving him small injections of morphine through a hypodermic needle. Obscure modern sources have falsely listed Wright's cause of death as a drug overdose. Halsey Miller, Jr., noted that "If he died from morphine we can blame his pill-peddlers," who often overzealously distributed medication in those days.

Wright was kept under close watch until Drs. Boger, Bennett, and Pepper performed a surgery on October 2. He came out "relieved and brighter" over what appeared to be a successful surgery. He rested peacefully throughout the night and appeared alert in the morning. Then, unexpectedly, he suffered a relapse and slowly lost consciousness as noon approached. According to the *Sporting News'* E.J. Lanigan, at 12:30, Wright, with his wife Isabelle, Harry, Jr., and four daughters at his side, raised a pair of fingers and said "Two men out!"[88] The hand then fell limp beside him and he died ten minutes later.

"No death among the professional fraternity has occurred which elicited such painful regret," noted Henry Chadwick. In one of numerous exuberant eulogies, he further stated that

> To every worthy young ball player he was a father figure to a son, and those of older growth, who were deserving of his regard he was the true friend and counselor.... [By] his sterling integrity of character alone he presented a model every professional ball player can copy from with great gain to his individual reputation, and to public esteem and popularity. Let us trust that in the coming time one may look upon his like again.[89]

Colonel Rogers had the most flowery of all encomiums. Perhaps it seems that he would be unlikely, but if one understands the complexity of Rogers, it is clear that he was a man that delighted desperately, if not sincerely, in public proprieties, regardless of private inclinations. "Had he not greatness?" Rogers intoned at the November 14 League meeting.

> Not, perhaps, in its ordinary significance, as worshipped in the glare, glitter, and tinsel of public life, accompanied by hurrahs and drums and

trumpets, but in the higher meaning he was truly great: great because he was good. Good to every one! Good at all times! Good in word, act, and deed! Who can recall one harsh or unkind syllable uttered by Harry Wright? Who can accuse him of one mean or dishonest transaction? When did he ever forget the Golden Rule? How many are the witnesses of his fairness, his impartiality, his effort to do the right because it was right, his silence when he could not praise; his proclivity for smoothing asperities and his preaching the perennial gospel of peace.... And so this man of amiable manners and sympathetic heart, serene tempered self controlled and self abrogated, so illumed the atmosphere of his surroundings that every one felt the better for the breathing of it and for the guidance of its kindly light.[90]

The number of grieving personal friends and base ball associates, fans aside, was estimated in the thousands. One thousand were in attendance for Wright's funeral at the home of Philadelphia scorekeeper Frank C. Hough. Hundreds lined up along the sidewalk before the service began to file past the black satin-lined casket and past the elaborate floral bouquets. The most notable was a bed of roses sent by the Philadelphia club with a base ball field in the middle and the reassuring words, "Safe at Home."

At the November League meeting, Hough, on behalf of the Philadelphia-based Scorers' Association, made the unprecedented proposition that all major league clubs reserve a day before the official commencement of the championship season to raise money for a monument in Wright's honor. It was agreed that all clubs within the National Agreement and any other willing clubs would set aside all gate receipts for the Wright family's benefit. At an April 1 meeting of the Harry Wright Memorial Association it was decided that April 13, 1896, would be the day.

Harry Wright Day turned out to be a national celebration of base ball. In Rockford, Illinois, A.G. Spalding and the old Forest City ballplayers arrived by train to join a mile-long parade through the heart of the city with bands, militia, cyclists, equestrians, former ballplayers, civic societies, and citizens of Rockford. In Cincinnati, the Reds of 1896 took on the Reds of 1882 and held a banquet afterwards at the Gibson House. Henry Chadwick, who had made a rare venture away from his home in Sag Harbor, Long Island, was the guest of honor. Between him and the long guestlist of base ball brethren, the evening was spent reminiscing noisily about the good old days.

In Indianapolis, the occasion was much more boisterous. The Pittsburgh Pirates' Jake Beckley lived up to his team's reputation for dirty play by getting thrown out of the game in the 6th. As he was escorted from the grounds by a policeman, the Pittsburgh bench attacked umpire Murphy with a slew of catcalls. Murphy was so upset that he threatened to eject the entire team from the grounds if they didn't "shut up."

Drizzling rain and frigid air kept attendance down and prevented the clubs from making the $3,349.78 necessary to pay for the monument. Between the games of April 13 and subsequent tributes by other leagues and clubs on April 28, May 9, and May 15, the totals broke down as follows:

Philadelphia v. Athletics, at Philadelphia	$1,220.30
New York v. Metropolitans, at New York	322.00
Chicago v. Kansas City, at Kansas City	99.75
Indianapolis v. Pittsburgh, at Indianapolis	246.24
Harvard v. John Morrill's nine, at Boston	238.80
Boston v. Springfield, at Derby, Connecticut	69.62
Washington v. Departmental Picked Team, at Washington	127.25
Cincinnati '96 v. Cincinnati '82, at Cincinnati	365.20
Louisville '96 v. Unknowns, at Louisville	128.95
New Haven v. Victor, at Bridgeport, Connecticut	10.00
Brockton v. Harvard Second Nine, at Brockton, Massachusetts	33.75
Spalding and other veterans, at Rockford, Illinois	309.17
Total	$3,171.08

The extra $178.70 needed was made up by the National League.

The monument was originally intended to be placed in Fairmount Park, but commissioners did not permit it. Instead it was placed at the gravesite in West Laurel Hill Cemetery where Wright was buried.

Several League officials were expected at the unveiling on a Thursday afternoon in mid–June 1897, but only Reach and Rogers showed up. A large number of on-lookers were there for the short ceremonies to hear letters from a number of managers and a short, complimentary speech by Rogers, perhaps a rereading of his earlier cited eulogy. They stood under the shadows of the trees and the 14-foot high bronze statue. A slightly enlarged 6' 6" statue of Wright stood atop a 7' 6" granite pedestal. He was dressed in the everyday wear of his later days, with his linen duster in one hand and glasses in the other.

The generosity shown by the National League in this instance was in part a return of the last gesture towards the game by Harry Wright. When Wright's will was read in Philadelphia on October 10, 1895, it was found that in addition to awarding an estate of $13,500 to his family, he had also included an amendment added five days before his death, on September 28. To the National League and the American Association he left the volumes of memoranda that he had built up and thought to save over the past three decades in base ball. They were dedicated "in the sincere hope and wish that they [the NL and AA] may use them as a nucleus or beginning of a historical collection of memoranda bearing upon our grand national game of base ball, in the services of which I have passed the greater part of my life."[91] Indeed, without this one last contribution some of the greatest volumes to cover the history of base ball would have been diminished.

VII.

It took a long time before the Wright name faded from the base ball society. George Wright accompanied the Chicago and New York nines on their around-the-world tour of 1888-9. He joined the group in San Francisco, where he was escorted by Sammy. From there the players climbed aboard the ship that they sailed into the Pacific Ocean. Along the ride, George took time to teach the men cricket, not in his brother's way of verbal instruction, but by actually playing it on the decks of the ship. A cricket alley was set up by sailors under George's supervision with a sail from the ship as a backstop. An awning already set up kept the ball from going overboard.

The tour moved through Alaska, Australia, parts of Africa, and Europe before returning to the U.S. A stop was even made in Sheffield, where George had a photo taken of the players beside the train on the countryside hills. On the evening of April 13, back in the States, a banquet was held in Boston to hail George as the first professional cricketer to travel around the world. Spalding, Anson, and Ward were among those in attendance.

In the years after his older brother's death, George stayed involved with base ball, but unenthusiastically at first. He remained involved with cricket as a bowler for Boston's Longwood Cricket Club and even traveled up to Ottawa for an October 1897 contest.

George's most significant deviation from base ball was golf. He had ordered a set of clubs from a Scottish distributor across the Atlantic not knowing what their purpose was. After receiving them, a man from Scotland happened to be stopping by who was familiar with the game. He explained the foreign sport and promised to send back a rule book when he got home. George studied that book, honed his skills, and in 1890 got permission to construct the first American golf course, at Franklin Park in Hyde Park, Massachusetts. This caused a fiery disagreement among executives that supported it and park patrons that didn't, but eventually the course was built.

As the years went on, George identified with base ball once more. In June 1897 he played a game in Boston with the likes of Spalding, Morrill, Murnane, O'Rourke, and brother Sammy, against a team of Australians. In 1907 he was part of the Mills Commission that erroneously cited Abner Doubleday as the inventor of base ball, in Cooperstown, New York. (George's role, like others on the panel, was basically a nominal one aimed to give the Commission's findings prestige and credibility.) Five years later, at the 1912 Olympics in Stockholm, the 65-year-old umpired an exhibition game between the U.S. and Sweden. However, his favorite project was an effort to encourage Boston area schools to give rewards for outstanding base ball players, as they did with gymnastics and military drills. Like many older base ball fans, he had grown to regard the play of children as a purer representative of his spirit of play than that of professionals. Gazing sentimentally at a wooden picture of the Elysian Fields, he wrote, "It was here I spent most of my boyhood days. Oh, that I were a boy again!"[92]

Despite his preference for the sandlot style of play, George still appreciated a major league ballgame. Much of his last years were spent at Boston's Fenway Park and Braves Field, as well as other parks occasionally. He once attended a Cleveland Naps v. New York Yankees game with Albert Spalding. The two sat together and clapped vigorously for the excellent plays of Nap Lajoie. Afterwards, they were greeted by some of the ballplayers, namely Dan Brouthers of the second "Big Four," a group that, much like Boston's revolvers of 1874, jumped from Detroit to Buffalo in 1885.

In 1919, George was invited to a World Series game in Cincinnati where the Reds were taking on the heavily favored Chicago White Sox. The crooked play that he saw on behalf of the Black Sox was a surprise to a man who had proclaimed four years before that "Baseball is on a higher moral plane than it ever has been before."[93] If his brother Harry had been around it is likely that he would have been blindsided too, but in 1874 he had recognized the vulnerabilities that brought the Black Sox scandal about. "[I]s it any wonder," he asked rhetorically, "that some [ballplayers] fall from grace and that others are made dissatisfied … when they learn … they could have done much better."[94]

Oblivious to the disgrace that was going on before him, George spent a nostalgic day at Redland Field with the only other living members of the 1869 Cincinnati Red Stockings, Cal McVey and Oak Taylor. George kept his neighbors in the box seats mesmerized throughout the game with stories of the Western tour of 50 years before. The ballplayers, he said, were so scared of a Sioux raid that they slept with pistols ready under their pillows at night.

Soon after, George began splitting his time between Boston and Florida.

Wright's plaque at the Baseball Hall of Fame hangs third from the right in the bottom row of this picture. Notably, it misstates the year of his British tour as 1876, not 1874. (Author's Collection.)

From day to day, he would play golf in suitable weather or take his grandchildren to the park. Often he'd stop by the ballpark and get in for free with his Number One Lifetime Pass granted years before.

In September 1936 George began experiencing trouble with inflammation of his heart. This persisted for nearly a year until on August 19, 1937, he contracted pneumonia. The combination was too much for the 90-year-old man. He died two days later, just a few weeks long enough to have experienced his induction into the Baseball Hall of Fame.

Harry Wright's election to Cooperstown took another 16 years, until 1953. He was finally selected by the Veterans Committee that had been established the previous year to replace an older version. Its first choice was Ed Barrow in the 1952 vote.

Perhaps no one was more upset with the delay in electing Wright to the Hall of Fame than Harry Wright, Jr. Harry had looked up to his father since his boyhood often spent on the field with Wright's Philadelphia ballclub. In his teenage years, third baseman Ed Meyer took Harry, Jr., under his wing and attempted to polish him into a major leaguer. But Wright, Sr., insisted that his son go to school and get an education. He enrolled at Spring Garden University in Philadelphia to study art and then took advanced classes at the University of Pennsylvania. But Harry, Jr., spent too much time playing base ball for the professional Caledonia club and then coaching a team later on the side. After college, he managed three different clubs in Merchantville, Pennsylvania, and then Mount Holly's Boy's Baseball Club. The latter team had great success in local play and even against the stiffest competition in Philadelphia and South Jersey. Once coaching was done with, he also spent quite a bit of time scouting for major league clubs.

Harry, Jr., also enjoyed painting, a talent he shared with Sister Carrie. His collection numbered about 200 water color and pencil sketches, and included several prize-winning pieces. His favorite, and most valuable, paintings were of landscapes.

But Harry, Jr.'s love of art never eclipsed his love for base ball, his father, and the connection of the two. His third floor studio was full of memorabilia from Harry Wright's days in the game, a "shrine," one reporter described it as, to his father's legacy. He had become embittered by Wright's obscurity in the emerging times of power stretched from Ruth to Mantle. In Harry, Jr.'s eyes this was inconceivable. "I have never known anyone in my life who could compare with him," he stated reverently. "Father to me was next to God."[95]

"Idolization of Harry Wright," noted Halsey Miller, Jr., "was the normal thing among the family."

Appendix A:
The Cincinnati Red Stockings' 1868 Club Song

The Cincinnati Baseball Club Song.
By a member.
(Air — "Bonnie Blue Flag")

We are a band of baseball players
　From "Cincinnati City";
We come to toss the ball around,
　And sing to you our ditty.
And if you listen to our song
　We are about to sing,
We'll tell you all about baseball
　And make the welkin ring.

CHORUS.
Hurrah! Hurrah!
　For the noble game, hurrah!
"Red Stockings" all will toss the ball,
　And shout our loud hurrah.

Our Captain is a goodly man,
　And Harry is his name;
Whate'er he does, 'tis always "Wright,"
　So says the voice of fame.
And as the Pitcher of our nine,
　We think he can't be beat;

In many a fight, old Harry Wright
　Has saved us from defeat.

CHORUS.

The man who catches Harry's balls,
　It passes all belief,
He's so expert in catching "fouls"
　We have dubbed him "chicken thief."
And if a player's on his first,
　He'd better hold it fast;
With "Johnny Hat" behind the bat,
　The balls are seldom passed.

CHORUS.

In many a game that we have played,
　We've needed a First Base,
But now our opponents will find
　The "basket" in its place.
And if you think he "muffs" the balls,
　Sent into him red hot,

You'll soon be fooled by "Charlie
  Gould,"
    And find he "muffs" them not.

CHORUS.

We travel on to Second Base,
    And Brainard there is found;
He beats the world in catching "flies,"
    And covering the ground.
And as the Pitcher of our nine,
    Whene'er 'tis best to change,
The man will find that plays behind,
    That "Asa" has the range.

CHORUS.

And lest the boys should thirsty get
    When after balls they've ran,
We take with us, where'er we go,
    A jolly "Waterman."
Upon Third Base he stops the ball,
    And sends them in so fine,
That all have said that jolly "Fred"
    Is home upon the nine.

CHORUS.

Our Shortstop is a man of worth,
    We hope he'll never die;
He stops all balls that come to him;
    He's grim death on the "fly."
The many deeds he has performed,
    We will not here relate,
But tell you now that "Johnny How"
    As a player is first-rate.

CHORUS.

The infield now is traveled o'er;
    The out comes next in line,

And "Moses Grant" is brought to view,
    Right Fielder in our nine.
He knows the place, he plays right well,
    To none the palm he'll yield;
He's bound you shan't catch "Moses
  Grant"
    A "napping" in right field.

CHORUS.

There is a man upon our nine,
    To him a verse we'll sing;
You all have heard of him before,
    His name is Rufus King.
Just now he plays as Center Field,
    Sometimes as Second Base;
We all have proof that merry "Ruf"
    Is worthy of his place.

CHORUS.

Come, fill your glasses to the brim
    With joyous, sparkling wine,
And drink a toast to all that's "Left"
    Of the 'riginal First Nine.
Of all the men who first essayed
    Upon that nine to play,
There's only one, and that's "Johnson,"
    Who holds a place to-day.

CHORUS.

To win the game we play to-day,
    We earnestly shall try,
And hope our expectations won't
    Be captured on the "fly."
We shall expect a quick return
    To toss the ball around;
We'll welcome all to games of ball
    Upon our "Union Ground."

CHORUS.

Appendix B:
The Chronology of Harry Wright's Managerial Career

Year	Team	Games	Wins	Losses	Winning Percentage	Standing
1876	Boston	70	39	31	.557	4
1877		61	42	18	.700	1
1878		60	41	19	.683	1
1879		84	54	30	.643	2
1880		86	40	44	.476	6
1881		83	38	45	.458	6
1882	Providence	84	52	32	.619	2
1883		98	58	40	.592	3
1884	Philadelphia	113	39	73	.348	6
1885		111	56	54	.509	3
1886		119	71	43	.623	4
1887		128	75	48	.610	2
1888		131	69	61	.531	3
1889		130	63	64	.496	4
1890		133	78	54	.591	3
1891		138	68	69	.496	4
1892		155	87	66	.569	4
1893		133	72	57	.558	4
18 years		1917	1042	848	.551	

177

Bibliography

Books and Articles

Appel, Marty. *Slide, Kelly, Slide: The Wild Life and Times of Mike "King" Kelly.* Lanham, Md.: Scarecrow Press, 1996.

Biesel, David. *The Baseball Encyclopedia: The Complete and Official Record of Major League Baseball Revised and Updated.* New York: Macmillan, 1974.

Blum, John et al. *The National Experience: A History of the United States.* San Diego: Harcourt Brace Jovanovich, 1989.

Brock, Darryl. *The Wright Way.* Sports Heritage, March/April 1987.

Di Salvatore, Bryan. *A Clever Base-Ballist: The Life and Times of John Montgomery Ward.* New York: Pantheon, 1999.

Guschov, Stephen D. *The Red Stockings of Cincinnati: Base Ball's First All Professional Team.* Jefferson, N.C.: McFarland, 1992.

Ryczek, William J. *Blackguards and Red Stockings: A History of Baseball's National Association, 1871–1875.* Jefferson, N.C.: McFarland, 1992.

_____. *When Johnny Came Sliding Home: The Post–Civil War Baseball Boom, 1865–1970.* Jefferson, N.C.: McFarland, 1996.

Seymour, Harold. *Baseball: The Early Years.* New York: Oxford University Press, 1989.

Sowell, Mike. *July 2, 1903: The Mysterious Death of Hall-of-Famer Big Ed Delehanty.* New York: Macmillan, 1992.

Spalding, Albert. *America's National Game.* Lincoln: University of Nebraska Press, 1992.

Voigt, David Quentin. *American Baseball: From Gentleman's Sport to the Commissioner System.* Norman: University of Oklahoma Press, 1966.

Newspapers, Periodicals, and Microfilm Files

The Harry Wright Correspondence
The Henry Chadwick Diaries, Volumes 23 and 24
The Henry Chadwick Scrapbooks
The Sporting Life
The Sporting News

Notes

1. A Base Ball Edison

1. Stephen D. Guschov, *The Red Stockings of Cincinnati* (Jefferson, North Carolina: McFarland & Co., Inc., Publishers, 1998), p. 84
2. Harold Seymour, *Baseball: The Early Years* (New York: Oxford University Press, 1989), p. 38.
3. *Chadwick Scrapbooks.*
4. *Harry Wright Correspondence,* letter of 1882 or 1883 to *Cincinnati Commercial Gazette.*
5. *HWC,* December 29, 1874, to William Hulbert.
6. *Chadwick Diaries, Volume 23.*
7. *Ibid.*
8. *Chadwick Scrapbooks.*
9. *Ibid.*
10. *Pittsburgh Telegram,* May 3, 1877.
11. *The Sporting News,* August 4, 1894.
12. *HWC,* March 28, 1873, to Nick Young.
13. William J. Ryczek, *When Johnny Came Sliding Home: The Post–Civil War Boom, 1865–1870* (Jefferson, North Carolina: McFarland & Co., Inc., Publishers, 1998), p. 178.
14. *The Sporting News,* October 12, 1895.
15. *Chadwick Scrapbooks.*
16. *HWC,* March 23, 1875, to Hulbert.
17. *Chadwick Scrapbooks.*
18. April 8, 1963, letter from Carrie Wright to Halsey Miller, Jr.
19. *The Sporting News,* October 19, 1895.
20. Author's correspondence with Halsey Miller, Jr.; January 22, 2001.
21. *The Sporting Life,* December 19, 1883.
22. *HWC.*
23. Ryczek, *When Johnny Came Sliding Home,* p. 54.
24. Hall of Fame Library File on Harry Wright; unidentified source.
25. Guschov, *The Red Stockings of Cincinnati,* p. 11.
26. *Ibid.*
27. *Chadwick Scrapbooks.*
28. *Ibid.*
29. *Ibid.*
30. *Ibid.*
31. *The Sporting News,* January 14, 1893.
32. *The Sporting News,* October 17, 1891.
33. *The New York Times,* July 7, 1876.
34. *Chadwick Scrapbooks.*
35. *Ibid.*
36. *Ibid.*
37. *HWC,* October 12, 1878, to Robert Morrow.

38. *Chadwick Scrapbooks.*
39. *Ibid.*
40. Ryczek, *When Johnny Came Sliding Home*, p. 13.
41. Guschov, *The Red Stockings of Cincinnati*, p. 32.
42. *Ibid.*
43. Guschov, *The Red Stockings of Cincinnati*, p. 8.
44. *Ibid.*
45. Darryl Brock, *The Wright Way; Sports Heritage*, March/April 1987, p. 38.
46. *Chadwick Scrapbooks.*
47. Ryczek, *When Johnny Came Sliding Home*, p. 72.
48. *Ibid.*

2. The Queen City

1. *Chadwick Scrapbooks.*
2. Ryczek, *When Johnny Came Sliding Home*, p. 5.
3. Guschov, *The Red Stockings of Cincinnati*, p. 12.
4. Ryczek, *When Johnny Came Sliding Home*, p. 149–150.
5. Ryczek, *When Johnny Came Sliding Home*, p. 172.
6. Guschov, *The Red Stockings of Cincinnati*, p. 17–20.
7. Brock, *The Wright Way*, p. 41.
8. *Ibid.*
9. *HWC.*
10. *The Sporting News*, March 19, 1887.
11. *HWC*, April 15, 1874, to William Cammeyer.
12. *Ibid.*
13. Ryczek, *When Johnny Came Marching Home*, p. 166
14. Guschov, *The Red Stockings of Cincinnati*, p. 25.
15. Guschov, *The Red Stockings of Cincinnati*, p. 33.
16. Guschov, *The Red Stockings of Cincinnati*, p. 147.
17. Guschov, *The Red Stockings of Cincinnati*, p. 31.
18. Guschov, *The Red Stockings of Cincinnati*, p. 85.
19. Guschov, *The Red Stockings of Cincinnati*, p. 41.
20. Guschov, *The Red Stockings of Cincinnati*, p. 43.
21. Guschov, *The Red Stockings of Cincinnati*, p. 87.
22. Guschov, *The Red Stockings of Cincinnati*, p. 86.
23. *Chadwick Scrapbooks.*
24. Guschov, *The Red Stockings of Cincinnati*, p. 36.
25. *HWC.*
26. Guschov, *The Red Stockings of Cincinnati*, p. 51.
27. Guschov, *The Red Stockings of Cincinnati*, p. 58.
28. *Ibid.*
29. Ryczek, *When Johnny Came Sliding Home*, p. 183.
30. *Ibid.*
31. *Ibid.*
32. Guschov, *The Red Stockings of Cincinnati*, p. 59.
33. Ryczek, *When Johnny Came Sliding Home*, p. 180.
34. Guschov, *The Red Stockings of Cincinnati*, p. 100.
35. Guschov, *The Red Stockings of Cincinnati*, p. 61.
36. Guschov, *The Red Stockings of Cincinnati*, p. 63.
37. *HWC.*
38. Guschov, *The Red Stockings of Cincinnati*, p. 62.
39. Guschov, *The Red Stockings of Cincinnati*, p. 67.
40. Ryczek, *When Johnny Came Sliding Home*, p. 186.
41. Guschov, *The Red Stockings of Cincinnati*, p. 78.
42. Ryczek, *When Johnny Came Sliding Home*, p. 188.
43. Ryczek, *When Johnny Came Sliding Home*, p. 189.
44. Ryczek, *When Johnny Came Sliding Home*, p. 210.
45. Ryczek, *When Johnny Came Sliding Home*, p. 190.
46. *Chadwick Scrapbooks.*

47. Ryczek, *When Johnny Came Sliding Home*, p. 190.
48. Ryczek, *When Johnny Came Sliding Home*, p. 190–91.
49. Ryczek, *When Johnny Came Sliding Home*, p. 192.
50. Guschov, *The Red Stockings of Cincinnati*, p. 84.
51. Guschov, *The Red Stockings of Cincinnati*, p. 88.
52. HWC, letter of 1882 or 1883 to *Cincinnati Commercial Gazette*.
53. *Chadwick Scrapbooks*.
54. *Ibid*.
55. Ryczek, *When Johnny Came Sliding Home*, p. 193.
56. Guschov, *The Red Stockings of Cincinnati*, p. 84.
57. Guschov, *The Red Stockings of Cincinnati*, p. 93.
58. Ryczek, *When Johnny Came Sliding Home*, p. 198.
59. Guschov, *The Red Stockings of Cincinnati*, p. 97.
60. Guschov, *The Red Stockings of Cincinnati*, p. 15.
61. *The Sporting News*, February 19, 1887.
62. HWC.
63. Guschov, *The Red Stockings of Cincinnati*, p. 104.
64. Guschov, *The Red Stockings of Cincinnati*, p. 105.
65. Ryczek, *When Johnny Came Sliding Home*, p. 209.
66. Guschov, *The Red Stockings of Cincinnati*, p. 108.
67. Guschov, *The Red Stockings of Cincinnati*, p. 111.
68. *Ibid*.
69. Guschov, *The Red Stockings of Cincinnati*, p. 112.
70. Guschov, *The Red Stockings of Cincinnati*, p. 111.
71. Guschov, *The Red Stockings of Cincinnati*, p. 112.
72. Ryczek, *When Johnny Came Sliding Home*, p. 232.
73. Guschov, *The Red Stockings of Cincinnati*, p. 113.
74. Guschov, *The Red Stockings of Cincinnati*, p. 147.

75. Guschov, *The Red Stockings of Cincinnati*, p. 116.
76. Guschov, *The Red Stockings of Cincinnati*, p. 118.
77. Ryczek, *When Johnny Came Sliding Home*, p. 232.
78. *Ibid*.
79. Ryczek, *When Johnny Came Sliding Home*, p. 233.
80. Guschov, *The Red Stockings of Cincinnati*, p. 121.
81. HWC.
82. Ryczek, *When Johnny Came Sliding Home*, p. 233.
83. Guschov, *The Red Stockings of Cincinnati*, p. 118.
84. Ryczek, *When Johnny Came Sliding Home*, p. 233.
85. Ryczek, *When Johnny Came Sliding Home*, p. 236.
86. Guschov, *The Red Stockings of Cincinnati*, p. 124–25.
87. Guschov, *The Red Stockings of Cincinnati*, p. 125.
88. Guschov, *The Red Stockings of Cincinnati*, p. 126.
89. Ryczek, *When Johnny Came Sliding Home*, p. 221.
90. *Ibid*.
91. HWC.
92. Guschov, The Red Stockings of Cincinnati, p. 127.
93. *Ibid*.
94. Ryczek, *When Johnny Came Sliding Home*, p. 229.
95. HWC.
96. Ryczek, *When Johnny Came Sliding Home*, p. 193.
97. Guschov, *The Red Stockings of Cincinnati*, p. 133.
98. Guschov, *The Red Stockings of Cincinnati*, p. 134–35.
99. Guschov, *The Red Stockings of Cincinnati*, p. 137.

3. Dynasty in the Rough

1. Ryczek, *When Johnny Came Sliding Home*, p. 237.

2. Guschov, *The Red Stockings of Cincinnati*, p. 136.
3. Ryczek, *When Johnny Came Sliding Home*, p. 238.
4. *Ibid.*
5. *Chadwick Scrapbooks.*
6. Guschov, *The Red Stockings of Cincinnati*, p. 22.
7. Ryczek, *When Johnny Came Sliding Home*, p. 246.
8. Ryczek, *When Johnny Came Sliding Home*, p. 250.
9. William J. Ryczek, *Blackguards and Red Stockings: A History of Baseball's National Association, 1871–1875* (Jefferson, North Carolina: McFarland & Co., Inc., Publishers, 1992), p. 12.
10. *HWC*, April 29, 1873, to Hicks Hayhurst.
11. Ryczek, *Blackguards and Red Stockings*, p. 3.
12. *HWC.*
13. *HWC*, January 5, 1878.
14. Ryczek, *Blackguards and Red Stockings*, p. 104.
15. *HWC.*
16. *Ibid.*
17. *Ibid.*
18. *Ibid.*
19. *Ibid.*
20. *Chadwick Scrapbooks.*
21. *The Sporting News*, September 10, 1887.
22. *HWC.*
23. *Ibid.*
24. *HWC*, December 26, 1871, to Hayhurst.
25. *HWC.*
26. Ryczek, *Blackguards and Red Stockings*, p. 114.
27. *Chadwick Scrapbooks.*
28. *Ibid.*
29. *HWC.*
30. *Ibid.*
31. *Ibid.*
32. *Ibid.*
33. *Ibid.*
34. *Ibid.*
35. Ryczek, *Blackguards and Red Stockings*, p. 113.
36. *HWC.*

37. Ryczek, *Blackguards and Red Stockings*, p. 125.
38. Ryczek, *Blackguards and Red Stockings*, p. 117.
39. *HWC.*
40. *Ibid.*
41. *Ibid.*
42. *Ibid.*
43. *Ibid.*
44. *Ibid.*
45. *Ibid.*
46. Ryczek, *Blackguards and Red Stockings*, p. 159.
47. *HWC.*
48. *Chadwick Scrapbooks.*
49. *Ibid.*
50. Guschov, *The Red Stockings of Cincinnati*, p. 148.
51. Ryczek, *Blackguards and Red Stockings*, p. 163.
52. Ryczek, *Blackguards and Red Stockings*, p. 162.
53. *Chadwick Scrapbooks.*
54. *Ibid.*
55. *Ibid.*
56. *HWC.*
57. *Chadwick Scrapbooks.*
58. *Ibid.*
59. *Ibid.*
60. *Ibid.*
61. *HWC.*
62. Ryczek, *Blackguards and Red Stockings*, p. 163.
63. *HWC.*
64. Ryczek, *Blackguards and Red Stockings*, p. 143.
65. Ryczek, *Blackguards and Red Stockings*, p. 173.
66. *Chadwick Scrapbooks.*
67. *HWC.*
68. Ryczek, *Blackguards and Red Stockings*, p. 189.
69. *HWC.*
70. Albert Spalding, *America's National Game* (Lincoln: University of Nebraska Press, 1992), p. 208.
71. Ryczek, *Blackguards and Red Stockings*, p. 204.
72. National League Constitution.
73. *HWC.*
74. *HWC*, January 6, 1875, to Young.

75. *Chadwick Scrapbooks.*
76. *HWC.*
77. Guschov, *The Red Stockings of Cincinnati*, p. 148.
78. Guschov, *The Red Stockings of Cincinnati*, p. 149.
79. *HWC.*
80. *Chadwick Scrapbooks.*
81. Brock, *The Wright Way*, p. 38.
82. *Chadwick Scrapbooks.*
83. *Ibid.*
84. Guschov, *The Red Stockings of Cincinnati*, p. 17.
85. *Chadwick Scrapbooks.*
86. *The Sporting Life*, July 5, 1890.
87. *HWC.*
88. *Ibid.*
89. *Ibid.*
90. *Chadwick Scrapbooks.*
91. *Pittsburgh Telegram*, May 3, 1877.
92. *HWC.*
93. *HWC*, February 24, 1878, to Harry Wright from James Devlin.
94. *HWC.*
95. *Ibid.*
96. *Ibid.*

4. Uncle Harry

1. *HWC.*
2. *Ibid.*
3. *Chadwick Scrapbooks.*
4. *HWC.*
5. *Ibid.*
6. *Chadwick Scrapbooks.*
7. *HWC.*
8. *Ibid.*
9. *Ibid.*
10. David Quentin Voigt, *American Baseball: From Gentleman's Sport to the Commissioner System* (Norman: University of Oklahoma Press, 1966), p. 78.
11. Voigt, *American Baseball*, p. 79.
12. *Chadwick Scrapbooks.*
13. *Ibid.*
14. *Ibid.*
15. *Ibid.*
16. *Ibid.*
17. *Ibid.*
18. *Ibid.*
19. *Ibid.*
20. *The Sporting Life*, December 12, 1883.
21. *Chadwick Scrapbooks.*
22. Marty Appel, *Slide, Kelly, Slide: The Wild Life and Times of Mike "King" Kelly* (Lanham, Md.: Scarecrow Press, Inc., 1996), p. 57.
23. *Ibid.*
24. Appel, *Slide, Kelly, Slide*, p. 58.
25. *Ibid.*
26. *The Sporting News*, June 16, 1888.
27. *The Sporting News*, September 4, 1884.
28. *The Sporting News*, March 17, 1886.
29. *Chadwick Scrapbooks.*
30. *Ibid.*
31. *Ibid.*
32. *Ibid.*
33. *The Sporting News*, March 9, 1887.
34. *Chadwick Scrapbooks.*
35. *The Sporting News*, January 13, 1893.
36. *Chadwick Scrapbooks.*
37. Voigt, *American Baseball*, 194.
38. *The Sporting News*, March 5, 1887.
39. *Chadwick Scrapbooks.*
40. *Ibid.*
41. *The Sporting News*, September 9, 1886.
42. *Chadwick Scrapbooks.*
43. *The Sporting News*, September 9, 1886.
44. *Ibid.*
45. *The Sporting News*, September 13, 1886.
46. *Chadwick Scrapbooks.*
47. *HWC.*
48. *The Sporting News*, August 11, 1888.
49. *Chadwick Scrapbooks.*
50. Mike Sowell, *July 2, 1903* (New York: Macmillan, 1992), p. 93.
51. Sowell, *July 2, 1903*, p. 97.
52. Sowell, *July 2, 1903*, 100.

53. Hall of Fame Library File on Harry Wright; unidentified source.

54. *Chadwick Scrapbooks.*

55. *The Sporting News*, November 16, 1889.

56. *Chadwick Scrapbooks.*

57. *Ibid.*

58. *Ibid.*

59. *Ibid.*

60. *Ibid.*

61. Brock, *The Wright Way*, p. 41.

62. *The Sporting News*, May 3, 1890.

63. *Chadwick Scrapbooks.*

64. *Ibid.*

65. *Ibid.*

66. *Ibid.*

67. *Ibid.*

68. *Ibid.*

69. Guschov, *The Red Stockings of Cincinnati*, p. 149.

70. *Chadwick Scrapbooks.*

71. *The Sporting News*, March 9, 1889.

72. *Chadwick Scrapbooks.*

73. *The Sporting News*, July 29, 1893.

74. Author's correspondence with Halsey Miller, Jr.; January 22, 2001.

75. *Chadwick Diaries*, Volume 23.

76. *The Sporting News*, October 14, 1893.

77. *The Sporting News*, October 8, 1892.

78. *The Sporting News*, December 2, 1893.

79. *Chadwick Diaries*, Volume 23.

80. *The Sporting News*, December 16, 1893.

81. *The Sporting News*, January 10, 1894.

82. Hall of Fame Library File on Harry Wright; unidentified source.

83. *Ibid.*

84. *Chadwick Scrapbooks.*

85. *Ibid.*

86. *Ibid.*

87. *Chadwick Diaries*, Volume 23.

88. *The Sporting News*, October 12, 1895.

89. *Chadwick Diaries*, Volume 23.

90. *Ibid.*

91. *The Sporting News*, October 12, 1895.

92. Brock, *The Wright Way*, p. 37.

93. Brock, *The Wright Way*, p. 94.

94. *HWC.*

95. Author's correspondence with Halsey Miller, Jr.; January 11, 2001.

Index